The *Ndebele* Pattern

The bold geometric designs and vivid colours used by the Ndebele people are the inspiration for the book's design, which was created by designer Rosemary Collingwood. The Ndebele people of South Africa created their own unique style of artistic expression with beadwork, pottery and mural art in the 18th century. The bold, coloured patterns of the traditional Ndebele houses, with their symbolic forms, are believed to have been adapted and developed from Sotho and Pedi traditions that are centuries old.

Traditionally, it is the women who paint the outside walls of their houses. Initially, they used natural paints in natural ochre tones, but nowadays the colours are more bold and lively due to the use of synthetic paints. Modern patterns often show more complex scenes than the initial pure rectangular patterns. The designs are not only regarded as decoration: the vibrant symbols and patterns portray the Ndebele heritage as well as the house owner's status, hopes and emotions. Today still much in use, these designs are an example of the proud cultural heritage of South Africa.

Living
in *South Africa*

**A guide to moving to, working in and
enjoying life in South Africa**

Created and written by
Regina Gräff
Derryn Campbell

Welcome

....

LIVING IN SOUTH AFRICA is an expat guide born out of our desire to share our insights into daily life in South Africa and to ensure the transition of moving to this beautiful country is a rewarding and fulfilling experience. The book will provide you with a detailed and unique overview of South Africa, the provinces and the people, welcoming you to this wonderful country.

Regina Gräff

Regina is a German expatriate and teacher. She is the editor of *the* award-winning website *ExpatCapeTown.com*. On her blog and forum she shares her experiences and insights into life in South Africa with expats from all over the world. Regina lived and worked in the USA, Australia, Singapore and various European countries before moving to South Africa with her family in 2005.

Derryn Campbell

Derryn is a passionate South African and the creator of the best-selling book *Awesome South Africa*. The book, which is a collection of fun facts and trivia on South Africa, was short-listed for the Nielsen Bookseller's Choice Award. Derryn is a co-founder of Awesome SA, a movement that encourages South Africans to positively influence the future.

....

Foreword by Nkosazana Dlamini-Zuma

Nkosazana Dlamini-Zuma is a former anti-apartheid activist and a medical doctor by training. She was appointed by former President Nelson Mandela as Minister of Health. Subsequently she has been the Minister of Foreign Affairs and the Minister of Home Affairs. In 2012 Dr Dlamini-Zuma was appointed as chairperson of the African Union. She has worked tirelessly in the pursuit of creating a better life and world for all, and is a shining role model for all South Africans.

Foreword

South Africa is an awesome country! Blue skies and stunning scenery, combined with a vibrant mix of cultures make this country one of the world's favourite destinations. Whilst our people are diverse, we are united in our 'South Africanness' and you will be touched by their warmth and friendliness.

Positioned at the foot of Africa where two oceans meet, this is the cradle of humankind, with a very rich and proud history. South Africa remains well-endowed with mineral, energy and other natural resources. South Africa is the strongest economy in Africa and represents a frontier for global economic growth and stability, now and into the future.

Despite our country's beauty and wealth, there are many challenges and there is much work to be done. I encourage you to join us as we strive to improve the quality of life of all South Africans.

Nelson Mandela said, 'It is what we make out of what we have, not what we are given, that separates one person from another.'

This book is the perfect introduction to our amazing country. The authors have conveyed their deep passion for South Africa and its people. The book is filled with vital information, practical tips and social insights, which includes both local and foreign perspectives. I trust that adjusting to living in our country will be easier and more fulfilling as a result of this book.

I welcome you to our Rainbow Nation and invite you to make the most of your time here, embrace the country, explore the beautiful continent of Africa and enjoy all it has to offer.

Nc Zuma

Nkosazana Dlamini-Zuma

Why do I love South Africa?
By Ian Macdonald

I love her for the perfection of her days
The crisp Karoo morning
The Joburg winter noon
The late summer Cape Town sunset
The star-filled Free State night
• • •
I love her for her people
For our warm smiles
For our resilience
For our I-am-because-we-are
• • •
I love her because she delights my senses
Highveld thunderbolts
Jacarandas in bloom
Sunday braais
African sun
Icy sea
I love her raw power,
her intensity, her strength
• • •
I love her because of how she makes me feel
Sometimes angry, sometimes joyous
Sometimes fearful, sometimes love-filled
Sometimes frustrated, sometimes hopeful
Always alive
• • •
I love her because she intrigues me
And challenges me
The Chinese have a curse:
'May you live in interesting times'
I see it as a blessing

I love her because she helps me keep things in perspective
By reminding me how privileged I am
Every day

• • •

I love her for being a microcosm of the world
A world in one country
For what we can teach the world
About compromise
And sharing
And forgiveness
And tolerance
And hope

• • •

I love her because she's imperfect
And full of opportunity
And potential unfulfilled

• • •

I love her because she has come so far
And has so much further to go
And whether we ever get there
Will all depend on us

• • •

I love her because she's been so good to me
And she inspires me to return the favour

• • •

I love her because she's my country
No matter what, I love her because she's my home
And where my soul is at rest

CONTENTS

'My humanity is bound up in yours, for we can only be
human together.' ~ *Desmond Tutu*

SOUTH AFRICA BASICS

FACTS

South Africa is one of the most diverse, most fascinating and most popular destinations in the world. People from all over choose to settle in this awesome country, which is rich in spectacular scenery, natural wonders, economic opportunities and, above all, home to a multicultural, diverse and passionate people. 'South Africa is a country in which one can expect the unexpected. An inspiration for all' Kofi Annan, former UN Secretary-General, remarked about the southernmost country on the African continent.

According to many surveys, South Africa is named among the world's leading holiday and expat destinations due to its great variety of attractions. The country is blessed with a sunny and, in most parts, comfortable climate. So it is no wonder that it has attracted many foreigners through the centuries and is a top tourism, business and expat destination. The stunningly beautiful landscape, richness in natural resources, steady economic growth and hospitality of the people offer plenty of possibilities to those who want to experience life in South Africa and settle here, even if only for a little while.

While travellers and visitors praise the country for its high quality and value-for-money services and its award-winning accomodation options, expats also value highly the good education, housing and healthcare options on offer. According to the 2012 HSBC Expat Explorer survey, the major cities in South Africa, Johannesburg and Cape Town, are among the most liveable cities in the world and the country is rated ninth best in the world for expat experiences.

South Africa is known to extend a hearty welcome and friendly atmosphere to all its visitors. Cape Town, Africa's leading beach destination and one of *National Geographic*'s 'places of a lifetime' was recently named as the best city in the world to visit. There are, however, many other great places to stay and live. They are are less known but not less beautiful.

 Name

Republic of South Africa (RSA)

Country Code: SA (or ZA: Dutch/ Afrikaans)

 General

Population 51.8 million

Time Zone: GMT +2 hours

 Languages

English, Afrikaans, isiZulu, isiXhosa, isiNdebele, Sepedi, Sesotho, Setswana, siSwati, Tshivenda, Xitsonga

 Capital Cities

Pretoria (administrative), Cape Town (legislative), Bloemfontein (judicative)

People from all over the world come to the country to work and live here. They come as volunteers or on special permits to gain new insights and experience. 'Swallows', retired visitors mainly from Europe, flee the cold winter temperatures in the northern hemisphere and visit the country every summer for several months at a time. Many have invested in the country and consider South Africa their 'home away from home'. Most of them find a new perspective on life when they experience the discrepancies in lifestyles beween various population groups, which are still stark.

Background knowledge, common sense and taking some special precautions are advised when living in South Africa and especially when planning to venture off the beaten track.

The first chapter in this book will give you some background into the land, its culture and its inhabitants so you will settle in more easily. Knowing the most important facts about the country and its people will help to create a better understanding of how and why things are done in South Africa. Now enjoy your journey and make the best of your stay.

Why South Africa?

Prime housing options

Attractive schooling facilities

First-class private healthcare

Healthy food and diet options

Easy integration into communities

Excellent work/life balance

Rich scenery and pleasant climate

(Source: HSBC Expat Explorer, 2012)

 Borders

Namibia,
Botswana,
Zimbabwe,
Mozambique,
Lesotho,
Swaziland

 Political

Date of Full
Democracy:
27 April 1994
Government:
Constitutional
Democracy

 Connect

Internet Country
Code: .za
International Dialling
Code: +27

 Currency

1 Rand = 100 Cents
Notes: R200, R100,
R50, R20, R10

Timeline
of South Africa's
History

Ancient
History

**Hominid &
human fossils**
in South Africa date back
3.3 million years

Rock paintings
of the Bushmen (San)
date back 15 000 years

**The
Khoikhoi and San**
lived in the area of
present-day South Africa
for more than 4 000 years

**The Kingdom of
Mapungubwe**
reigns in the 11th century.

At this time, the
**first trade in gold and
ivory is recorded.**
Various precious artefacts
of the skilled craftsmen
date back to more than
900 years ago

Before the 15th century,
according to old maps,
Arabs, Indians and Chinese
are said to have explored
the African coastline

1652

**The first
Dutch settlement
is established**
at the Cape when
Jan van Riebeeck
sets up a refreshment
station for the Dutch
East India Company

1508

Englishman
**Sir Francis Drake
rounds the Cape**
and commented
on his voyage:
*'This Cape is a most
stately thing, and
the fairest Cape we
saw in the whole
circumference of
the earth'*

1488

The Portuguese
explorer,
**Bartholomeu Diaz
rounds the Cape**
and lands in Algoa Bay
(today Port Elizabeth)

Explorers
and Early
Settlement

1688

French
Huguenots arrive
at the Cape
and soon assimilate
the Dutch customs and
language

1795

The British
occupy the Cape
and the first fights
with the Dutch Boers
occur

1808

Slavery is
abolished
in South Africa

1815

King Shaka reigns
as Zulu king
and the forced migration
mfecane starts

1820

British settlers arrive in
the **Eastern Cape**

1907

Chinese labourers
are imported to work in
South African mines

1936

The Land Act
reorganises agricultural
land ownership
in favour of whites

1905

The
Cullinan diamond,
the largest rough
diamond in the world
is found

1910

The
Union of South Africa
is established,
combining the
British colonies with the
Boer republics

Louis Botha is elected
first prime minister.
Except in the Cape
Province and Natal, black
people are denied the
right to vote

1931

South Africa
abolishes the
gold standard

1899

The second
Anglo-Boer War
begins,
and fighting lasts
for three years

1930

White women
in South Africa get
the right to vote

1912

The ANC
(African National Congress)
is founded and
starts campaigning for
black rights

UNITY IN DIVERSITY

1927

The first
conservation area,
the Kruger Park,
is established.

The first
Immorality Act
prohibits sexual relations
between unmarried white
and black people

1893

Gandhi arrives
from India
and starts his 22-year
passive resistance
against discrimination

1913

The
Natives Land Act
confines black ownership
of land to only roughly
8% of the country

1886

Gold
is discovered
in the Witwatersrand near
today's Johannesburg,
and the gold rush starts

Expansion
and
Exploration

1914

South African troops
invade
German South West
Africa (Namibia)

1923

Discriminatory **pass laws**
force blacks to carry
passbooks to regulate their
movement in white areas

Apartheid and Resistance

1948

The National Party wins the general election;

the apartheid era begins

1949

Inter-racial marriages are prohibited

1950

The first of three **Group Areas Acts** creating separate residential and business areas for the different races are passed

1950

The first **National Resistance Day** is held in protest

1951

Homelands ('Bantustans') are established for black ethnic groups

1952

Pass laws restricting the movement and employment of black people are made more stringent

1961

South Africa becomes **a republic** and leaves the Commonwealth

1960

In a referendum a **narrow majority** of white voters vote for a republic

1960

The Sharpeville Massacre occurs, the ANC and PAC are banned and

Albert Luthuli becomes the first African to win a Nobel Peace Prize

1959

The **Pan African Congress (PAC)** is founded

1957

Coloured voters are taken off the common voters' roll

1955

The ANC's **Freedom Charter** is adopted, and **women march** to the Union Buildings in 1956 to protest against passes

1966

Prime Minister **Hendrik Verwoerd** (one of the architects of apartheid) is assassinated

1974

The UN starts **sanctions against** South Africa

1975

South Africa **invades Angola**

1976

The Soweto Riots begin when scholars protest against compulsory Afrikaans in schools

1984

The new **Tri-cameral Constitution** is adopted, allowing coloureds and Indians to vote for separate legislative houses

1991

President FW de Klerk openly opposes the apartheid system

and leads the way to the unbanning of struggle organisations and parties

1990

Nelson Mandela is released from prison

and the ANC is re-established

1987

Many countries announce **stronger sanctions** against South Africa

1986

The **trade union COSATU** (Congress of South African Trade Unions) is formed; the pass laws are abolished

1985

South Africa declares a **'state of emergency'**

Independence
and
Democracy

1993

FW de Klerk and Nelson Mandela receive the **Nobel Peace Prize**

1994

The **first free and democratic elections** are held on 27 April. The Government of National Unity is formed with Nelson Mandela as president

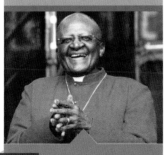

1996

The **Truth** and **Reconciliation Commission** is established and works until 2003 under the chairmanship of Archbishop Desmond Tutu to uncover the horrors of the apartheid years

---

2014

Cape Town is World **Design Capital**

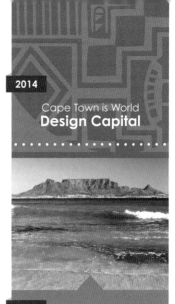

2012

Table Mountain

is voted as one of the 7 Wonders of Nature

2010

The **Soccer World Cup** is hosted in nine cities

2006

South Africa allows gay partnerships and legalises **same-sex marriages**

1997

The **new constitution** is approved by the National Assembly;

Nelson Mandela

retires

COAT OF ARMS

The coat of arms exemplifies creativity, strength, growth, fertility and unity, which inspire the nation to shine as brightly as the rising sun. The emblem also refers to the Khoisan people, who were the first inhabitants of the region.

Secretary Bird

The bird is a symbol of protection and a messenger bringing grace to the earth. The uplifted wings refer to the ascendance of the nation.

Spear & Knobkierie

Symbolise authority and defence. They are shown lying down to depict peace.

Ears of Wheat

As the emblem of fertility, they symbolise growth and development.

Motto

'!ke e: /xarra //ke', which means 'Unity in Diversity'

The motto derives from the ancient /Xam language of the San people and includes three of the four click sounds of the African language. It calls for the nation to unite in a common sense of belonging and national pride.

Rising Sun

A symbol of the rebirth and the source of life, light and the wholeness of humanity.

Protea

An emblem of the beauty of the land, it symbolises the flowering of the nation.

Shield & Figures

The shield shows both identity and spiritual defence. The two figures symbolise unity.

The images of the two people greeting each other are taken from the Linton Panel, a famous example of South African rock art now on display in Cape Town's Natural History Museum.

Elephant Tusks

The tusks symbolise wisdom and strength, moderation and eternity.

CONSTITUTION

South Africa's constitution is one of the most democratic and progressive constitutions in the world and enjoys high acclaim internationally. The constitution is the country's supreme law, and it was adopted after the first democratic elections in 1994 and came into effect in 1997.

We, the people of South Africa,
Recognise the injustices of our past;
Honour those who suffered for justice and freedom in our land;
Respect those who have worked to build and develop our country; and
Believe that South Africa belongs to all who live in it, united in our diversity.

We therefore, through our freely elected representatives, adopt this Constitution as the supreme law of the Republic so as to heal the divisions of the past and establish a society based on democratic values, social justice and fundamental human rights; Lay the foundations for a democratic and open society in which government is based on the will of the people and every citizen is equally protected by law; Improve the quality of life of all citizens and free the potential of each person; and Build a united and democratic South Africa able to take its rightful place as a sovereign state in the family of nations.

**May God protect our people.
Nkosi Sikelel' iAfrika.
Morena boloka setjhaba sa heso.
God seën Suid-Afrika.
God bless South Africa.
Mudzimu fhatutshedza Afurika.
Hosi katekisa Afrika.**

Bill of Rights

Everyone has a **basic human dignity,** which must be respected. You **cannot be discriminated against. Affirmative action and fair discrimination** are allowed. Everyone has the **right to life.** You have the right to use the **language of your choice** and practise your **own culture.** You have the right to a **basic education** in the official language of your choice. Your **right to privacy** includes your body, home and possessions. When arrested, you have the **right to remain silent,** to be brought before a court within 48 hours and the right to legal representation. You have the **right to think, believe and worship** however you may choose. You have the right to resolve legal disputes in a court or another impartial tribunal. You have the right to form, join and maintain **cultural, linguistic and religious groupings** of your own choice.

National **Anthem**

The South African anthem is a hymn of peace and reconciliation. It is the only anthem in the world that is made up of two anthems and combines five out of the eleven official languages (isiXhosa, isiZulu, Sesotho, Afrikaans and English).

The anthem is a combination of 'Nkosi sikelel' iAfrika' (God bless Africa) and 'Die Stem' van Suid Afrika' (The Call of South Africa). 'Nkosi sikelel' iAfrika' is a church hymn composed by Enoch Sontonga in 1897. The song was formerly used in the anthem of the ANC (African National Congress from 1925) and was sung during apartheid times as an act of defiance. Today this hymn is also used in the national anthems of Tanzania and Zambia. 'Die Stem' was written by CJ Langhoven in Afrikaans in 1918 and was the previous South African anthem. Now the new anthem is sung proudly by all South Africans at political meetings, national celebrations and at school assemblies.

Learn the text and
join in when everybody stands up and sings proudly.

National
Symbols

National **Flower**

King Protea
(Protea cynaroides)

This pink-coloured flower has the shape of a large artichoke (*cynara*). It grows on tall bushes and varies in size and colour. Proteas are most prominent in the Western Cape.

National **Tree**

Real Yellowwood
(Podocarpus latifolius)

This broad-leaved evergreen tree species grows up to 40 m (131 ft) in height and is not only among the tallest trees in the world but also the oldest. This tree species is protected in South Africa and antique furniture made of its wood is highly valued.

National **Animal**

Springbok
(Antidorcas marsupialis)

These small gazelles or antelopes grow up to 75 cm (2.5 ft) in height and are known for their jumps (Afrikaans: *spring* means jump and *bok* means buck or antelope). They can leap up to 4 m (13 ft) in height and 15 m (50 ft) in length.

Nkosi sikelel' iAfrika	*Lord, bless Africa*
Maluphakanyisw' uphondo lwayo,	*May her spirit rise high up*
Yizwa imithandazo yethu,	*Hear thou our prayers*
Nkosi sikelela, thina lusapho lwayo.	*Lord bless us.*
Morena boloka setjhaba sa heso,	*Lord, bless Africa*
O fedise dintwa le matshwenyeho,	*Banish wars and strife*
O se boloke, O se boloke setjhaba sa heso,	*Lord, bless our nation*
Setjhaba sa South Afrika – South Afrika.	*Of South Africa.*
Uit die blou van onse hemel,	*Ringing out from our blue heavens*
Uit die diepte van ons see,	*From our deep seas breaking round*
Oor ons ewige gebergtes,	*Over everlasting mountains*
Waar die kranse antwoord gee.	*Where the echoing crags resound.*
Sounds the call to come together,	*Sounds the call to come together,*
And united we shall stand,	*And united we shall stand,*
Let us live and strive for freedom,	*Let us live and strive for freedom,*
In South Africa our land.	*In South Africa our land.*

National **Fish**

Galjoen
(Dichistius capensis)

Endemic to South African waters, this small fish is well known by anglers as it keeps mostly to shallow waters. Its colour changes from black when near rocks to silver bronze when in sandy areas. The galjoen is also known as black bream or black fish.

National **Bird**

Blue Crane
(Anthropoides paradiseus)

This elegant bird gets up to one metre tall and has a long neck, long legs and light blue-grey wings. This endangered crane species is almost entirely restricted to South Africa and there are only about 25 000 of these birds still living in South Africa.

National **Flag**

*The flag was
first flown in 1994*

The flag was introduced when Nelson Mandela became the country's first ever democratically elected president. It is the only flag in the world with six colours. The flag should be flown with the red on top and the black on the left.

PUBLIC HOLIDAYS

South Africa has 12 public holidays per year, more than most other countries around the world! Although religious holidays of the various different faiths are celebrated throughout the year, only the Christian holidays of Christmas in December and Easter in March or April are recognised as official public holidays. Followers of other faiths still celebrate their religious holidays, like Eid, Diwali or Rosh Hashanah, and some offices or schools might be closed for these holy days. The remembrance public holidays, which commemorate the country's history, are explained below. As a general rule, when a public holiday falls on a Sunday, the following Monday becomes a public holiday. Christmas Day and Easter are the only days in South Africa when almost all shops are closed. On any of the other public holidays, the Sunday shopping hours usually apply.

Public Holidays

New Year's Day	1 January
Human Rights Day	21 March
Good Friday	Easter Friday
Family Day	Easter Monday
Freedom Day	27 April
Workers' Day	1 May
Youth Day	16 June
National Women's Day	9 August
Heritage Day	24 September
Day of Reconciliation	16 December
Christmas Day	25 December
Day of Goodwill	26 December

Human Rights Day
21 March

In 1960, 69 people were killed in Sharpeville in a demonstration against apartheid. The event was marked as a turning point in the fight for democracy. On this day in 1994, the Human Rights Commission was officially launched and the new Bill of Rights was instituted. The holiday highlights the value of the rights of all South Africans affirming human dignity, equality and freedom.

Freedom Day
27 April

In 1950 the apartheid government instituted the Group Areas Act. Under this law, non-whites were forced to live in areas separate from whites and from other non-whites. On this day people celebrate the end of apartheid and the beginning of democracy in South Africa. They recommit to ensuring democracy and living equality for all.

Workers' Day
1 May

Workers' Day is celebrated worldwide by socialist and labour movements. Workers' Day became official in South Africa after the first democratic elections in 1994, when the government recognised the role played by trade unions, the Communist Party and labour groups who fought against apartheid.

Heritage Day
24 September

After 1994 a holiday was created that would forge a new identity for all South Africans and create unity from diversity. Heritage Day highlights the histories of all racial groups and recognises the contributions of all the men and women who have contributed to the heritage and culture of the nation.

Youth Day
16 June

In 1976 learners around the country demonstrated against the apartheid system's unfair education conditions. In Soweto, police opened fire on 20 000 students, killing 12-year-old Hector Pieterson and 61 others. The day marks the valuable contribution of all young people in the establishment of democracy and the role of education in the future.

Day of Reconciliation
16 December

The Day of Reconciliation focuses on South Africa's triumph in overcoming the conflicts of the past and building a new nation. The constitution recognises South Africans' diversity - South Africans celebrate their harmony and recommit to continued reconciliation and nation building with an emphasis on equality, mutual respect and a shared future.

National Women's Day
9 August

On this day in 1956, 20 000 women, white and black, marched to the Union Buildings in Pretoria to protest against further restrictions in the apartheid laws. Petitions with more than 100 000 signatures were delivered to Prime Minister Strijdom's door. Women's Day celebrates the contribution made by women to society and the achievements made for women's rights.

PEELE

South Africa and its history teach us that the freedom and integrity of the people cannot be undermined and that people of so many different cultural backgrounds can indeed live together in harmony when all learn to speak with one strong voice against oppression and exploitation. Despite the deep scars from the turbulent past, most South Africans today are optimistic about the future. Like other countries worldwide, South Africa experiences problems including environmental, crime and health issues, although the people managed the recent economic recession with strengths that were praised by many.

Many different ethnic groups live together in South Africa, each with their various traditions and cultures. Archbishop Desmond Tutu coined the term 'The Rainbow People of God' for the South African people and their rich cultural diversity. President Nelson Mandela subsequently described South Africa as the 'Rainbow Nation' to reflect the multicultural heritage of a united South Africa in contrast to the apartheid ideology. Affirmative action measures apply in many instances and a significant amount of controversy around racial policies and practices is still evident.

The African (Black) population group consists of four major ethnic subgroups: The Nguni, the Sotho-Tswana, the Venda and the Tsonga people. The largest group are the Nguni people, which includes the Zulu, Xhosa, Swazi and Ndebele. The Sotho-Tswana group comprises the Southern Sotho (Basotho), the Northern Sotho (Pedi) and Western Sotho (Tswana) people, who are mainly in the Free State and neighbouring Lesotho. The Venda mainly live in the Limpopo Province in the far north of South Africa near the Zimbabwean border. The Tsonga live mainly in the north-east of the country bordering Swaziland and Mozambique.

The Caucasian (White) are descendants of settlers mainly from the European countries. The majority of English speakers are descendants from the British settlers and the Afrikaners are

Population	Age Distribution	Life Expectancy	Languages
51.8 million 60.7% urban population 40.2 people per km² Growth rate: 1.2%	Two thirds of the population is younger than 30 years	Life Expectancy at birth (2013) - males: 57.7 years - females: 61.4 years	11 Official Languages: Afrikaans, English and nine indigenous languages

The Soweto Gospel Choir

the descendants of Dutch, German and French settlers who came into the country in the 17th century. The Afrikaner heritage is upheld with various traditions, particularly in the farming communities. There are also other immigrant groups, such as the Italians, Portuguese, Greeks and Jews.

Today the term 'Coloured' is used for anyone of mixed racial ancestry. Originally it was the name given to the descendants of the early slaves who were brought from East and Central Africa and South-East Asia, or descendants of the indigenous Khoisan and whites. The Cape Coloureds spoke Malaysian and settled mainly in or around Cape Town. The coloured people of the Western Cape have the most diverse ancestry in the world and show 'the highest levels of intercontinental admixture of any global population' (Tishkoff, 2009).

Of the Indian (Asian) people, many are descendants of the indentured labourers who were brought to South Africa in the 19th and 20th centuries as sugar cane cutters in KwaZulu-Natal. The various Indian cultures are still very much alive in their communities. The Chinese population is growing in many parts of the country, particularly in recent years.

Ethnic Groups

African (Black)
79.2%
41 000 938 million

Coloured
8.9%
4 615 401 million

Caucasian (White)
8.9%
4 586 838 million

Indian (Asian)
2.5%
1 286 930 million

(Source: Statistics SA, Census 2011)

 Poverty

50% live below the poverty line

 HIV/Aids

Prevalence:12.3% of the total population receive anti-retroviral (ARV) drugs

 Unemployment

25% are officially unemployed

 Literacy

89% of the adult population can read and write

The small group of the **Venda**, with only 880 000 Tshivenda speakers, live in northern Limpopo. They are known for their rich traditions and for their culture of respect and morality. Artists are well respected in their communities where tribal meetings still play an important role.

The **Xhosa**, the second biggest ethnic group with 7.7 million speakers, live mainly in the Eastern and Western Cape. A patriarchal society, they have strong cultural traditions. They use clay paint on their faces for many purposes. Their language is recognisable by its click sounds.

The **Basotho** people live mainly in the kingdom of Lesotho and the Free State. There are 3.2 million Sesotho speakers. They are easily identified by the straw hats and coloured patterned blankets they traditionally wear. These blankets denote their cultural identity.

Most of the 3.7 million **Pedi** live in Mpumalanga and Limpopo, and they are renowned for their crafts and rich history. They speak Sepedi or Sesotho sa Leboa (North Sotho) Their unique music and the *kibo* dance originate from their rich cultural traditions.

The **Zulu**, South Africa's biggest ethnic group, with 9.2 million, live mostly in KwaZulu-Natal. They call themselves the 'people of the heavens'. Their language, isiZulu, is understood by almost half the South African population. The Zulu still have their own king and have strong religious beliefs. Their origins can be traced back as far as 1550.

The **Khoisan**, which are comprised of the Khoikhoi and the San (Bushmen), were displaced from their land by black migrants and white settlers. Of these early civilizations only a few people are now found. Most of these people belong to the Nama and live in the Northern Cape. Today there are only between 30 000 and 55 000 San people and they still live a semi-nomadic lifestyle. In recent years, they have been given back ownership of parts of their land.

Indigenous
Cultures

The 3.4 million **Tswana**-speaking people live predominantly in the north-western regions of the country. Their ancient stone settlements date back to 1600. Their culture is based on village democracy, where they openly discuss local affairs within the community.

The **Ndebele** have their roots mainly in Mpumalanga and Limpopo. Their homes are recognised by colourful geometric patterns, which are done freehand. Their beadwork shows creative craftmanship. There are 600 000 isiNdebele speakers in South Africa.

Most of the 1.5 million **Tsonga** live in the Limpopo lowveld. They also include the Shangaans and other smaller population groups. They had chiefdoms and the line of succession is through brothers not sons. A huge drum announces special occasions and is used to call villagers to meetings. They are also famous for the traditional gumboot dance.

The **Swazi** live in the Mpumalanga region bordering Swaziland. SiSwati is spoken by 1 million South Africans. Their celebrations are well known for their praise singing and dancing, and their annual reed dance attracts hundreds of visitors.

IMMIGRANTS

Although this is a listing of the largest and oldest immigrant communities in the country, in recent years South Africa is home to immigrants with all sorts of cultural backgrounds, such as Russians, Greeks, Taiwanese, Nigerians and Ghanaians. Numerous asylum seekers and illegal immigrants from African countries such as Somalia, Nigeria and Zimbabwe have also made South Africa their home.

Portuguese

Bartholomew Diaz (or Bartolomeu Dias) from Portugal was the first European explorer to set foot on the southern African continent in 1488. Because of the storms that prevailed around the Cape Peninsula when he passed he only managed to land in Mossel Bay, where he erected a *padrao* or cross. A statue in Cape Town of Bartholomew Diaz commemorates the event. In the 20th century many of the Portuguese immigrants came from the island of Madeira and settled near the coast, where they built fishing villages. When the Portuguese withdrew from their African colonies after 1976, many of their people came to South Africa.

Germans

Most of the German immigrants came during the 19th century and settled mainly in KwaZulu-Natal, where there are still many German communities. These early settlers were missionaries, farmers and artisans who set up flourishing communities in rural areas. After the Crimean War, German mercenaries coming to the Cape were supported in settling in Africa. Today, the fourth or fifth generations often do not speak German as they are completely assimilated into Afrikaner or English cultures. You can still notice the German influence in the towns of Hermannsburg, Wartburg and Wupperthal.

Jewish

Although non-Christian settlers were banned in the early Cape Colony, some of the first European settlers were of Jewish faith. Only after religious freedom was granted in the Cape Colony in 1803 did more Jewish settlers arrive. The Jewish settlers often were highly skilled businessmen and brought with them trading and financial expertise. They helped create the infrastructure for trade and helped the republic prosper. Many Jewish settlers came from Eastern Europe during World War II. The Jewish were well known for opposing the apartheid regime. Vocal freedom fighters were Helen Suzman, Joe Slovo and Denis Goldberg.

Indians

Most of the Indians in South Africa came as indentured labourers to work on the sugar cane fields from as early as the1860s and eventually settled in the region around Durban. In the 1920s, traders mainly from Gujarat arrived in the country as so-called 'passenger Indians' who paid their own fare for the voyage to South Africa. This population group still has a distinct ethnic identity, and today South Africa has the world's largest population of Indian descent outside of India. About 80% of the 1.15 million Indians live in KwaZulu-Natal, and most of them belong to Tamil or Hindi speaking communities. Mahatma Gandhi arrived in Durban in 1893. By the time he left in 1914 he had developed his philosophy of passive resistance. His statue stands in Pietermaritzburg, KwaZulu-Natal.

French

After the Edict of Nantes was revoked in 1687 French Protestants, known as the Huguenots, came to South Africa, fleeing Europe for religious reasons. The French brought knowledge and skills in agriculture and viticulture and helped the fledgling vineyards in the Cape Colony reach new heights when they brought their vines with them. Best known for its French influence is Franschhoek, which means 'French corner'. Nowadays, the only remaining reminders of the French influence are Afrikaans family names such as Du Plessis, Le Roux, Marais, Du Toit and others.

Italians

Italians settled in the country from as early as the 1860s when they fled from the struggles for independence in Italy. Later, many Italians were brought to South Africa as prisoners of war during World War II. The skilled Italian craftsmen and engineers were sought after to help build the infrastructure of the country, such as the Du Toit's Kloof Pass in the Western Cape, the Orange River Irrigation System in Upington and the railway lines in KwaZulu-Natal. In more recent years, many Italians have arrived to enrich the country with their contributions to the culinary scene.

Dutch

The first Dutch settlers arrived in Table Bay in the 1650s. Larger numbers arrived during the 17th and early 18th centuries from the Netherlands. Having been promised free passage and their own piece of land, many arrived with high hopes. The Dutch held control of the Cape for well over a century before relinquishing it to the British early in the 19th century. During the Great Trek movement in the 1830s and 1840s many Dutch immigrants moved inland to establish their own communities. The local Dutch identity developed into that of the Afrikaner. Cape Dutch architecture is very prominent and many streets and towns, such as Stellenbosch, were named after Dutch settlers. A statue of the first European to settle at the Cape, Jan van Riebeeck, stands on Heerengracht Street in Cape Town.

Chinese

The first Chinese in the country were very small groups of convicts and company slaves of the Dutch East India Company who settled in the Cape in the 17th century. Between 1880 and 1920 many Chinese were imported to colonial South Africa as indentured labourers to work in the gold mines, but virtually all were returned to China. The few Chinese who stayed behind set up shops and became traders. These Chinese were considered 'coloured' and subjected to discriminatory apartheid laws. South Africa's only Chinese township is located in Port Elizabeth. Today there are estimated to be over a million Chinese immigrants living in South Africa, the majority of whom immigrated during the last two decades as entrepreneurs and investors.

British

In 1795 the British took military control of the Cape in order to protect their interests in India. They later withdrew, but returned in 1806 and annexed the Cape as a British colony, bringing in some 5000 settlers. British rule upset many of the Dutch settlers, who moved eastwards and then, after the arrival of more British settlers in 1820, migrated into the interior during the Great Trek. In the late 1840s and early 1850s another immigration programme brought more British settlers to Natal. With the discoveries of diamonds, gold and coal, more English speaking people came to South Africa. At the end of the second Anglo-Boer War in 1902 Britain assumed control of the whole of South Africa.

LANGUAGES

South Africa is a multilingual society and many people speak at least one language over and above their home language. There are 11 official languages, but you will encounter many South African residents and descendants of immigrants who can also speak languages other than the official ones. Almost all young people can speak either English or Afrikaans. Road signs, directions, printed advertising material, forms and timetables are published in these two languages. In rural areas, however, you might encounter those that speak only the local language and some knowledge of local languages will come as a big advantage.

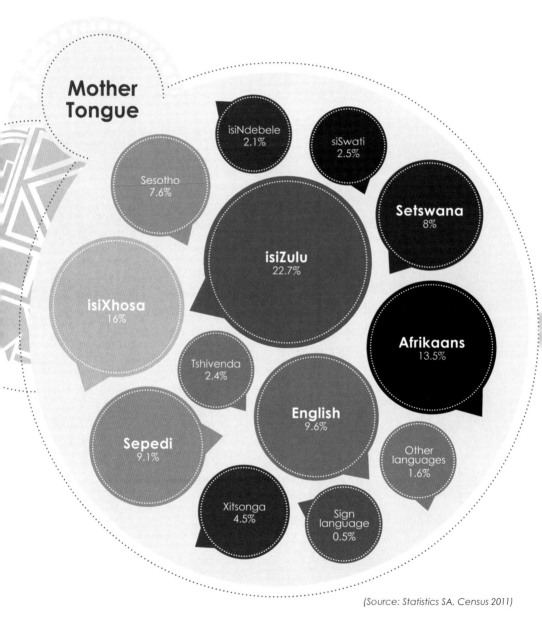

Mother Tongue

- isiNdebele 2.1%
- siSwati 2.5%
- Sesotho 7.6%
- Setswana 8%
- isiZulu 22.7%
- isiXhosa 16%
- Afrikaans 13.5%
- Tshivenda 2.4%
- English 9.6%
- Sepedi 9.1%
- Other languages 1.6%
- Xitsonga 4.5%
- Sign language 0.5%

(Source: Statistics SA, Census 2011)

Afrikaans

Afrikaans was officially recognised in 1925. It replaced Dutch as one of the two official languages and is the third most common language in South Africa. It is the first language of more than 60% of South African whites, more than 80% of the coloured population and also for some smaller sections of the black population. With 7 million speakers, it is the home language for only 13.5% of the overall South African population. Most of its speakers live in the Western Cape, Gauteng and the Free State. Afrikaans is also the dominant language in the Northern Cape, where it is spoken by almost 70% of the population on a daily basis.

Afrikaans is the only Germanic language with roots outside Europe's borders. The language stems from the High Dutch spoken in the Netherlands in the 1600s and evolved over time into a new language with inflections, vocabulary and structures influenced by the various cultural groups living in the Cape settlement. Afrikaans and modern Dutch actually share around 85% of their vocabulary; but the Afrikaans vocabulary also includes many words derived from other languages including German, French, English, Malay and various indigenous African languages. English is certainly a dominant influence and many people mix Afrikaans and English when talking.

English

English is the most widely spoken and understood language in South Africa. It is the main language taught as first and second language in schools and the primary language in business, commerce and government. However, only 9.6% of all South Africans refer to it as their home language. Most English home language speakers are found in KwaZulu-Natal, Gauteng and the Western Cape.

South African English is a dialect, which is spoken throughout South Africa, with unique slang words and its own tone and meanings. South Africans speak English, but that does not mean you will always understand what is said. Many of the slang words come from Afrikaans, European and African languages.

Languages at **Work**
Interaction with Supervisors

English: **40**%
Afrikaans: **28**%
isiZulu: **11**%

Languages at **School**
Medium of Teaching

English: **80**%
Afrikaans: **16**%
isiZulu: **6**%

(Source: PanSALB, 2002)

Afrikaans is the youngest language in the world and is spoken as first or second language by around 20 million speakers worldwide, most of them living in South Africa, Namibia, Botswana and Zimbabwe.

Indigenous African Languages

Nguni languages are isiZulu, isiXhosa, isiNdebele and siSwati, and Nguni speakers, who make up almost half of the South African population, tend to understand each other when speaking any of the Nguni languages.

isiZulu, the language spoken by the Zulu people, is the most widely spoken African language in South Africa and is the home language of almost a quarter of the South African population. isiZulu speakers mainly live in the KwaZulu-Natal and Gauteng provinces.

isiXhosa, the mother tongue of 16% of South Africa, is the most widely spoken home language in the Western and Eastern Cape. It is also the most widely dispersed home language and you will find isiXhosa speakers in all provinces. Like isiZulu, this language is spoken with three basic click sounds, which developed from the Khoisan language. The language uses tone and inflection to distinguish words. The language has 13 dialects.

The Sotho languages are Sepedi (Northern Sotho), Sesotho (Southern Sotho) and Setswana. People speaking one of these languages are able to converse with somebody speaking one of the other Sotho languages. The spread of these languages is limited mainly to the Limpopo and the North West provinces.

The indigenous Khoi, Nama and San languages are recognised in the constitution but are not official languages. One of the old Khoisan languages, /Xam is honoured on the South African coat of arms. The numbers of speakers of these languages are in decline and, although the language is not taught at any schools, some communities strongly uphold the traditions of the 'click' languages. A few thousand Nama speakers are located in Namaqualand and along the Orange River in the Northern Cape. Around 5 000 Khoisan speakers live in the region around Kimberley, where there is even a Khoisan radio station.

How to **Say Hello**

Goeie Môre — Good morning in Afrikaans

Molo — isiXhosa

Sawubona — isiZulu and siSwati

Dumela — Sepedi, Sesotho and Setswana

Ndaa — Tshivenda

Lotjhani — isiNdebele

Avuxeni — Xitsonga

Pidgin Languages

In South Africa, *Fanagalo* and *Tsotsitaal* are recognised pidgin languages. *Fanagalo* is a pidgin dialect spoken mainly by mine workers. The language is based on various indigenous languages and is mostly used to facilitate communication between the workers and their supervisors. It is a simplified version of isiZulu and isiXhosa and incorporates English and Portuguese words as well.

Tsotsitaal is a language mix from Afrikaans, English and African languages. Its name derives from the word '*tsotsi*' meaning gangster and '*taal*' meaning language in Afrikaans. This language is a very dynamic pidgin with a constantly evolving vocabulary. It is spoken mainly in the townships to ease communication between different African language groups. *Tsotsitaal* is also known and referred to as *Iscamtho*.

RELIGION

The constitution affords every South African freedom of conscience, religion, thought, belief and opinion. About 80% of South Africa's population describe themselves as being Christian. Other religions include Islam, Hinduism, Judaism, Buddhism and other beliefs.

Whilst the Christian religious holidays of Easter and Christmas are official public holidays, religious holidays are respected and celebrated across the cultures. Religious traditions are openly practised and many belong to religious communities and attend regular meetings and services. More than 56% of the population attend regular services in church, compared to an average of 26% churchgoers in other countries in the world. Friday prayers are observed by the country's Muslim population.

The City of Grahamstown has more than 40 churches and is known in South Africa as the 'City of Saints'. It is said that the Juma Masjid Mosque in Durban, which can accommodate about 6 000 worshippers, is the largest mosque in the southern hemisphere. The Nan Hua Buddhist Temple in Bronkhorstspruit is believed to be the largest Buddhist temple outside Asia.

The indigenous religions of the country include that of the San people and the African traditional religion. The San people believe there is a good and powerful God and they pray through a healer who is known as a shaman. They also perform important religious rituals, such as the trance dance. The African traditional religion is associated with ancestor worship.

The Zion Christian Church (ZCC), with roughly 5 million members, has the biggest following of all churches in the country. The ZCC headquarters are located in Zion City Moria in Limpopo province. Every Easter more than one million followers from all over the country make an annual pilgrimage to the ZCC headquarters. The members of this church can be easily recognised as they often wear a metal Star of David on a green ribbon pinned to their clothing.

St Michael and St George Cathedral in Grahamstown

Juma Masjid Mosque in Durban

Nan Hua Buddhist Temple in Bronkhorstspruit

The Union Buildings in Pretoria are the seat of the national government and house the offices of the South African president. The building was designed by Sir Herbert Baker in 1908.

GOVERNMENT AND POLITICS

South Africa has been a constitutional democracy since its first free elections in 1994, after the abolition of apartheid. South Africans over the age of 18 are eligible to vote, provided they are registered on the voters' roll. South African citizens living abroad can register to cast their votes in national elections in the foreign representations of South Africa.

Elections are held every five years in South Africa, when the voters elect the National Assembly by a system of proportional franchise. The National Assembly elects the president, who is normally the leader of the majority party.

Government is a three-tier system of national, regional and local governments. South Africa's government differs from other Commonwealth nations in that it is defined in the constitution as having 'distinctive, interdependent and interrelated' authorities.

Also unique to the country is that, in addition to the three-tier democratic system, the constitution allows for a system of traditional leadership that includes its own legislation pertaining to indigenous traditional law. Currently there are provincial houses of traditional leaders in six provinces: the Eastern Cape, KwaZulu-Natal, the Free State, Mpumalanga, Limpopo and the North West.

Seven kingships are acknowledged in South Africa on the basis of the Traditional Leadership and Governance Framework Act. In 2010 a separate Department of Traditional Affairs was added to the cabinet. The kings in South Africa have a cultural role and are seen as the custodians of the indigenous culture and traditions of their communities. The seven kingships are those of the abaThembo, amaXhosa, amaMpondo, amaZulu, amaNdebele wakwa Ndzundza, amaNdebele wakwa Manala and VhaVenda. Although the kingships all are funded and supported by the South African taxpayers and donations, the king of the amaZulu, King Zwelithini Zulu, is regarded by many as the most prominent.

There are two houses of parliament: the National Assembly and the National Council of Provinces. The head of state is the president, who is elected by the National Assembly, which consists of about 400 members and is presided over by the speaker. The cabinet consists of the president, the deputy president and the ministers. The president can select any number of ministers from the members of the National Assembly. Therefore, the number of ministries has varied since 1994. Currently there are 34 ministries in operation in South Africa.

In South Africa there are nine provincial parliaments, 283 municipalities and nine metropolitan municipalities. These are responsible for infrastructure and public services such as electricity, water and sanitation. They also oversee budgets for community services, such as recreational and cultural services and educational facilities, the municipal police services and social welfare institutions. Municipalities also impose property rates. The nine metropolitan municipalities are: Buffalo City (East London), City of Cape Town, Ekurhuleni (East Rand), City of eThekwini (Durban), City of Johannesburg, Mangaung Municipality (Bloemfontein), Msunduzi Municipality (Pietermartizburg), Nelson Mandela Metropolitan Municipality (Port Elizabeth) and City of Tshwane (Pretoria).

There are currently thirteen parties represented in the South African government. The majority of the 400 seats in parliament are currently held by the ANC (African National Congress). The party holds 66% of the seats and also has the majority of power in eight of South Africa's nine provinces. The biggest opposition party, the Democratic Alliance or DA, holds less than 17% in the National Assembly. However, the DA is the strongest party in the Western Cape, where it controls most of the local municipalities.

Parliament meets in both Cape Town and Pretoria, although the seat of government is in Pretoria. Cabinet meetings take place in Cape Town while parliament is in session there from January until June and in Pretoria the rest of the year.

Parties in Parliament

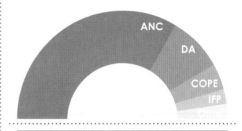

ANC
DA
COPE
IFP

400 Seats in the National Assembly 2012

African National Congress (ANC)
264 seats

Democratic Alliance (DA)
67 seats

Congress of the People (COPE)
30 seats

Inkatha Freedom Party (IFP)
18 seats

Other
21 seats

Parliament Buildings in Cape Town

COUNTRY

South Africa is the southernmost country in Africa and one of the biggest countries on the continent. The country covers a larger land area than France and Spain combined. South Africa shares borders with Namibia, Botswana and Zimbabwe in the west and the north, with Mozambique and Swaziland in the east and with the mountain kingdom of Lesotho, which is completely surrounded by South Africa.

Three distinct landscape forms dominate: the highveld or interior plateau, the escarpment and the coastal plains. Most of the country lies on a plateau with heights of 1 200 metres or more above sea level. The high plateau, which is renowned for the desert plains and bushveld or savannah vegetation, stretches up north and reaches west to the Kalahari desert and south to the Karoo. The escarpment, including the mountain ranges, divides the highveld from the lowveld. These mountain ranges, with their awe-inspiring waterfalls and dramatic rock formations, boast spectacular scenery.

South Africa has eight magnificent World Heritage Sites and boasts many iconic places such as Table Mountain, which was chosen as one of the world's New 7 Wonders of Nature. Some of the oldest rock formations in the world are found in the Barberton Mountains in the Northern Drakensberg, which make the mountain range older than the Himalayas or the Alps. The Blyde River Canyon in Mpumalanga is the third largest canyon in the world after the Grand Canyon in the USA and the Fish River Canyon in Namibia. There are numerous other geographical superlatives, which are shown in the table below.

Longest River	**Highest Waterfall**	**Oldest Mountains**	**Highest Peak**
The Orange (Gariep) River is 2 250 km (1 398 miles) long	The Tugela Falls are 948 m (3 110 ft) high and are Africa's highest waterfalls	The Barberton Mountains are more than 3.2 billion years old	Mafadi Peak at 3 451 m (11 322 ft) is located in the Drakensberg

Hole in the Wall, Eastern Cape

South Africa's climate is influenced by the country's topography and the currents of the Atlantic and Indian oceans along the coast. The country lies between 22 degrees and 34 degrees south latitude and is thus mostly south of the Tropic of Capricorn. Overall, South Africa has a temperate climate and the conditions are predominantly warm and sunny. However the climatic conditions vary according to seasons and location. South Africa has on average 8.5 hours of daily sunshine. According to the UK's National Physical Laboratory, Cape Town has the fifth best blue sky in the world.

South African standard time is UTC plus 2 hours. The country has only one time zone and does not adhere to daylight saving so there are considerable differences in daylight time between east and west. Sunrise and sunset in Cape Town are about an hour later than in Durban. The longest day of the year, the summer solstice on 21 December, has around 14.5 hours of sunshine and the winter solstice around 21 June has 10.5 daylight hours.

Climate

Temperate

The highveld experiences wide temperature ranges with distinct seasons.

Subtropical

In the south-eastern parts of South Africa, temperatures are warmer with high humidity levels.

Desert

The north-western parts of the country experience a dry desert climate with dramatic temperature variations.

Mediterranean

In the south-west a mild Mediterranean climate prevails. Winter rainfall occurs in this region.

 Oldest Caves

The Sudwala Caves were first inhabited over 200 million years ago

 Largest Canyon

The Blyde River Canyon is the largest green canyon in the world

 Largest Estuary

The iSimangeliso Wetland is the largest estuarine system in Africa

 Longest Caves

The Cango Caves are the longest underground caves in Africa

TEMPERATURES AND SEASONS

Spring
Sep, Oct, Nov

Summer
Dec, Jan, Feb

Autumn
Mar, Apr, May

Winter
Jun, Jul, Aug

The seasons in South Africa are opposite to those in the northern hemisphere. There are four noticeable seasons but the coastal regions of South Africa experience less seasonal change than the interior.

The rainy season in most parts of South Africa is during summer, with the exception of the Western Cape, which is a winter-rainfall area. There is a saying that in some regions of South Africa you can experience four seasons in one day, especially during spring and autumn. Be prepared for the quick weather changes by dressing in layers.

The summers are mostly hot throughout the country, while the winters are generally mild during the day. Temperatures in summer mostly range between 25 °C/77 °F and 35 °C/95 °F during the day and between 15 °C/59 °F and 25 °C/77 °F at night. Even in winter, daytime temperatures throughout the country often reach 20 °C/70 °F.

Warm days, humidity and rainshowers can be experienced throughout the year along the coast between Eastern Cape and KwaZulu-Natal. The temperatures in this region are on average 6 °C/43 °F higher than in other parts of the country. As the northern coastline in KwaZulu-Natal and the north-eastern region receive more precipitation and are more humid, precautions against malaria should be taken there.

Seasonal **Temperature**	City	Summer min/max °C		Winter min/max °C	
	Bloemfontein	15	31	-2	17
	Cape Town	16	26	7	18
	Durban	21	28	11	23
	East London	18	26	10	21
	Johannesburg	15	26	4	17
	Kimberley	18	33	3	19
	Polokwane	17	28	4	20
	Port Elizabeth	18	25	9	20
	Pretoria	18	29	5	20
	Richards Bay	21	29	12	23
	Upington	20	36	4	21

WEATHER PHENOMENA

The 'Cape Doctor' is a strong south-easterly wind that is common from November until February along the Western Cape coast. It eases the heat of summer but sometimes makes sunbathing on the beach a breezy occasion. Beaches along Cape Town's southern seaboard, such as Camps Bay and Clifton, as well as Kalk Bay on the False Bay side are usually protected from the south-easterly winds. When the 'Cape Doctor' winds are blowing, Table Mountain has its famous 'table cloth', which is a blanket of clouds spreading over the mountain plateau. Northerly and north-westerly winds predominate in the Western Cape between April and September. A heavy cloud above Lions Head, which lies to the west of Table Mountain, usually predicts rain.

Electrical storms occur mainly in spring and summer. These strong thunderstorms are frequent on the highveld. The sight of lightning followed by thunder is very spectacular but can be rather frightening. As with all thunderstorms, take due care. Thunderstorms can also be associated with hail. Cover should be sought during hailstorms as they have been known to cause significant damage to motor vehicles.

Tornados can be observed in the mountainous areas of KwaZulu-Natal, Gauteng, the Free State and the northern parts of the Eastern Cape during the early evening in mid-summer. Damage is usually minimal. Cyclones affecting the southern Indian Ocean are occasionally experienced off the east coast. The impact of tropical storms with rough seas and flooding is, however, usually not severe.

Frost and very low winter temperatures occur mainly in the country's interior and at high altitudes at night. In the interior, temperatures can drop below 0 °C/32 °F during crisp and clear winter nights. In winter, the higher mountain ranges in the Drakensberg mountains and the Western Cape mountain peaks experience some snowfall, though it is seldom thick or long-lasting. The main ski resorts are in the southern Drakensberg mountains and in neighbouring Lesotho.

Table Cloth over Table Mountain

Electrical Storm in Gauteng

Snow in the Drakensberg

World Heritage Sites

iSimangaliso Wetland Park

The largest of the estuary systems in Africa with more than 220 km of coastline, the region around the St Lucia Wetlands is renowned for its pristine sand beaches, coral reefs, reed and papyrus wetlands. This area supports five ecosystems and is the habitat for more than 6 500 animal and plant species. Lake Sibaya, in the wetland, is South Africa's largest freshwater lake. The reefs of Sodwana Bay are among the world's top diving sites.

uKhahlamba Drakensberg Park

This combined natural and cultural heritage site has the largest and most concentrated collection of cave paintings and rock art in the Sub-Saharan region. The San people lived in this region for over 4 000 years and their paintings shed light on their spiritual life. The region is also known for its biodiversity and many endemic species. Many globally threatened species find a safe refuge in the area.

Robben Island

The island, off Cape Town, was used during various times as a maximum security prison. Many political prisoners were held here, the most famous being Nelson Mandela. The island symbolises the triumph of the human spirit, freedom and democracy over oppression and has a museum complex where former political prisoners give insightful tours to visitors.

Cape Floral Kingdom

Although the smallest of the six floral kingdoms in the world, the Cape Peninsula is one of the biodiversity hotspots as almost 70% of all the plant species are endemic. There are more plant species in the area per square metre than anywhere else in the world. These species include the fynbos and renosterveld vegetation. The Cape Floral Kingdom stretches from Cape Point to Grahamstown and up to the Olifants River.

Vredefort Dome

Over 2 000 million years old, this 190 km wide crater represents the oldest meteorite impact site in the world. It is also considered to be the world's largest and most deeply eroded impact site. The multi-ring landscape includes fabulous inner centre rings and hills around Vredefort and the outer ring near Johannesburg, roughly 120 km from the impact site.

Richtersveld

This unique arid landscape is still home to the nomadic Nama, often referred to as Bushmen, who are descendants of the Khoisan people. This group lived in the area for hundreds of years but were dispossessed after the European settlers arrived in the late 18th century. The land was redistributed to the people in 1990 and the Richterveld community conservancy was awarded heritage status in 2007.

Mapungubwe

Once the site of the first and largest kingdom in southern Africa and abandoned more than 400 years ago, this area still shows evidence of the once powerful trade centre that linked the African subcontinent with the East. By the end of the 13th century Mapungubwe was the most important settlement in Africa. A wealth of archaeological artefacts, such as glass beads and gold, and ruins of palaces, display the extraordinary skills of the indigenous people.

The Cradle of Humankind

This cultural heritage site is home to some of the world's most important fossil finds of our human ancestors, the hominids. Various caves in the area offer valuable insights into the evolution of mankind. The Sterkfontein Caves are home to the oldest and most continual paleontological dig in the world. The pre-human skull, known as 'Mrs Ples', dates back 2.3 million years, and the almost complete hominid skeleton called 'Little Foot' is more than 4 million years old. 'The Taung Child', a fossilised skull of a young child, was discovered in Taung in 1924 and is considered the first find linking the origins of humankind to the African continent.

FLORA

South Africa is renowned for its spectacular landscape and flora, and is one of the most biologically diverse countries in the world. After Indonesia and Brazil, the country houses the richest diversity of plant and animal species in the world. The vast majority of the land area in South Africa is used for crop cultivation or grazing of livestock. Less than 10% of the area is conserved. Some endemic species are under threat.

The country has eight biomes or unique ecological zones as shown in the map below: the Nama Karoo, succulent Karoo, fynbos, desert, Albany thicket, savannah, grassland and forest.

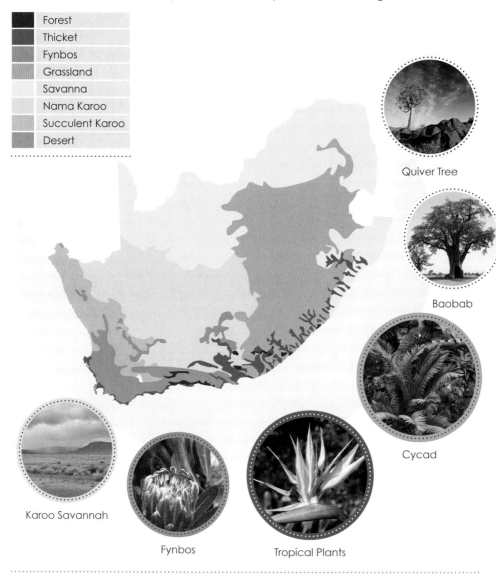

Forest
Thicket
Fynbos
Grassland
Savanna
Nama Karoo
Succulent Karoo
Desert

Quiver Tree

Baobab

Cycad

Karoo Savannah

Fynbos

Tropical Plants

South Africa is the only country in the world with an entire plant kingdom, the Cape Floral Kingdom, inside the country's borders.

FAUNA

In South Africa there are more animal species than in Europe and Asia or North and South America combined. There are more than 800 species of birds and almost 300 mammal species in the country. Some of the species found here are on the South African Endangered Species List. Endangered species such as the honey badger, the wild dog and the black rhino often find refuge in the many national parks and private game concessions.

Several dedicated conservation organisations such as the WWF and the Endangered Wildlife Trust are involved in creating awareness and protecting the rare local species.

Living in South Africa does not mean living in the wilderness. So, contrary to popular belief, lions do not roam the streets. However, living in one of South Africa's cosmopolitan cities can bring you close to nature, and you can experience an array of possible wildlife encounters. For example, baboons or monkeys live in certain city suburbs, and there are plenty of stray animals or creepy crawlies of all sizes. In rural areas or near townships, goats and cows graze on the roadside or cross the roads. You can even find cows lazing on the beaches of the Wild Coast in the Eastern Cape.

There are 175 species of scorpions in South Africa, most of which are harmless. In general, scorpions with a long thin tail are not venomous, but the smaller black scorpions with a short thick tail are poisonous. Anyone bitten by a scorpion should get immediate medical attention.

The most common spiders in South Africa are rather harmless but look very scary, such as the huge and hairy rain spider or the baboon spider (African tarantula). There are, however, some dangerous spiders, such as the button spider, which is small. Its venom can be harmful to adults and deadly to children.

There are more than a hundred species of snakes in South Africa. Although most of them are not poisonous, some are deadly, such as the neuro-toxic Cape cobra, the green boomslang, the puffadder and the green or black mamba. Cape cobras and puffadders can be encountered in the suburbs, especially if you live close to the sea and dunes or live near a national park.

South Africa is Home to...

The Oldest Creature
The coelacanth is a fish species that already lived 65 million years ago.

The Tallest Mammal
The giraffe grows up to 6 m tall and its neck, containing seven vertebrae, can be 2 m long.

The Fastest Mammal
The cheetah can run with speeds up to 113 km/h in short sprints and is a threatened species.

The Smallest Mammal
The pygmy shrew is only 8 cm long (including tail) and weighs less than 4 g.

Buffalos can often be spotted near waterholes in many of South Africa's national parks. They are usually in herds and are feared due to their aggressiveness.

Elephants are the largest land-based animals growing up to 3.7 m tall (shoulder height). They can become very protective and aggressive when they have young in the herd. Elephants live in tight-knit family herds and have an excellent memory.

Big Five

The term 'Big Five' was coined by game hunters to describe the power and strength of these five animals and the danger these trophy animals posed when being hunted on foot. Nowadays, these five animals are usually the ones that people most want to see when they visit South Africa.

Lions are only encountered in national parks and private game reserves. These animals live in prides, which are dominated by one male lion. You often see families with young lion cubs and you can hear lions roar from miles away at dawn and dusk when staying in one of the camps inside the national parks.

Rhinoceros are an endangered species in South Africa, as they are poached for their precious horn. There are white and black rhinos, and both are massive and strong. They cannot see well but have an excellent sense of smell.

Leopards are mostly restricted to game reserves and there are only a few left that roam freely in remote areas. They hunt at night and hide in or under trees during the day, so they are difficult to spot. They live mainly on craggy hillsides or rocky areas.

Baboons and monkeys

do roam in some of the suburbs, especially in rural areas or close to nature reserves. Both can get quite vicious when they feel threatened and can attack and bite. Take care when taking food on a hike in an area where chacma baboons or vervet monkeys are known to roam. In areas where baboons or monkeys live, never leave food visible in your house when doors or windows are open and never feed wild animals.

African penguins can sometimes be seen wandering through the streets near nesting spots in the Western Cape. At some beaches, such as Boulders Beach, you can swim and splash in the waters while the penguins swim right next to you.

Wildlife

Ostriches are the largest flightless birds and grow up to 2.7 m tall. They roam freely in many rural areas. Do not approach them or scare them. If an ostrich gets panicky and approaches you, lie flat on the earth. Ostriches can only kick forward, yet their kicks are powerful and can kill.

Crocodiles and **hippos** can occasionally be seen in some of KwaZulu-Natal's and Mpumalanga's rivers. They are found abundantly in the wetlands of, iSimangaliso where you also might encounter the hippopotamus wandering through the streets at night.

Buck and zebra
are common on farms and in rural areas.

RESOURCES

General Info

General Information: www.southafrica.info
Government Information: www.info.gov.za
Government Services: www.services.gov.za
Parliament: www.parliament.gov.za
Public Protector: www.publicprotector.org
Smart Cape: www.smartcape.org.za
SA Good News: www.sagoodnews.co.za
South Africa Government: www.gov.za
South Africa Tourism: www.southafrica.net
South Africa Yearbook: www.gcis.gov.za
Statistics SA: www.statssa.gov.za

Geography

Dept of Mineral Resources: www.dmr.gov.za
Dept of Environment: www.environment.gov.za
News: www.environment.co.za
Geological Society: www.gssa.org.za
Geo Council: www.geoscience.org.za
Heritage Sites: whc.unesco.org
Chamber of Mines: www.bullion.org.za

Parks & Reserves

National Parks: www.sanparks.co.za
KZN Parks: www.kznwildlife.com
Ezemvelo KZN Wildlife: www.ekznw.co.za

Biodiversity

Animal Welfare: www.nspca.co.za
Biodiversity Institute: www.sanbi.org
Cape Nature: www.capenature.org.za
Endangered Wildlife Trust: www.ewt.org.za
IUCN Redlist: www.iucnredlist.org
Rhinos: www.savetherhino.org
Spiders: www.spiderclub.co.za
Snakes: www.capesnakeconservation.com
Wildlife & Environment: www.wessa.org.za

Religion

Buddhist Retreat: www.brcixopo.co.za
Christian: www.christianrepublic.co.za
Council of Churches: www.sacc.org.za
Jewish Community: www.jewishsa.co.za
Muslim Portal: www.muslims.co.za
Hindu: www.sahms.org.za

Weather

Forecast: www.southafricanweather.co.za
Tides Reports: www.sanho.co.za
Surf Report: www.wavescape.co.za
Weather Service: www.weathersa.co.za
Wind Report: www.windreport.co.za

Recommended Reading

Campbell, Derryn (2010) *Awesome South Africa*. Durban: AwesomeSA Publishers

Friedman, Roger & Gool, Berry (2011) *The South African Story with Archbishop Desmond Tutu*. Johannesburg: Penguin

Joyce, Peter (2010) *Cultures of South Africa*. Cape Town: Sunbird Publishers

Harrison, Philip (2005) *South Africa's Top Sites: Arts & Culture*. Cape Town: Spearhead Press

Hopkins, Pat & Slabbert, Denise & Ngwenya, Bongiwe (2009) *South African Fact Book*. Johannesburg: Penguin

Marsh, Rob (2013) *All about South Africa*. Cape Town: Struik

Norman, Nick & Whitefield, Gavin (2009) *Geological Journeys: A Traveller's Guide to South Africa's Rock and Landforms*. Cape Town: Struik

Parker, Alexander & Richman, Tim (2012) *50 Flippen Brilliant South Africans*. Johannesburg: Jacana

SASOL Guides (1999) *First Field Guide Series: Various titles*. Cape Town: Struik

Sinclair, Ian, Hockey, Phil, Tarboton, Warwick & Ryan, Peter (2011) *SASOL Birds of Southern Africa*. Cape Town: Struik

Swart, Chris & Tilde (2000) *A Field Guide to Tracks & Signs of Southern and East African Wildlife*. Cape Town: Struik

Sycholt, August (2009) *EcoGuide: South African Destinations*. Pretoria: Briza Publishers

The Wildlife Guide of Southern Africa (2000) *A Field Guide to the Animals & Plants of the Region*. Cape Town: Struik

Van Lill, David (2013) *See South Africa*. Cape Town: Tafelberg Publishers

History

Apartheid: www.apartheidmuseum.org
District Six: www.districtsix.co.za
Heritage Resources: www.sahra.org.za
Justice & Reconciliation: www.ijr.org.za
Archives: www.national.archives.gov.za
National Arts Council: www.nac.org.za
National Library: www.nlsa.ac.za
Nelson Mandela: www.nelsonmandela.org
South African History: www.sahistory.org.za

Languages

General: www.africanlanguages.com
Language Board: www.pansalb.org.za
Languages Info: www.salanguages.com
EduSA: www.edusouthafrica.com
Sign Language: www.sled.org.za
Translations: www.translators.org.za
Various Languages: www.omniglot.com

Theme Parks

Gold Reef City: www.goldreefcity.co.za
Ratanga Junction: www.ratanga.co.za
Ushaka: www.ushakamarineworld.co.za

Arts & Culture

Dept of Arts & Culture: www.dac.gov.za
Heritage Council: www.nhc.org.za
General: www.everyculture.com
Art History: www.rebirth.co.za
Indian: www.indianspice.co.za
Ndebele: www.inkundla.net
San People: www.san.org.za
Sesotho: www.sesotho.org
Setswana: www.setswana.blogspot.com
Traditional Leaders: www.contralesa.org
Xhosa: www.xhosaculture.co.za
Zulu: www.zulu-culture.co.za

Cultural Villages

Botshabelo: www.botshabelo.org
Cata Village: www.cata.org.za
!Khwa ttu San Centre: www.khwattu.org
Lesedi African Village: www.lesedi.com
Ndebele: www.ndebelevillage.co.za
Phezulu: www.phezulusafaripark.co.za
Shangana: www.shangana.co.za
Xhosa: www.khaya-la-bantu-cultural-village.com
Zulu: www.shakaland.com

Movies to Watch

- *Invictus*
- *Sarafina*
- *Themba*
- *Tsotsi*
- *Zulu*
- *Spud*
- *Jock of the Bushveld*
- *Cry the Beloved Country*
- *Shuks Tshabalala's Survival Guide to South Africa*
- *Mandela: Long Walk to Freedom*

Tutu, Desmond (2006) *The Rainbow People of God*. Cape Town: Double Storey

Uys, Isabel (2009) *The South African Aid*. Pretoria: Protea Books

Books for Children

Clark, Nadine (2007) *Get Bushwise Series*. Cape Town: Struik

Latimer, Alex (2012) *The South African Alphabet*. Johannesburg: Penguin

Mandela, Nelson (2002) *Madiba Magic – Mandela's Favorite Stories*. Cape Town: NB Publishers

Mhlope, Gcina (2004) *Stories of Africa*. Durban: University of KZN Press

Stewart, Dianne & Heale, Jay (2008) *African Myths & Legends*. Cape Town: Struik

Books to Read

Coetzee, JM: *Disgrace*
Courtenay, Bryce: *The Power of One*
Gordimer, Nadine: *Burger's Daughter*
Krog, Antjie: *Country of My Skull*
Malan, Rian: *My Traitor's Heart*
Mandela, Nelson: *Long Walk to Freedom*
Mpe, Phaswane: *Welcome to our Hillbrow*
Otter, Steven: *Khayelitsha*
Paton, Alan: *Cry the Beloved Country*
Plaatje, Sol: *A Native Life in South Africa*
Schreiner, Olive: *The Story of an African Farm*
Van de Ruit, John: *Spud*

'Adventure is in the hearts and minds of all of us. It's a
matter of turning the key.' ~ *Kingsley Holgate, explorer*

PROVINCES

South Africa is divided into nine provinces. Each province has its own legislature, premier and executive council.

The nine provinces were formed in 1994 out of the four provinces (Transvaal, Orange Free State, Cape and Natal) that existed during the apartheid regime. The apartheid homelands in which most of the black population was forced to live during apartheid were also abolished in 1994.

All the provinces are divided into districts consisting of either metropolitan or district municipalities. These municipalities are responsible for infrastructure and public services, such as electricity, water, sanitation and municipal police services, in addition to imposing property rates and overseeing the community services budgets.

As you can see in the following chapter, each province has a very distinct landscape, people, economy and climate.

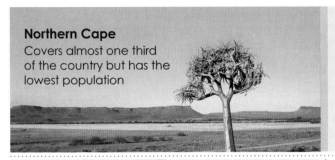

Northern Cape
Covers almost one third of the country but has the lowest population

Northern Cape (NC)
Capital: Kimberley
Population: 1.1 million
Population Density: 3/km²
Population Share: 2.2%
Area Share: 30.5%
Unemployment: 27.4%
Informal Housing: 13.1%
Private Schooling: 4.1%

Gauteng
The smallest province with the highest earning and population density

Gauteng (GP)
Capital: Johannesburg
Population: 12.3 million
Population Density: 675/km²
Population Share: 23.7%
Area Share: 1.4%
Unemployment: 26.3%
Informal Housing: 18.9%
Private Schooling: 16.7%

KwaZulu-Natal (KZN)
Capital: Pietermaritzburg
Population: 10.3 million
Population Density:109/km²
Population Share: 19.8%
Area Share: 7.7%
Unemployment: 33.0%
Informal Housing: 8.3%
Private Schooling: 4.6%

Limpopo (LP)
Capital: Polokwane
Population: 5.4 million
Population Density: 43/km²
Population Share: 10.4%
Area Share: 10.3%
Unemployment: 38.9%
Informal Housing: 5.2%
Private Schooling: 4.3%

Eastern Cape (EC)
Capital: Bhisho
Population: 6.6 million
Population Density: 39/km²
Population Share: 12.7%
Area Share: 13.8%
Unemployment: 37.4%
Informal Housing: 7.7%
Private Schooling: 4.5%

Mpumalanga (MP)
Capital: Mbombela/ Nelspruit
Population: 4.0 million
Population Density: 53/km²
Population Share: 7.8%
Area Share: 6.3%
Unemployment: 31.6%
Informal Housing: 10.9%
Private Schooling: 5.8%

North West (NW)
Capital: Mahikeng
Population: 3.5 million
Population Density: 34/km²
Population Share: 6.8%
Area Share: 8.7%
Unemployment: 31.5%
Informal Housing: 21.2%
Private Schooling: 5.5%

Western Cape (WC)
Capital: Cape Town
Population: 5.8 million
Population Density: 45/km²
Population Share: 11.2%
Area Share: 10.6%
Unemployment: 21.6%
Informal Housing: 18.2%
Private Schooling: 7.5%

Free State (FS)
Capital: Bloemfontein
Population: 2.7 million
Population Density: 21/km²
Population Share: 5.3%
Area Share: 10.6%
Unemployment: 32.6%
Informal Housing: 15.7%
Private Schooling: 6.4%

Western Cape
The province with the highest employment rate

WESTERN CAPE

The Western Cape is the oldest province in the country, and Cape Town, at the foot of Table Mountain, is often fondly referred to as the 'Mother City'. In 1652 the Dutch East India Company established a refreshment station at Table Bay for ships en route to South-East Asia. More European settlers arrived, and in the early 1800s the settlement was annexed by Britain as the Cape Colony. The oldest traces of *homo sapiens* in the region date back much further. Footprints of our ancestors found on Langebaan Beach some 150 km north of Cape Town show that people have lived in the area for more than 117 000 years.

The province today is comparable in size to England and consists of six districts: City of Cape Town, West Coast, Cape Winelands, Overberg, Eden district and Central Karoo. The Western Cape, with its many tourist attractions, is considered by many to be the most developed province and is currently the only province governed by the Democratic Alliance party. However, in terms of economic output, it is second to the fast-paced Gauteng province.

Popular tourist routes include the Cape Wine route, which leads through Stellenbosch, known for its university, and Franschhoek, home to the early French settlers. Worcester, Robertson and many smaller towns lie on the scenic Route 62.

The landscape varies widely, from arid semi-desert in the Karoo to the lush green valleys along the popular Garden Route. Mountain ranges include the Swartberg, Cederberg and Hottentots Holland mountains. The area has a Mediterranean climate with mild, wet winters, although in the mountain ranges and inland areas there are occasional snowfalls and temperatures can fall below zero, especially on winter nights.

Cosmopolitan Cape Town is one of the most popular tourist attractions in the world and tourism in the Western Cape is a strong contributor to the economy.

 Capital

 Population

 Education

 Languages

Capital	Population	Education	Languages
Cape Town 3.7 million inhabitants	5.8 million 45 people per km² 94% are urban households	Most highly educated workforce in the country High school graduation rate is at 80% Literacy rate of 95%	Afrikaans 50% isiXhosa 25% English 20% English is spoken and understood by most

Table Mountain, Western Cape

WEEKEND BREAKS

(1) West Coast: Go fishing or enjoy watersports on Langebaan Lagoon

(2) Winelands: Taste the wine and fresh produce on the friendly wine farms

(3) Garden Route: Enjoy the beaches and lagoons along the lush Southern Cape

(4) Cederberg: Hike in the mountains and admire ancient San rock paintings

(5) Oudtshoorn: Visit the Cango Caves, and the town's ostrich farms

(See map on next page)

BUSINESS SECTORS

The major contributors to the economy of the region are the financial, business, real estate, manufacturing and agriculture sectors. The Western Cape's manufacturing sector has a variety of industries and is the second largest sector, contributing around 15% to the provincial GDP. The agricultural sector is strong, especially in fruit and vegetable farming. Ceres is the headquarters of the country's fruit juice production and the Cape Winelands are growing in importance as one of the main producers of new world wines. Fruit and wine provide more than 55% of South Africa's export produce.

The province has several well-developed port facilities, with an upgraded container terminal in Cape Town and solid port operations in Mossel Bay. At Saldanha Bay more than 58 million tonnes of cargo, including various minerals, steel coils and coking coal were handled in 2011. The port in Saldanha also handles bulk crude oil and is a base for maintenance and repair in the oil industry.

Cape Town, as South Africa's most popular city with award-winning beaches and tourist magnet Table Mountain, is a city which thrives on its reputation of being the centre of the country's knowledge industry. Many local and international high-tech companies and the IT industry, as well as the service industry with its rapidly growing call centres are located in the city. The film industry is equally strong with various international TV and movie productions, as well as advertising being handled here. Fashion, design and arts are supported by the regional government and thus this sector is thriving. Cape Town was voted the Design Capital of the World for 2014.

Koeberg Nuclear Power Station in Melkbosstrand, 30 km north of Cape Town, is operated by Eskom, the state owned electricity producer. It is the only power plant in Africa using nuclear energy.

Health	Climate	Infrastructure	Economy
No malaria HIV prevalence 18.2%. Second highest doctor per patient ratio after Gauteng	Mediterannean climate around Cape Town with winter rainfall Inland is drier with hot days and cold nights	Well-developed highways. Cape Town International Airport and George Airport Metrorail and MyCity bus service	Finances, IT services, manufacturing and agriculture are main sectors Contributes 14% to the country's GDP

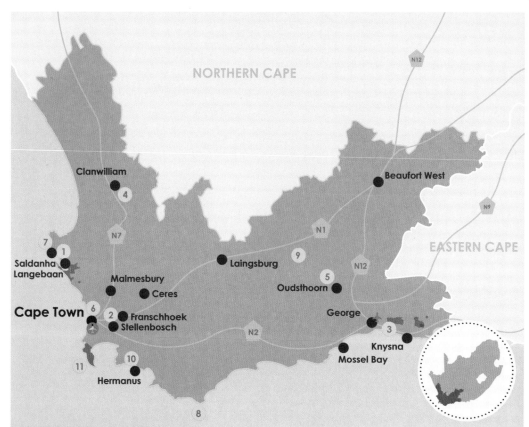

NORTHERN CAPE

Clanwilliam
4

Beaufort West

N12

N9

EASTERN CAPE

7
1
Saldanha
Langebaan

N7

Laingsburg

9

N1

5
Oudtshoorn

Malmesbury
Ceres

Cape Town
6
2 Franschhoek
Stellenbosch

N12

George
3

N2

Knysna
Mossel Bay

11

10

8

Hermanus

The V&A Waterfront in Cape Town is one of the most popular tourist attractions in the world. It has many amenities, such as shopping and restaurant facilities, and offers a variety of activities and entertainment, with an aquarium and upmarket craft market. Medical suites and office buildings can be found here as well.

The Saldanha Port is South Africa's largest natural deep-water port. Modern harbour facilities support the handling of bulk crude oil and the export of iron ore from the Sishen mine in the Northern Cape. Saldanha Bay is the only iron ore handling port in South Africa and a heavy metal smelter is located nearby.

The wine estates in Constantia and the Cape Winelands around Stellenbosch, Franschhoek and the Breede River Valley are known for award-winning wines. More than 200 wineries are located in the Stellenbosch area alone. KVW in Paarl, founded in 1918, is the biggest wine co-operative in the world.

⑧ Cape Agulhas

At this most southerly point of the African continent the cold waters of the Atlantic Ocean and the warm waters of the Indian Ocean meet.

③ Knysna

This lively town with its turquoise lagoon and adjacent islands is a popular holiday resort along the Garden Route. Many craft shops, entertainment facilities and animal sanctuaries are found in the vicinity.

④ Cederberg

The gigantic rock formations attract rock climbers, hikers and mountain bikers. Meander through crags and boulder fields in the Cederberg and admire the various rock painting sites.

⑤ Oudtshoorn

The town in the Little Karoo is home to the world's largest ostrich population and is known for its 'feather palaces' (stately homes) from the bygone era of the early 20th century, when ostriches were farmed for their feathers.

⑨ Karoo National Park

South Africa's largest ecosystem is located in the semi-desert and arid savannah and is home to the endangered Cape Mountain Zebra.

⑥ Table Mountain

Cape Town's most famous landmark was voted one of the 'New 7 Wonders of Nature'. Either hike up on various trails or ride to the top on the Swiss-made cable car. On clear days you can see up to 100 km away. Enjoy magnificent views on a circular walk on the 1 063 m plateau.

The *fairest* Cape of all

⑩ Hermanus

In the 'whale watching capital' of South Africa, southern right whales can be spotted from the beach between May and October. A 'whale crier' blows a horn when whales are spotted in the bay.

① Langebaan

The fishing village and its lagoon are popular with holiday makers from all over the world as Langebaan is one of the world's top kitesurfing venues and known for its huge waves and continuous winds.

⑪ Cape Point

The southernmost point of the Cape Peninsula is often referred to as the 'Cape of Good Hope' or the 'Cape of Storms'. Ostriches, zebras, springbok and various antelopes can be sighted in the nature reserve.

CITIES AND TOWNS

Stellenbosch

Stellenbosch

South Africa's second oldest town is a university town with a young and vibrant flair. Local designer boutiques and a lively restaurant and bar scene attract locals and tourists alike. One of South Africa's foremost universities offers various faculties with classes taught in Afrikaans and English. The town is located centrally in the Cape Winelands and offers many options for activities, such as visiting historic buildings and museums, tasting local specialties at the numerous wine estates or exploring the nearby nature reserves. There are various cultural and culinary festivals in the area throughout the year. Modern amenities in and around the town make this place popular with people from all backgrounds and nationalities.

Cape Town

Cape Town, or *Kaapstad* as Afrikaans signs will show, is the capital of the Western Cape province and the legislative capital of the country. The business hub of the region, Cape Town's city centre has undergone massive refurbishment in recent years and offers many first class facilities to its visitors and inhabitants. A modern bus rapid transport link from the city centre to various suburbs has been established and will be extended in coming years. Many tourist attractions can be found in and around town. Excellent educational institutions are found all over the province, with some of the best tertiary facilities in Africa. Cape Town is renowned for the entrepreneurial spirit of its inhabitants and the city's contribution to the provincial economy is strong. Nearby towns Blouberg, Gordons Bay and Somerset West are sought-after locations for retirement. Hout Bay, once a small fishing village at the foot of Chapman's Peak Drive, is popular for its relaxed lifestyle, as is the Constantia valley for its wine estates and affluent suburbs.

George

The second biggest city in the province, George, was founded in 1776 when the Dutch East India Company built an outpost for timber production. The town was later named after the British King George III. The thriving town is the centre of the popular Garden Route, which links Cape Town with Port Elizabeth. A popular holiday destination, it is also a well-established conference venue and is the business hub of the region with a well-developed infrastructure. George is renowned for its world-class golf courses such as the Fancourt and the Le Grand George course. Many towns along the Cape southern coast, among them Knysna, Wilderness, Sedgefield and Plettenberg Bay, are popular holiday resorts.

RESOURCES

Province, District and Municipalities

Western Cape Government:
www.westerncape.gov.za
Cape Town: www.capetown.gov.za
Winelands: www.capewinelands.gov.za
Eden: www.edendm.co.za
Karoo: www.skdm.co.za
Overberg: www.odm.org.za
West Coast: www.westcoastdm.co.za

Business and Industry

www.capetownchamber.com
www.westerncapebusiness.co.za
www.thedti.gov.za
Cape Business News: www.cbn.co.za
Trade and Investment: www.wesgro.co.za

National Parks/National Heritage

Cape Nature: www.capenature.org.za
Table Mountain: www.tablemountain.net
National Parks: www.sanparks.org

Tourism and Attractions

www.capetown.travel
www.tourismcapetown.co.za
www.gardenroute.co.za
www.winelands.co.za
www.thecapecountrymeander.co.za
www.capewestcoastpeninsula.co.za
www.stellenbosch.travel
www.robertsonr62.com
www.waterfront.co.za
www.robben-island.org.za

Annual Events

Cape Minstrel Carnival in January
Cape Argus Cycle Race in March
Hermanus Whale Festival in September

Knysna Oyster Festival in July

Local Websites

www.cape-town-family-holiday-magic.com
www.expatcapetown.com
www.george.co.za
www.mothercityliving.co.za
www.whatsoncapetown.com

'Good Hope'
Provincial motto

Recommended Reading

Briggs, Philip (2012) *Top 10 Cape Town and the Winelands.* London: Dorling Kindersley

Fraser, Sean (2010) *Seven Days in Cape Town.* Cape Town: Random House Struik

Jacana Maps (2006) *Garden Route Guide.* Johannesburg: Jacana

Lundy, Mike (2003) *Weekend Trails in the Western Cape.* Cape Town: Human & Rousseau

Schoeman, Chris (2013) *The Historical Karoo.* Cape Town: Random House Struik

MAIN CITIES AND TOWNS

Stellenbosch

Municipality: Stellenbosch
Population: 156 000
Elevation: 136 metres
Airport: Cape Town
International Airport
20 km SW of the town

Cape Town

Municipality: City of
Cape Town
Population: 3.5 million
Elevation: 16 metres
Airport: Cape Town
International Airport
20 km E of the city

George

Municipality: George
Population: 194 000
Elevation: 205 metres
Airport: George Airport
9 km NE of the town

EASTERN CAPE

The Eastern Cape is a fast growing tourism destination. This is South Africa's second largest province and includes the former homelands of the Transkei and the Ciskei. Home to the second largest ethnic group in South Africa, the Xhosa people, here cultural traditions are still practiced alongside modern day life. Historically this province was frontier land where the European settlers clashed with the local Xhosa people. The province played an important role during apartheid. Many of South Africa's freedom fighters, such as Steve Biko, Oliver Tambo and Nelson Mandela, were raised and educated here.

The provincial capital Bhisho, approximately 80 km from East London, is a small town within the Buffalo City Metropolitan Municipality, which incorporates East London. East London and Port Elizabeth are the two main business hubs of the province. Today many expats live in the province because of the presence of the automotive manufacturers there.

The Eastern Cape is the only one of all nine South African provinces that has all seven ecological zones or biomes in its boundaries. While tourism is concentrated mainly on the coastal regions and around the numerous malaria-free game reserves, the hinterland offers rural hillside villages and the only ski resort in the country.

The province is renowned for its unspoilt coastline and is named the Sunshine Coast. The landscape varies greatly, ranging from rolling hills to the semi-desert landscape of the Karoo and the rough rocky southern Drakensberg mountains. The climate thus ranges from a Mediterranean climate at the coast to mountain climates in the high-lying regions and dry and hot conditions in the semi-desert regions.

 Capital

 Population

 Education

 Languages

Capital	Population	Education	Languages
Bhisho 137 000 inhabitants	6.8 million 39 people per km² Almost two thirds live in rural areas. With migration outflow of 27.8%	One third of the population have not had formal schooling Lowest literacy rate of all provinces at 59%	isiXhosa 83% Afrikaans 9% English 4% English and Afrikaans are understoon by many

Mazeppa Bay, Eastern Cape

(See map on next page)

WEEKEND BREAKS

1 **Addo National Park:** See the Big Five on a self-drive tour

2 **Tsitsikamma National Park:** Go hiking in the forest or kloofing along the coast

3 **Jeffreys Bay:** Surf at this surfer's mecca

4 **Grahamstown:** Visit the historical monuments in the 'City of Saints'

5 **Wild Coast:** Experience unspoilt nature and the Hole in the Wall

BUSINESS SECTORS

The automotive industry provides 30% of the jobs in the province's manufacturing sector and accounts for 32% of gross added value. Half of South Africa's passenger vehicles are made in the Eastern Cape and 51% of the country's motor exports originate here. Many international car manufacturers, such as DaimlerChrysler, Volkswagen, Delta (General Motors) and Ford (Samcor), as well as original equipment manufacturers, such as Bridgestone, are located in the province. As the powerhouse of the provincial economy, Nelson Mandela Bay contributes more than 35% to the province's GDP with the automotive industry being the major contributor. Coega Industrial Development Zone (IDZ) presents one of the most modern industrial development opportunities and is South Africa's premier location for new industrial investments. Major investments are also made by Nestlé, Cadbury, Dulux, Goodyear and Johnson & Johnson among other internationally operating enterprises located in the province.

Agriculture comprises deciduous fruit (Langkloof), citrus fruit (Addo/Kirkwood) and the second largest producer of chicory (Alexandria) in the world. The Eastern Cape has more livestock than any other province and produces a quarter of the nation's milk. Wool-producing Merino sheep and mohair-producing Angora goats contribute significantly to the economy. South Africa produces about 55% of the world's mohair.

Game conservation plays an important part in the province and it has many private world-class game reserves. Tourism is centred mainly around Port Elizabeth, which is the easternmost point of the picturesque Garden Route with the nearby Addo National Park, as well as along the Wild Coast. The annual National Arts Festival in Grahamstown (Africa's largest cultural event), the birthplace of Nelson Mandela in Qunu, and the country's only ski resort near Rhodes are also major drawcards for local and foreign tourists.

Health	Climate	Infrastructure	Economy
Bilharzia prevalent in the rural eastern districts HIV prevalence of 27.6%	Hot and dry during the summer Winter rainfall Snowfall in winter in highlying areas	Established main roads, underdeveloped in rural areas Airports in Port Elizabeth and East London	Major industries are the automotive industry, agricultural sector and tourism Contributes 7.7% to the country's GDP

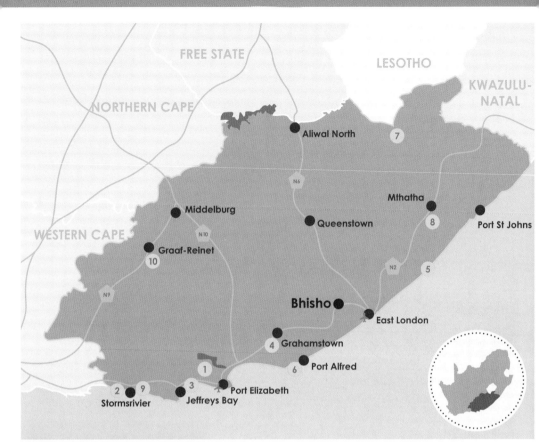

FREE STATE

LESOTHO

KWAZULU-
NATAL

NORTHERN CAPE

Aliwal North

7

N6

Mthatha

Middelburg

Queenstown

8

Port St Johns

WESTERN CAPE

N10

Graaf-Reinet

10

N2

5

N9

Bhisho

East London

Grahamstown

4

1

6

Port Alfred

2

9

3

Port Elizabeth

Stormsrivier

Jeffreys Bay

The Automotive Industry has major manufacturing sites in the province. Volkswagen South Africa operates in Uitenhage, Ford and General Motors SA in Port Elizabeth and Mercedes-Benz in East London. Underdeveloped areas and highly developed industries clash in the province, which is considered to have most growth potential for investors.

The Wild Coast, a 250 km stretch from the Kei River Mouth to Port Edward is dotted with jagged cliffs, high waterfalls and sheltered wild beaches. Untamed nature and abundant wildlife is omnipresent. Cows can be seen lying on the beaches and driving becomes a challenge as a result of the many stray animals.

Addo Elephant Park is the tourist magnet of the region. The national park has a finely tuned ecosystem and is renowned for its large elephant herds and the unique flightless dung beetles. The park claims to provide game viewing of the 'Big Seven' which include the lion, leopard, elephant, buffalo and rhino as well as the great white shark and southern right whales.

The coastal town of Port Alfred and nearby Kenton-on-Sea are popular with holidaymakers due to their quaintness and pristine beaches. Explore the region's rivers on a canoe trip, dive through coral reefs or go on a horseback safari at one of the nearby private game reserves.

⑦ Tiffindell

South Africa's only ski and snowboarding resort is situated at 2 700 m near Rhodes. For over 100 days in the year, snow is guaranteed at this small resort.

⑧ Qunu

Nelson Mandela, who is affectionately called 'Madiba' by the locals, was born and raised in the area.

② Tsitsikamma Forest

This coastal forest is South Africa's oldest rainforest. Various trails lead along a picturesque coastline. Admire the breath-taking scenery when hiking along the coastal 'Dolphin Trail' or 'Otter Trail'.

Birthplace of
Madiba,
Father of
the Nation

③ ⑤ Jeffreys Bay

Africa's biggest surfing event takes place here every July, attracting surfers from all over the world. This surfer's mecca boasts many swim- and surfwear outlets. The main beach, called 'Dolphin Beach', is rated among the best in the province and entertainment is provided for the whole family. Dolphins are sighted here all year round.

⑨ Bloukrans Bridge

The 216 m high arch bridge over the Bloukrans River on the picturesque Garden Route is the world's largest single-span concrete arch bridge and the world's highest bungee jump bridge.

⑩ Graaff-Reinet

One of the oldest towns in the country, Graaff-Reinet is situated on the Sundays River and called the Gem of the Karoo. This town has kept its original 19th century feel and boasts more than 200 national monuments.

CITIES AND TOWNS

Port Elizabeth

Port Elizabeth

Port Elizabeth, the province's major city, is also referred to as PE or 'The Bay'. South Africa's fifth largest city is located centrally on the Eastern Cape coast, midway between Cape Town and Durban. The city was founded by British settlers in 1820 and is now part of the Nelson Mandela Bay Metropolitan Municipality, which also includes Uitenhage and Despatch. Nelson Mandela Bay offers a wide range of modern amenities to its population. Many prestigious educational institutions and private schools are located in the region. The long white beaches, the Boardwalk entertainment complex, which has a large variety of shops and restaurants, and the Bayworld Aquarium are the major attractions in this relaxed seaside resort. Due to the welcoming atmosphere towards strangers, Port Elizabeth is often nicknamed 'The Friendly City'.

East London

South Africa's only river port, East London has grown in importance in recent years. It is located in the Buffalo City Metropolitan Municipality together with the provincial capital Bhisho and the industrial hub of Berlin. The East London Industrial Development Zone (ELIDZ) is the main industrial district in the area. Many international companies, such as DaimlerChrysler South Africa, East London's biggest employer, are located there. The city offers a range of modern amenities, some excellent private schools and various tourist facilities. The beaches around East London, such as Gonubie Beach or Nahoon Beach, are recognised as some of the most beautiful in the country.

Grahamstown

Nicknamed 'City of Saints' because of its numerous churches of various denominations, Grahamstown is home to the prestigious Rhodes University. The university town is located in the historic heartland of the province and is known for its Victorian architecture and excellent educational and cultural life. The city is also dubbed 'Festival City' as it hosts the National Arts Festival, South Africa's biggest and longest running cultural festival, and the Sci Fest. These events attract thousands of visitors every year. Various nature reserves, such as the Great Fish River Reserve, offer excellent bird viewing and hiking. There are also many private game farms in the area that offer abundant game viewing.

RESOURCES

Province, District and Municipalities

Eastern Cape Province:
www.ecprov.gov.za
Nelson Mandela Bay:
www.nelsonmandelabay.gov.za
Buffalo City/East London:
www.buffalocity.gov.za
Alfred Nzo/Drakensberg:
www.andm.gov.za
Amathole Municipality:
www.amathole.gov.za
Cacadu Municipality: *www.cacadu.co.za*
Chris Hani District Municipality:
www.chrishanidm.gov.za
OR Tambo Municpality:
www.ortambodm.org.za
Grahamstown: *www.makana.gov.za*

Business and Industry

Eastern Cape Development Corporation:
www.ecdc.co.za
Nelson Mandela Bay Business Chamber:
www.nmbbusinesschamber.co.za
www.easterncapebusiness.co.za
East London IDZ: *www.elidz.co.za*
Coega IDZ: *www.coega.co.za*

Tourism and Attractions

www.ectourism.co.za
www.nmbt.co.za
Rhodes: *www.rhodesvillage.co.za*
National Parks: *www.sanparks.org*
Tiffindell Ski Resort: *www.tiffindell.co.za*
www.visiteasterncape.co.za
www.jeffreysbaytourism.org

Annual Events

Grahamstown SciFest in March
Grahamstown National Arts Festival in June
Nelson Mandela Bay Splash Festival in
March

Local Websites

www.eastlondon.org.za
www.grahamstown.co.za
www.mype.co.za
*www.portelizabethdailyphoto.blogspot.
com*

'Development through Unity'
Provincial motto

Recommended Reading

Brett, Michael (2012) *Getaway Guide
Eastern Cape & Wild Coast.* Cape Town:
Sunbird Publishers

Grogan, Tony (2005) *Tony Grogan's Eastern
Cape.* Cape Town: Don Nelson

Magona, Sindiwe (2006) *Mud Chic:
Lifestyle and Inspiration from the People of
the Eastern Cape.* Cape Town: Quivertree

Van Wyk, Chris (2013) *Celebrating Steve
Biko.* Johannesburg: Wits University Press

MAIN CITIES AND TOWNS

Port Elizabeth

Municipality: Nelson
Mandela Bay Metro
Population: 1.2 million
inhabitants
Elevation: 16 metres
Airport: Port Elizabeth
Airport 4 km S of the city

East London

Municipality: Buffalo City
Population: 755 000
inhabitants
Elevation: 133 metres
Airport: East London
airport 15 km SW of the
city

Grahamstown

Municipality: Makana
Population: 120 000
inhabitants
Elevation: 551 metres
Airport: Port Elizabeth
Airport 170 km SW of
the town

NORTHERN CAPE

The Northern Cape is South Africa's largest province, extending over almost one third of the country, yet it is the least populated and is home to only 2.2% of all South Africans. The province, bordering Namibia and Botswana to the north, is renowned for its Kalahari desert scenery, rough coastline, the mighty Orange River, its vast open spaces, numerous national parks and the stunning flower displays in Namaqualand in spring. The landscape ranges from arid desert areas in the Kalahari and the Karoo to rugged mountain terrain along the Orange River and in the southern parts of the province, where 4x4 vehicles become a necessity.

With only a few major cities, more than 70% of the province's population live in the many small towns and villages and on remote farms. The region's economy is based mainly on agriculture and mining. The Northern Cape has the highest unemployment rate of all the provinces, so almost one third of the population live in poverty. There are five distinct regions and district municipalities: Namaqualand (Namakwa) along the West Coast of South Africa, the Green Kalahari (Siyanda) and the Kalahari (John Taolo Gaetsewe) region to the north as well as the Karoo (Pixley Ka Seme) and the Diamond Fields region (Frances Baard) in the east of the province.

The area is rich in cultural history. It has prehistoric rock paintings and former mission stations, such as the Moffat Mission and the Pella Mission stations. The region offers insights into South Africa's unique cultures and you can still meet some of the last remaining San (Bushmen). The Anglo-Boer War left its mark on the province and numerous former battle sites can be found around Kimberley. Several places celebrating the cultural and natural heritage can be visited during the year. The most active month is September when various festivals take place and the countryside is clothed in a riot of colour during the wildflower season.

The Northern Cape's climate is typical of all desert and semi-desert regions and has extremely high temperatures in summer and very low average minimum temperatures on winter nights.

Capital	Population	Education	Languages
Kimberley 167 000 inhabitants	1.1 million 3 people per km² Mainly rural households	11% of adults have not been to school Only 30% of pupils finish secondary school Literacy rate of 83%	Afrikaans 54% Setswana 33% isiXhosa 5% Khoi and Nama Afrikaans and English understood by most

WEEKEND BREAKS

1. **Orange River:** The country's longest river is renowned for water rafting

2. **Kimberley:** Step back in time in this historic town and visit the Big Hole

3. **Kgalagadi Transfrontier Park:** Game viewing at its best

4. **|Ai-|Ais/Richtersveld Transfrontier Park:** Experience this World Heritage Site

5. **Namaqualand:** Wonder at the colourful spring flowers in bloom

(See map on next page)

BUSINESS SECTORS

Mining plays an important role in the development and prosperity of the province and is the dominant business sector contributing more than 30% to the regional GDP. While the province is most famous for diamonds, with 95% of the country's diamond output originating there, the platinum mines are also a major contributor to the GDP. The Northern Cape accounts for more than 80% of the country's iron ore production, 85% of the manganese production and 90% of the lead production. Aggeneys, Kathu and Okiep are among the main mining centres of the province. Mining giants Mittal Steel, AngloAmerican and Assmang operate the biggest mines in the region. AngloAmerican, being one of the world's largest mining companies, is the largest private sector employer in the country with 76 000 permanent employees and more than 20 000 contractors.

Agriculture and agri-processing of regional crops, among them grapes, dates, olives and citrus fruits, are prevalent. Many small wine estates can be found along the Orange River close to Upington. The Orange River Wine Cellars is the second biggest wine co-operative in the world. Sheep and lamb farming are the main source of income in the dry Karoo. The Vaalharts region produces almost half the country's cotton yield. Over 300 tons of rooibos tea is cultivated annually near Calvinia. Most of the local produce is exported. Due to the abundant sunshine, the province is earmarked for major renewable energy projects, such as the solar projects near Upington. Wind farms are proposed for sites near De Aar and Copperton and many of the renewable energy sources, which are expected to supply 40% of the country's energy needs by 2030, are located in the province.

Tourism is also one of the economic drivers, with the Orange River being the main attraction, particularly for wild water enthusiasts.

Health	Climate	Infrastructure	Economy
No malaria occurrence HIV prevalence of 16.2%	Hot to very hot in summer Mild to cold in winter Very dry all year round	12% of the roads are tarred Wide net of gravel roads Major airports in Upington and Kimberley	Agriculture, diamond, iron ore and manganese mining Lowest contributor to the country's GDP at 2.2%

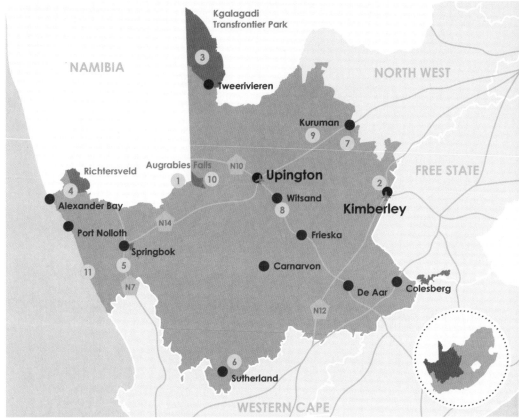

Kgalagadi
Transfrontier Park

NAMIBIA

3

Tweerivieren

NORTH WEST

Kuruman
9
7

Richtersveld
Augrabies Falls
N10
1
10
Upington

4
Witsand
8

Alexander Bay

FREE STATE

2

Kimberley

N14

Port Nolloth

Frieska

Springbok

Carnarvon

11
5

N7

De Aar
Colesberg

N12

6
Sutherland

WESTERN CAPE

The Kgalagadi Transfrontier Park extends into Namibia and Botswana where border fences have been removed to allow the abundant wildlife, which includes 19 species of carnivore, gemsbok and springbok, to roam freely. Sand and gravel roads for game watching run along wide river beds. 4x4 vehicles are recommended.

The Big Hole mine in Kimberley is the biggest man-made hole in the world with a perimeter of 1.6 km. Diamond mining operations, which produced more than 14.5 million carats or 2.72 tons of diamonds, over a 43-year period were stopped in 1914. Today the site houses a full-scale open-air museum.

The SALT or Southern African Large Telescope in Sutherland is the largest single optical telescope in the Southern hemisphere and the Square Kilometre Array Radio Telescope (SKA), which is currently under construction near Carnarvon, will be the world's biggest telescope. The Karoo desert provides clear views of the sky undisturbed from city lights and pollution.

⑦ Wonderwerk Caves

The caves reach as far as 139 m in depth and are among the oldest inhabited caves in the world. Stone tools found in the cave in 2008 date back more than 2 million years.

⑧ Witsand

Experience 'Roaring Sands' and huge dunes, that are roughly 9 km long and up to 30 m high, at Witsand Nature Reserve near the town of Kuruman.

⑩ Augrabies Falls

The 56 m high Augrabies Falls, also called 'the place of big noise' in the local Khoikhoi language. They carry three times more water than the Niagara Falls. Admire the impressive waterfalls and the 18 km long gorge while taking a 4x4 drive along the scenic circular route through the national park.

Place of the
Nama People

⑨ Sishen

The Sishen iron ore mine in Kathu near Kuruman is one of the largest opencast mines in the world and the iron ore railway linking Sishen with the port of Saldanha Bay in the Western Cape is one of the longest iron ore carriers in the world, covering a distance of 861 km.

⑤ Namaqualand

In spring, wildflowers paint the otherwise dry landscape in flamboyant colours, especially in the Namaqua National Park. Daisies and other spring flowers in bright pinks, yellows and oranges form vast carpets of colour attracting visitors from all over the world to this spectacular display.

④ San People

The mountainous desert of the Richtersveld is home to the last remaining San (Bushmen) people. Descendants of the Khoisan, they were evicted from their own lands and were almost wiped out.

⑪ West Coast

Alexander Bay and Port Nolloth are important fishing centres along the western coastline where abalone, kelp, oyster and lobster are cultivated. Alexander Bay is a popular West Coast holiday resort and the driest place in South Africa, with an annual rainfall of only 46 mm.

CITIES AND TOWNS

Kimberley

Kimberley

Kimberley is the provincial capital of the Northern Cape. As one of South Africa's major mining towns it is often referred to as the 'Diamond Capital of the World' or 'The City that Sparkles'. The discovery of the 83.5 carat 'Star of Africa' diamond in Kimberley in 1869 was the starting point for the economic growth of the country. The ensuing diamond rush brought diggers and diamond dealers from around the world to the region. During the diamond rush in the late 1800s, the mining town was home to the most millionaires in the world. English businessman and imperialist Cecil Rhodes founded the diamond trading company De Beer which is the world's largest producer of uncut diamonds. Today, Kimberley is a growing city with a thriving economy. The city has many modern buildings and some architectural gems that stem from Victorian times. Tourist attractions are: the Big Hole, Kamfers Dam with its flamingo nesting sites, the nearby Anglo-Boer War battlefields, art galleries and the Flamingo World casino complex.

Upington

Upington is located in the fertile Orange River valley and was originally a mission station established in 1875. The town, bustling with agricultural, tourism and service industries is a popular stopover for those travelling between Cape Town and Johannesburg. It is also a gateway for tourists travelling to the Kgalagadi Transfrontier Park or the Augrabies Falls National Park. Upington is known as one of the five sunniest places on earth with more than ten hours of sunshine per day. The town will be home to the world's largest Solar Park, which is currently being built. In addition a further 5 GW concentrated solar power plant is commissioned for the area in 2016. These projects, with international participation, are estimated to create about 200 000 jobs in the coming ten years. Housing projects to cater for the influx of workers have already been started. The deserted highways around Upington and the huge saltpans in the area are often used for filming, particularly vehicle commercials. A wide range of housing options, private health and education facilities and general amenities can be found in town.

Springbok

The busy town adjacent to the N7, the main artery between Cape Town and Windhoek/Namibia, caters for travellers and holiday makers. The nearby parks and nature reserves, such as Geogap Nature Reserve and Skilpad, are especially attractive during August and early September, when the spring flowers paint the landscape in vibrant colours.

RESOURCES

Province, Districts and Municipalities

Northern Cape Government:
www.northern-cape.gov.za
Khara Hais Municipality/Upington:
www.kharahais.gov.za
Namakwa District Municipality/Springbok:
www.namakwa-dm.gov.za
Frances Baard District/Kimberley:
www.francesbaard.gov.za
Gaetsewe District/Kgalagadi/Kathu:
www.taologaetsewe.gov.za
Siyanda: *www.zfm-dm.co.za*

Business and Industry

Northern Cape Chamber of Commerce
and Industry (NOCCI): *www.nocci.co.za*
Northern Cape Department of Trade and
Industry (DTI): *www.northern-cape.gov.za*
www.northerncapebusiness.co.za
www.idc.co.za

National Parks/National Heritage

San Parks: *www.sanparks.org*
Bushman Rock Art: *www.san.org.za*
South African San Institute: *www.sasi.org.za*
Richtersveld: *www.richtersveld.net*

Tourism and Attractions

www.experiencenortherncape.com
www.greenkalahari.co.za
www.thebighole.co.za
www.museumsnc.co.za
www.kalahari-adventures.co.za
www.felixunite.co.za
www.northerncape.org.za

Local Websites

www.kalaharibulletin.co.za
www.namaqualand.com
www.kathugazette.co.za

Annual Events

Orange River Canoe Marathon in March
Gariep Kunstefees, Kimberley in August/
September
Namakwaland Daisies in Bloom in August/
September
Kalahari Kuierfees, Upington in September

'Strive for a Better Life'
Provincial motto

Recommended Reading

Dean, CM (2005) *Journey through the
living Deserts of South Africa.* UK: Dean and
Associates

Naude-Moseley, Brent & Moseley,
Steve (2008) *Getaway Guide to Karoo,
Namaqualand and Kalahari: Out and
About in the Northern Cape.* Sunbird
Publishers

Manning, John (2008) *Ecoguide
Namaqualand.* Briza

Schadeberg, Jürgen (2002) *The San of the
Kalahari.* Protea Boekhuis

Solomon, Anne (1988) *The Essential Guide
to San Rock Art.* David Phillips Publishers

MAIN CITIES AND TOWNS

Kimberley

Municipality: Sol Plaatje
Population: 142 000
Elevation: 1 219 metres
Airport: Kimberley
Airport 7 km E of the city

Upington

Municipality: Khara Hais
Population: 71 300
Elevation: 810 metres
Airport: Upington Airport
7 km N of the town

Springbok

Municipality: Nama Khoi
Population: 11 000
Elevation: 925 metres
Airport: Upington Airport
380 km E of the town

GAUTENG

The smallest province of South Africa is situated on the highveld plateau. It is also the most densely populated province, housing more than 22% of the country's population and comprising six municipalities. Among them are three metropolitan municipalities: City of Tshwane (Greater Pretoria, the country's administrative capital and the seat of the South African government), Ekurhuleni (East Rand) and the country's business hub, the City of Johannesburg.

The region is also recognised as the 'cradle of humankind' and was first inhabited by the San and Khoikhoi people and later by people moving in from the northern parts of central Africa. In the 1800s the area gained more attention when the Transvaal Boer Republic was created. The discovery of gold and the ensuing gold rush led to the influx of fortune seekers from near and far. Today the province is still the melting pot of South Africa with people from all over the world making the province their home.

With a well-developed infrastructure, Gauteng is the economic powerhouse of the country and is considered the transport hub of southern Africa. OR Tambo International Airport, which caters for 19 million passengers a year, is one of only three airports in the world offering direct flights to all continents. The Gautrain Rapid Rail Link is a state-of-the-art rail service inaugurated in 2010. Its two service lines connect OR Tambo International Airport, Sandton, Johannesburg and Pretoria.

As the financial and technology centre of the country, Gauteng also has some highly acclaimed educational facilities including universities and international schools.

The dry inland climate in the province is influenced largely by the high altitude of the region, which is situated on the 1500 m – 1800 m high plateau. The temperatures get hot in summer while the winters are crisp and cold with snowfalls on rare occasions. The rainfall occurs in summer when late afternoon thunderstorms are frequent.

Capital	Population	Education	Languages
Johannesburg 3.9 million inhabitants	12.3 million 680 people per km² 24% are under age of 15, 4% are over 65 Urban households; 97% 26% are unemployed	Second highest matric pass rate of 81% after Western Cape Literacy rate of 94% 8.4% of adults have not received any schooling	Zulu 21% Afrikaans 14% Sesotho 13% English 13% English is spoken by most

Johannesburg, Gauteng

WEEKEND BREAKS

1. **Cradle of Humankind:** Visit Maropeng and Sterkfontein Caves

2. **Gold Reef City:** Theme park and tours dedicated to the gold rush times

3. **Soweto:** See the country's biggest township and cradle of freedom fighters

4. **Hartbeespoort Dam:** Enjoy watersports and the surrounding Magaliesberg

5. **Tswaing Meteorite Crater:** Nature walks and eco-tourism centre near Pretoria

(See map on next page)

BUSINESS SECTORS

Gold, platinum and uranium mining are the major contributors to the province's GDP. The Witwatersrand Basin is still the greatest unmined source of gold in the world and the gold reserves there are estimated to be 30 times richer than any other goldfields in the world. The shaft of the Western Deep mine is the world's deepest mining shaft, plunging some 3.6 km into the earth. South Africa's only gold refinery is Rand Refinery, which is located in Germiston. Major gold mines, operated by AngloGold Ashanti mines, Gold Fields and Harmony are major employers in the area. Coal mining is also done extensively in the region around Vereeniging and Vanderbijlpark.

The province houses one of the world's leading financial centres. The finance sector contributes more than 20% to the province's GDP. In recent years, Gauteng became renowned for its highly advanced knowledge industry with the high-tech corridor between Pretoria and Johannesburg. The region is seen as being one of the top global hubs for information technology. The province also houses more than 40% the country's biotechnology companies.

The manufacturing industry is located mainly in the Ekurhuleni district, which also houses the logistics centre near OR Tambo International Airport. Well-serviced industrial estates surround this major transport hub. Light industry operations can be found in this area as well.

Agricultural products are harvested mainly in the province's West Rand. Maize, cattle and vegetables are the main income sources in this area. Western Gauteng has large-scale commercial farming, but only a small amount of agri-processing takes place in the province.

Health	Climate	Infrastructure	Economy
No malaria HIV prevalence is 29.9% Highest doctor per patient ratio in the country	Dry highveld climate Hot summers with afternoon thunderstorms Dry cold winters with occasional snowfall	Developed highways several toll roads OR Tambo International and Lanseria airports Gautrain service	Highest per capita income Mining, finance and manufacturing Contributes 36% to the country's GDP

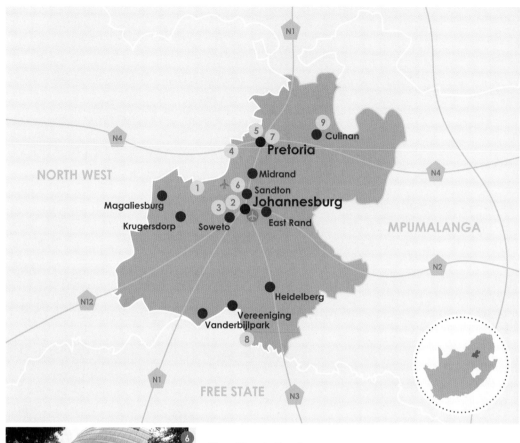

NORTH WEST

N1

N4

9
Culinan

5 7
4
Pretoria

Midrand

1 6
Sandton
3 2
Johannesburg

Magaliesburg

Krugersdorp

Soweto

East Rand

N4

MPUMALANGA

N2

N12

Heidelberg

Vereeniging
Vanderbijlpark

8

N1

FREE STATE

N3

The Stock Exchange in Johannesburg (JSE) is one of the biggest stock exchanges in the world. Many international companies and more than 70 national and international banking institutions have their South African headquarters in Johannesburg, either in the CBD or in the business hub of Sandton.

The Voortrekker Monument sitting on a hilltop in Pretoria/Tshwane is a national heritage site. The massive granite monument houses a huge domed 'Hall of Heroes' and a cenotaph commemorating the Voortrekkers who left the Cape Colony between 1835 and 1854. The monument is surrounded by a nature reserve with various game animals.

The gold rush in the Witwatersrand Basin brought prosperity to the country and gold is extensively mined in the province. Experience the pioneering history of the gold rush on a heritage tour in South Africa's foremost theme park at Gold Reef City. Go on a tour through a 226 m deep mine shaft, visit old mining houses and see artefacts of the bygone era.

❷ Apartheid Museum

Engage with the country's past and learn about the freedom struggle. The museum leads visitors on an emotion-filled journey through the country's apartheid times.

❽ Vaal Dam

The country's second biggest dam is a favorite location for watersports enthusiasts. The dam and river provide much of Gauteng's water supply.

❾ Cullinan Diamond

The world's largest rough diamond was found near Pretoria in 1905. The more than 3 106 carat diamond weighed more than 621 g and was cut into nine stones, of which the largest is known as the 'Star of Africa'.

Gauteng,
place of
gold

❸ Soweto

'Soweto' originates from the words So(uth) We(stern) To(wnships). Many of the county's freedom fighters came from the area.

Vilakazi Street in Soweto is famous for its two Nobel laureates, Nelson Mandela and Desmond Tutu, who once lived there.

❻ Sandton

Situated between Johannesburg and Pretoria, this is Africa's richest square mile. The growing business centre with more than 10 000 businesses is known for its excellent shopping, entertainment and lively Mandela Square.

❺ Tswaing Meteorite Crater

The crater landscape is also known as the 'Pretoria Saltpans' as its name derives from the Setswana 'place of salt'. It was created by a meteorite more than 220 000 years ago.

❶ Cradle of Humankind

The museums complex at Maropeng in the Cradle of Humankind uses exciting interactive displays to lead you through more than 3.5 million years of human history and lets you explore the past, present and future of our earth. Nearby Sterkfontein caves are where the oldest fossil hominids 'Mrs Ples' and 'Little Foot' were discovered.

CITIES AND TOWNS

Pretoria

Pretoria

South Africa's administrative capital, Pretoria, was founded in 1855 by Marthinus Pretorius. During the Boer wars, Pretoria played a major role and still today many sites, such as the monumental Voortrekker Monument, show evidence of this. Pretoria is also called the 'Jacaranda City' due to the purple blossoms of its thousands of jacaranda trees in spring. The city houses the national government headquarters and foreign missions. Many global players have their headquarters in this quiet city. International schools as well as various other prestigious private educational facilities are located in the city. Pretoria is also considered a major research centre and is home to four universities and seven of the eight national science councils. The city offers many attractions that include the Pretoria Art Museum, the Transvaal Museum, Freedom Park and various nature reserves, such as Groenkloof and Rietvlei.

Johannesburg

Johannesburg, also called 'Jozi' or 'Joburg', is the provincial capital of the province. Founded in 1886 during the gold rush, the city is also referred to as 'Egoli', which means 'City of Gold'. Since then it has grown from a mere mining town into the most populous city and busiest economic hub in southern Africa. Johannesburg is often compared to Los Angeles in the USA, with a similar urban sprawl that connects it with Pretoria, which lies roughly 50km north of the city. Johannesburg has a vibrant cultural scene and thriving nightlife. A lively arts and culture scene is developing especially in popular Newtown, the city's main theatre district. Braamfontein, Kensington, Rosebank and Melrose are famous for their vibey cafés, art galleries and antique stores. The East Rand, including Boksburg, Alberton, Germiston and Benoni, is known for its many lakes, dams and parks. Because of its international population, you will find many foreign cultural centres and international schools in the city and its surrounding suburbs. Johannesburg has excellent museums, and sports and cultural events take place regularly. With more than 10 million trees, Johannesburg is said to be the place with the largest urban man-made forest in the world.

Vanderbijlpark

One of the country's largest industrial towns, Vanderbijlpark is situated on the Vaal River and was purpose-built in the 1950s for housing the workers of the local steel mill. With the surrounding towns Vereeniging, Sasolburg and Meyerton around the river Vaal, the region is often referred to as the Vaal Triangle. Nearby Suikerbos Reserve with undulating hills and a mountain range reaching up to 1 900 m in height is a popular weekend getaway.

RESOURCES

Province, District and Municipalities

Gauteng: www.gautengonline.gov.za
Tshwane: www.tshwane.gov.za
Johannesburg: www.joburg.org.za
Randfontein: www.randfontein.gov.za
Sedibeng: www.sedibeng.gov.za
Ekurhuleni: www.ekurhuleni.gov.za

Business and Industry

Johannesburg Chamber of Commerce
and Industry: www.jcci.co.za
Gauteng Economic Development
Agency: www.ggda.co.za
Gauteng Enterprise Propeller:
www.gep.co.za
Gauteng Companies:
www.gautengcompanies.co.za
Business Directory: www.lookatjoburg.co.za

National Parks/National Heritage

www.cradleofhumankind.co.za
www.voortrekkermon.org.za
www.freedompark.co.za

Tourism and Attractions

Gauteng Tourism: www.gauteng.net
Johannesburg: www.joburgtourism.com
Sandton: www.sandtontourism.com
Maropeng: www.maropeng.co.za
Gold Reef City: www.goldreefcity.co.za
Montecasino: www.montecasino.co.za
www.worldofbeer.co.za
www.rhinolion.co.za
www.liliesleaf.co.za
www.lesedi.com

Annual Events

Joburg Open Golf Tournament in January
Johannesburg Rand Show in April
Johannesburg Arts Alive Festival in August
Mogale City Cradle Festival in August
Johannesburg Africa Fashion Week in
October

Local Websites

www.sandtoncentral.co.za
www.joburgexpat.com
www.joburghappenings.co.za
www.pretoria-south-africa.com
www.vaaltriangleinfo.co.za
www.jozikids.co.za
www.vaalmeander.co.za

'Unity in Diversity'
Provincial motto

Recommended Reading

Coetzer, Diane (2012) *Weekends Away in
and Around Gauteng.* Struik

Holland, Heidi & Roberts, Adam (2010)
From Joburg to Jozi. Penguin

Nuttall, Sarah & Mbembe, Achill (2008)
Johannesburg: The Elusive Metropolis. Wits
University Press

Temkin, Nicki (2011) *Chic Jozi.* Penguin

MAIN CITIES AND TOWNS

Johannesburg

Municipality: City of
Johannesburg
Population: 3.9 million
Elevation: 1 753 metres
Airport: OR Tambo, 21 km
E of the city,
Lanseria: 45 km N of city

Pretoria

Municpality: City of Tshwane
Population: 2.3 million
Elevation: 1 350 m
Airport: OR Tambo nearby
Johannesburg 57 km S of
the city,
Lanseria: 56 km SW of the city

Vanderbijlpark

Municpality: Sedibeng
Population: 97 800
Elevation: 1 485 metres
Airport: OR Tambo
nearby Johannesburg
90 km NE of the city

FREE STATE

The Free State is a rural province set between South Africa's two biggest rivers, the Orange (Gariep) River in the south and the Vaal River in the north. The province shares borders with six South African provinces as well as the neighbouring country of Lesotho. Before the end of apartheid the province was known as the Orange Free State.

The land is set mostly on the undulating plains between 1 000 m and 1 500 m above sea level and has widely dispersed towns and villages with only a few bigger cities. With a population of less than 3 million, the province is only sparsely populated and most of the people live in rural households. Rolling farmlands and impressive sandstone formations and cliffs dominate the landscape. The Golden Gate Highlands National Park in the Maloti Mountains bordering neighboring Lesotho is a major attraction.

The province is made up of five district municipalities, with the Mangaung region in the central Motheo district being the business and cultural hub of the Free State. The major industrial sites are located in and around the provincial capital of Bloemfontein, which lies in the Mangaung region, as well as in Welkom, Sasolburg and Harrismith. All of these have modern commercial facilities including advanced telecommunication systems, tertiary education institutions and private medical facilities.

The province has many acclaimed rock art sites, which are predominantly located in the Eastern Free State around Ladybrand, Ficksburg, Bethlehem and Clarens. The region belonged to the Independent Boer Republic in the 19th century and during the Anglo-Boer War many gruesome battles were fought here. Former battle sites can be visited in the province along the Battlefields Route.

The climate in the province is fairly dry due to the altitude of this high-lying area, and droughts can occur, especially in the southern and western parts. Wide temperature variations can be expected.

Capital	Population	Education	Languages
Bloemfontein 463 000 inhabitants	2.7 million 21 people per km² 71% are urban households	Third highest matric rate after Gauteng and Western Cape Literacy rate of 69%	Sesotho 64% Afrikaans 13% isiXhosa 8% Setswana 5% English is the main business language

WEEKEND BREAKS

1. **Clarens:** An artists' retreat in the foothills of the Maloti (Maluti) Mountains

2. **Vredefort Dome:** Largest meteorite impact site in the world

3. **Golden Gate National Park:** Fascinating sandstone rock formations

4. **Gariep Dam:** The lake is a paradise for watersport enthusiasts

5. **Lesotho:** Take a 4x4 trip to the Mountain Kingdom

(See map on next page)

BUSINESS SECTORS

The mining and chemical industries are dominant in the province's economy. The main business sector and the biggest employers in the province are the mines of the goldfields which consist of a more than 400 km-long gold reef with a mining area of almost 33 000 ha that stretches across the Free State and into Gauteng. There are 12 gold mines in the province. Welkom is the biggest mining centre. The province also has rich coal deposits and 80% of the country's betonite, which is used in cement. The gold mines also produce a substantial amount of by-products such as silver, uranium, platinum-group metals and sulfuric acid. Diamonds, clay and gravel are mined predominantly in the region around Koffiefontein. Large quarries in the province are run by Lafard, Corobrik and Raumix.

The chemical plants around Sasolburg in the north of the province are another economic driver. More than 85% of the economic output for manufacturing comes from the petrochemicals sector, and Sasolburg is the site of the first coal-to-petrol plant in the world. Sasol is one of the world leaders in the petrochemical industry producing synthetic fuels and synthetic lubrication oils. The remainder of the manufacturing output in the Free State is in the high-technology industries, which constitute the highest percentage of all provinces in the country.

The Free State has fertile farmlands which give rise to a thriving agricultural sector. The province is often called South Africa's 'bread basket' due to the fertile plains which provide more than half of the country's wheat and sorghum harvest, nearly half of the sunflower and maize crops and more than 30% of potatoes and groundnuts. Cattle and sheep farming accounts for almost one fifth of all red meat produced in the country. The agricultural sector provides employment to almost one fifth of the population of the province.

Health	Climate	Infrastructure	Economy
No malaria risk HIV prevalence of 32.9%	Moderate to hot temperatures in summer Occasional snow in winter Summer rainfall	Extensive road infrastructure Bloemfontein airport offers domestic flights	Mining, agriculture, manufacturing and tourism industry Contributes 5.5% to the country's GDP

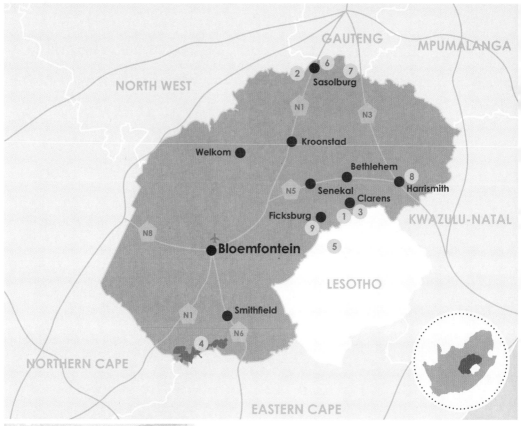

GAUTENG
MPUMALANGA
NORTH WEST
6
2 7
Sasolburg
N1
N3
Kroonstad
Welkom
Bethlehem
8
N5 Senekal Harrismith
Clarens
Ficksburg 1 3
9 KWAZULU-NATAL
N8
Bloemfontein 5
LESOTHO
N1 Smithfield
N6
4
NORTHERN CAPE
EASTERN CAPE

Gariep Dam, South Africa's largest dam on the Orange River, also called the Gariep River. Gariep is a San word meaning 'Great Water'. The 90 km long dam is a mecca for watersports. The Orange Fish River tunnel, which diverts water to the Great Fish River is the world's second longest water conduit.

Sasolburg The province is the main centre for the petrochemical industry in South Africa. The Sasolburg refinery is one of only two viable coal-derived oil refineries in the world. The city has a fantastic environmental awareness program and some 72 000 trees have been planted in the town.

Golden Gate Highland National Park in the foothills of the Maloti mountains owes its name to the park's sandstone cliffs, which sparkle like gold in the sunlight. The most famous formations are the Golden Gate and Sentinel Rock. The world's oldest dinosaur eggs, more than 200 million years old, were found in the area in 1978.

⑦ Vaal

The Vaal River bordering Gauteng is popular for watersport activities.
Parys, a small town on the river banks, is the main centre for whitewater rafting.

Heartland
of the
Basotho
people

⑨ Ficksburg

One of the agricultural centres of the province, the small town is known for its annual Cherry Festival in November, which attracts thousands of visitors each year. 90% of all cherries harvested in the country are from the area around Ficksburg.

② Vredefort Dome

The 42 km wide crater near Parys is the world's biggest and oldest meteorite impact site. It was formed about 2 billion years ago when a huge meteorite hit the earth. A museum complex called 'Deep Impact' informs about this World Heritage Site.

① Clarens

The quaint village at the foothills of the Maloti Mountains is a well-known artists' retreat and boasts numerous art galleries and craft centres. Many Stone Age caves and San rock art sites are found in the surrounding mountains.

⑧ Harrismith

This country town is situated midway along the Durban and Johannesburg route and is a good access point for the northern Drakensberg region.

Sunflowers

Sunflowers and grain fields as far as the eye can see. Undulating plains and farmland are typical for the region.

⑤ Maloti Drakensberg Route

The Maloti Route via Lesotho is the longest signed tourism route in South Africa leading through three provinces, the Eastern Cape, Free State and KwaZulu-Natal. The route passes through Basotho villages, magnificent mountain scenery and the town of Ladybrand, with its pretty sandstone buildings.

CITIES AND TOWNS

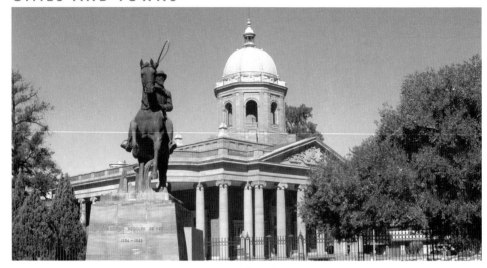

Bloemfontein

Bloemfontein

Bloemfontein, South Africa's sixth largest city, is the judicial capital of the country and home to the Supreme Court of Appeal. This Dutch/Afrikaans name means 'fountain of flowers' and Bloemfontein is also dubbed the 'City of Roses' due to the abundant number of rose bushes in the city's gardens. This modern city has many historic buildings and museums, such as the Oliewenhuis Art Museum, the National Natural History Museum and the Anglo-Boer War Museum. Bloemfontein forms part of the Mangaung Municipality ('place of cheetahs' in Sesotho). In 1912 the ANC was founded in Mangaung, and the party's recent annual conference was held there. The Bloemfontein Waterfront, nearby King's Park and the adjacent zoo are popular for weekend get-togethers. The 'Windmill' is a combined casino and entertainment complex.

Welkom

The province's second biggest city is in the heart of the country's goldfields, roughly 160 km north of Bloemfontein. Welkom, established after gold was discovered there in 1946, is one of the few completely pre-planned cities in the world. The planning was an ambitious project started by Sir Harry Oppenheimer, and South Africa's youngest city was officially recognised in 1955. Harmony Gold operates nine mines around the city and is the biggest local employer. It is interesting to note that there are no traffic lights in the city centre and traffic flow is regulated solely by traffic circles or roundabouts. The numerous suburbs all have their own modern amenities such as churches, schools and shopping centres. Flocks of flamingoes can be seen at Flamingo Pan and the nearby dams.

Sasolburg

The industrial town in the far north of the province was established in the 1950s to house employees of Sasol, the world's largest producer of synthetic fuel. The growing town is home to several nationalities who work in the refinery and for other major employers such as Karbochem. The town offers a wide range of modern amenities and educational facilities, from primary schools to tertiary education at the local college or nearby North West University and Vaal University of Technology in Vanderbijlpark. Riemland Eco-Park provides bird watching and game viewing opportunities for zebra, impala and other antelope species. The nearby towns of Oranjeville and Deneysville are both popular for watersport activities.

RESOURCES

District and Municipalities

Lejweleputswa: *www.lejwe.co.za*
Fezile Dabi: *www.feziledabi.gov.za*
Mangaung Metro (Bloemfontein):
www.mangaung.com
Metsimaholo (Sasolburg):
www.metsimaholo.gov.za

Business and Industry

Free State Development Corporation:
www.fdc.co.za
Free State Business Guide:
www.freestatebusiness.co.za
Mangaung Chamber of Commerce and
Industry: *www.bcci.co.za*
Welkom directory:
www.welkompublicity.co.za

National Parks / National Heritage

SANParks: *www.sanparks.org*

Tourism and Attractions

Free State Tourism:
www.freestatetourism.org
Bloemfontein Tourism:
www.bloemfonteintourism.co.za
Free State Venues:
www.freestatevenues.co.za
Maloti Route:
www.malotidrakensbergroute.com
Gariep Dam: *www.gariepdam.co.za*
N12 Treasure Route: *www.bloemhof.co.za*

Lesotho

Sani Pass: *www.sanilodge.co.za*
www.visitlesotho.travel
www.gov.ls

Annual Events

Macufe (Mangaung African Cultural)
Festival in October
Ficksburg Cherry Festival in October
Bloem Show in April

Local websites

www.bethulie.za.net
www.bloeminfo.co.za
www.goficksburg.co.za
www.harrismith.co
www.mangaung.info
www.sasolburg.net
www.vaaltriangleinfo.co.za

'Success through Unity'
Provincial motto

Recommended Reading

Bristow, David (2010) *Best Walks of the Drakensberg*. Random House Struik

Mitchell, Peter (2013) *The Eland's People*. Wits University Press

Mynhardt, Patrick (2003) *Boy from Behtulie*. Wits University Press

Uys, Isabel (2010) *The English-Afrikaans-Northern Sotho-Tswana Aid*. Pharos

MAIN CITIES AND TOWNS

Bloemfontein

Municipality: Mangaung
Metropolitan
Population: 463 000
Elevation: 1 382 metres
Airport: Bloemfontein
14 km N of the city

Welkom

Municipality:
Matjhabeng
Population: 406 000
Elevation: 1 333 metres
Airport: Bloemfontein
160 km S of the city

Sasolburg

Municipality:
Metsimaholo
Population: 141 000
Elevation: 1 500 metres
Airport: Johannesburg
OR Tambo 86 km N of
the town

NORTH WEST

South Africa's fourth biggest province is located mainly on the country's highveld and borders on neighbouring Botswana in the north. The province, which was established only after 1994, includes regions of the former Transvaal, the north-western parts of the Cape province and parts of Bophuthatswana, a former black homeland. It is split into four district municipalities around the major economic centres Rustenburg, Vryburg, Klerksdorp and Mahikeng, the province's capital. The North West province is rich in minerals, and platinum, gold, uranium and diamonds are mined here. Many international companies, such as Bosch, Samsung, BMW and Firestone have production sites in the province, the majority of which are located around Mahikeng.

The people living in the area are mainly Batswana with some Ndebele in the east and Sotho in the south. Various cultural villages have been established to keep the cultural heritage alive.

The North West province has a diverse landscape with bushveld predominating in the northern and eastern parts and grassland and arid savannah in the southern and western parts. The province has many endemic plant species and is home to various endangered animal species, such as the wild dog, cheetahs and rhinos. There are 14 national parks, over 40 wetland parks and many more nature reserves which make for excellent game viewing and birding sites. The Big Five game viewing is done extensively and the Pilanesberg National Park and Madikwe Game Reserve attract visitors from all over.

A major attraction in the region is Sun City, an enormous fun park set in the middle of the bushveld with a turquoise lagoon surrounded by an artificial sandy beach, a super bowl stadium for major concerts, a vast casino complex and a world-famous golf course. The Lost City, with its 'lost world theme' is a fantastic resort in Sun City and it has accommodation options for every budget. This tourist attraction has a huge wave pool with a man-made beach located at the centre.

 Capital

Mahikeng
842 000
inhabitants

 Population

3.5 million
34 people per km²
Mainly in rural
households

 Education

More than 15% of all
adults have never had
any formal schooling
Literacy rate of 70%

 Languages

Setswana 63%
Afrikaans 9%
isiXhosa 6%. English
is spoken and
understood by many

WEEKEND BREAKS

 Sun City: Fantasy entertainment and 'beach' resort in the African savannah

 Madikwe Game Reserve: Sight the rare wild dogs in this national park

 Hartbeespoort Dam: Watersport activities for outdoor enthusiasts

 Magalies Meander: Hike the 130 km Magaliesberg mountain range

(5) **Molopo Nature Reserve:** View game amidst grasslands and red dunes

(See map on next page)

BUSINESS SECTORS

Most of the province's economic activities happen in the southern and eastern regions of the province, with the mining industry mostly settled around Rustenburg and agriculture dominating the region around Vryburg and Klerksdorp. The mining industry contributes more than half of the province's GDP. The province has more than 80 mines, which employ one third of all the mine workers in South Africa. The North West is recognised as the world's richest platinum reserve and the region around Rustenburg and Brits produces 94% of the country's platinum. The so-called Platinum Corridor, which stretches from Pretoria to eastern Botswana, provides employment to over a third of the people of the province. Gold and uranium mining takes place around Klerksdorp and diamonds are mined mainly around Christiana and Bloemhof.

The manufacturing sector accounts for most of the other half of the province's GDP, where high tech equipment, automotive parts, and electronic and medical equipment are produced mainly in the municipalities of Brits, Rustenburg, Potchefstroom, Klerksdorp and Mahikeng.

The agricultural sector dominates in the region around Vryburg, which is also referred to as the 'Texas of South Africa' due to its large cattle herds. In the northern and western parts of the province cattle, game and sheep farming are major income sources. In the southern and eastern parts of the province various crops are farmed, mainly maize (corn), tobacco, sunflowers and cotton.

Tourism is an important factor around the province's game reserves and national parks. Sol Kerzner's Sun City entertainment complex is one of South Africa's major tourist attractions for locals and international visitors.

Health	Climate	Infrastructure	Economy
No malaria HIV prevalence of 31%	Moderate to high temperatures in summer with cold nights in winter Summer rainfall season	Well-developed road infrastructure Pilanesburg Airport near Sun City and Rustenburg Airport	Main industries are mining, agriculture, manufacturing and tourism Contributes 5% to the country's GDP

LIMPOPO

BOTSWANA

N3

2

5

Zeerust

7   1   Hartbeespoort   3

Rustenberg

Mahikeng   6   N4   4

GAUTENG

Lichtenburg

N14

Potchefstroom

10   Klerksdorp

Vryburg   9

8   N12

Bloemhof

FREE STATE

NORTHERN CAPE

Sun City is located 180 km north of Johannesburg and is a popular weekend destination for many Gauteng city dwellers. The resort is situated in the middle of the African bushveld and includes a casino complex as well as a golf course designed by Gary Player. The adjacent Pilanesberg nature reserve borders the entertainment complex and offers superb game drives.

Platinum mining is extensively carried out in the province. The area around Rustenburg and Brits is known as the 'Bushveld Igneous Complex' and contains the world's richest platinum reserves. Over 90% of the country's platinum resources are mined in the north-eastern parts of the province.

Madikwe Game Reserve is one of the country's prime malaria-free safari destinations with its vast plains of open woodland and grassland. The reserve, also known for its wild dog conservation programme, is located along the Botswana border and offers day and night game drives and bushwalks.

7 Groot Marico

Get away from the hustle and bustle of the city and experience typical farm hospitality in this little river-side town. *Mampoer* is brewed on many farms.

8 Taung

In this little town, which is called 'Place of the Lion', the significant fossil skull of a child was found. This world heritage site is the most southern hominid site in Africa.

9 Klerksdorp

This town still has many of the original buildings from the gold rush era. Nearby San rock engravings are worth a visit.

6 Hartbeespoort Dam

The dam and the area around Brits are popular for watersports facilities and numerous other attractions. A cableway offers stunning views over the area. Nearby Crocodile Junction houses one of the country's biggest arts and crafts markets.

5 Lesedi

The cultural village near Broederstroom consists of recreated homesteads of five of the traditional cultures: Pedi, Zulu, Xhosa, Basotho and Ndebele.

The **People** ^{of} *the Dew*

10 Vryburg

This large town, named after its 'free citizens' (*vryburgers*), is the industrial and agricultural hub of the southern part of the province. Situated in the middle of cattle farming land, it hosts one of the largest cattle markets in the southern hemisphere and also hosts the third largest annual agricultural show in South Africa.

4 Magaliesberg

The mountain range of the Magaliesberg stretches over 130 km between Rustenburg and Pretoria and is popular for bird watching, hiking and visits to animal sanctuaries.

1 Pilanesberg

The largest national park in the province is located in the crater of an extinct volcano, adjacent to Sun City. The game reserve is known for excellent wildlife viewing and elephant-back safaris.

CITIES AND TOWNS

Sun City

Mahikeng

Also commonly known as Mafikeng and formerly known as Mafeking, the capital of the North West is located close to the border with Botswana. The city has many facilities and a modern conference centre. It lies conveniently on the Cape Town to Zimbabwe railway and on the east-west corridor linking Maputo/Mozambique with Walvis Bay/Namibia. The city boasts many educational facilities, among them an international school and the main campus of the North West University. There are a number of tourist attractions and national monuments in town, several relating to the 217-day siege of the city during the Anglo-Boer War. On the outskirts of the city is Mahikeng Game Reserve, where on a two-hour circular self-drive many of the plains game can be seen, including giraffes, buffalos, gemsbok and white rhinos.

Rustenburg

The town set at the foot of the rolling hills of the Magaliesberg offers a range of modern facilities. Once home of former Transvaal president Paul Kruger, the town's name means 'place of rest' and it still keeps its relaxed country feel. Nearby is the ethnic homeland of a small community of around 100 000 Setswana speaking 'people of the dew', the so-called 'Royal Bafokeng Nation' which is ruled by a king. The Royal Bafokeng Nation has a very successful community investment project that derives income from royalties mining companies pay for the mining of platinum on the 'Merensky Reef' which lies on their territory. Mining companies must pay royalties for their mining rights. The country's foremost high altitude sports centre and the soccer stadium are named in honour of the local people. In the surrounding region there are various game reserves such as the Pilanesberg nature reserve and Kgaswane Game Reserve as well as the scenic Olifantsnek Dam.

Potchefstroom

Formallly called Potchefstroom, the town is often referred to simply as 'Potch'. This university town on the banks of the Mooi River is renowned for its colonial architecture and range of national monuments, including a 6 km long oak alley. Also labelled 'home of sports', the city accommodates one of the two premier high-altitude training centres in South Africa and the headquarters of several sports associations. The city is an important industrial growth point in the province, housing major industries of the chemical, steel and agricultural sectors. A variety of shopping, health and education facilities, including a university, can be found in the city. Nearby Boskop Dam and various nature reserves are popular for weekend breaks and leisure pursuits such as birdwatching and watersports.

RESOURCES

Province, District and Municipalities

North West Province: *www.nwpg.gov.za*
Bojanala Platinum District:
www.bojanala.gov.za
Ngaka Modiri-Molema District:
www.nmmdm.gov.za
Dr Kenneth Kaunda District:
www.kaundadistrict.gov.za
Rustenburg: *www.rustenburg.gov.za*
Mahikeng: *www.mafikeng.gov.za*

Business and Industry

North West Provincial Business Directory:
www.nwpbd.co.za
Invest North West: *www.inw.org.za*
North West Business Guide:
www.northwestbusiness.co.za
North West Development Corporation:
www.nwdc.co.za
Rustenburg Business Info:
www.rustenburg.biz

National Parks and National Heritage

www.sanparks.org.za
www.parksnorthwest.co.za

Tourism and Attractions

www.tourismnorthwest.co.za
Bill Harrop's Balloon Safaris:
www.balloon.co.za
www.hartiescableway.co.za
www.lesedi.com
www.magaliesmeander.co.za
www.n12treasureroute.com
Outdoor Adventure Centre:
www.oac.co.za
www.skydiverustenburg.co.za
www.sun-city-south-africa.com
Vredefort Area:
www.domeadventures.co.za

Local Websites

www.bafokeng.com
www.klerksdorp.co.za
www.marico.co.za
www.platinumweekly.co.za
www.potch.co.za
www.showmerustenburg.co.za
www.vryburg.com

Annual Events

Hartbeespoort Dam Race in March
Sun City Nedbank Golf Challenge in
December
Sun City Pigeon Race in February
Taung Cultural Calabash in September

'Peace and Prosperity'
Provincial motto

Recommended Reading

Bosman, Herman Charles (2000) *Old Transvaal Stories*. Human & Rousseau

Carruthers, Vincent (2012) *The Magaliesberg*. Protea Books

Mbenga, Bernard & Manson, Andrew (2010) *People of the Dew*. Jacana

MAIN CITIES AND TOWNS

Mahikeng

Municipality: Ngaka
Modiri-Molema
Population: 250 000
Elevation: 1 500 metres
Airport: Mahikeng 17
km N of the city

Rustenburg

Municipality: Rustenburg
Population: 550 000
Elevation: 1 170 metres
Airport: Johannesburg
OR Tambo, 173 km SE of
the city

Potchefstroom

Municipality: Tlokwe
Population: 162 762
Elevation: 1 350 metres
Airport: Potchefstroom,
Johannesburg OR Tambo,
146 km SE of the city

KWAZULU-NATAL

KwaZulu-Natal is a diverse province showcasing stunning beaches, historic battlefields and majestic mountain ranges. It was formed by combining the Zulu kingdom and the province of Natal, once a British colony and named by Portuguese navigators who came upon this coast on Christmas Day 1497. Larger than Portugal, the province has international borders with Lesotho to the west and Swaziland and Mozambique to the north. The province has a rich mix of cultural heritages and has the highest number of Indians in the country. Their vibrant cultural influence is strongly felt.

The province has several distinct regions. The north and south coasts lie in the coastal belt centred on Durban. The central interior of Natal is the Midlands region, with southern Natal and East Griqualand to the south and the Drakensberg district to the west. In the north-west is northern Natal with its battlefields, and in the north-east are Zululand and Maputaland.

The landscape along the coast is dominated by lush tropical vegetation and sugar cane fields while the rolling hills in the hinterland lead to South Africa's highest mountain range. The provincial capital, Pietermaritzburg, lies 90 km inland from Durban in the heart of the Midlands, with its rolling green hills and picturesque historic villages. Durban and Richards Bay on the north coast are the main business centres due to their busy ports, which are important links for the industries not only of the region but of the whole country. The N2 highway links Durban with the northern and southern coastlines and the N3 links the province with Gauteng and the Free State.

Due to their abundant beaches and 320 days of sunshine a year, the coastal resorts from Port Edward in the south to Kosi Bay in the north are popular with watersports enthusiasts from all over the world. The mountainous western region is a major drawcard for hikers and climbers. The weather in this region, however, is less predictable with sudden summer storms and frequent snow in winter, when temperatures can drop below 0 °C.

Capital	Population	Education	Languages
Pietermaritzburg 500 000 inhabitants	10.3 million 109 people per km² 30% live in Ethekwini Municipality (Durban)	Literacy rate of 89% Wide variety of excellent state and private schools Two regional universities	isiZulu 78% English 13% English is spoken by most

Durban, KwaZulu-Natal

WEEKEND BREAKS

1. **Midlands Meander:** Stroll through picturesque villages

2. **Hluhluwe-iMfolozi Park:** View the Big Five in stunning settings

3. **iSimangeliso Wetlands:** Visit pristine beaches and world-class diving sites

4. **uKhahlamba-Drakensberg:** Hike the spectacular Dragon Mountains

5. **Coastal Resorts:** Enjoy golden beaches, diving reefs and turquoise surf

(See map on next page)

BUSINESS SECTORS

Durban and Richards Bay are the two biggest metropolitan areas. Here more than 70% of the province's GDP is produced. Many international manufacturers have production sites in the province, among them Nestlé in Estcourt, Coca Cola in Durban, Kerry in Pinetown, Clover, Africa's largest dairy producer, in Mooi River and Ulster Carpets and Defy in Durban. Car manufacturer Toyota, Volvo trucks and MAN trucks have plants in Durban.

Paper manufacturer Mondi owns and manages one of the largest plantation units in the world with its sites in KwaZulu-Natal, and Sappi Saiccor is the world's largest manufacturer of chemical cellulose. Bell Equipment, situated in Richards Bay, manufactures the world's first and only production 50-tonne Articulated Dump Truck and operates internationally.

The province's agriculture, forestry and fishing sector contributes a 26% share to the national GDP. Sugar is the main agricultural product, providing more than 200 000 jobs. Thirteen of South Africa's 15 sugar mills are located in the province with the Sugar Terminal on Durban's Maydon Wharf currently being the largest in the world.

Although mining is a relatively small contributor to the province's GDP, KwaZulu-Natal boasts some world firsts and top businesses in this sector. Richards Bay is home to the world's largest sand mining and mineral-producing operations. Dredge mining operations are used to extract heavy minerals, such as rutile and zircon, from the sand dunes. Richards Bay Minerals (RBM) contributes almost a quarter of the global market in titianium, slag, rutile, high-purity pig iron, and zircon. Hulamin is the leading producer of semi-fabricated aluminium products in Africa and has its head-quarters in Pietermaritzburg.

Health	Climate	Infrastructure	Economy
Malaria risk along the north coast Highest HIV rate in the country with 39.5% prevalence	Mild to hot temperatures Very humid on coast Inland has cold winters and snow on mountain ranges	Main roads are tarred, A wide net of gravel roads in rural areas King Shaka International Airport north of Durban	Manufacturing, and services industry, agriculture, mining and tourism Contributes 16.5% to country's GDP

Kozi Bay
MPUMALANGA
SWAZILAND
FREE STATE
Pongola
Sodwana Bay
9
Newcastle
Vryheid
Hluhluwe
7
2
3
N11
N3
Ulundi
St Lucia
Ladysmith
Richards Bay
N2
Estcourt
4
Mooi River
5
LESOTHO
1
Ballito
Pietermaritzburg
Umhlanga Rocks
Durban
6
Kokstad
8
EASTERN CAPE
Port Shepstone
Margate

Durban's port is not only the largest port in South Africa, but also one of the ten largest in the world. It also houses the Sugar Terminal on Durban's Maydon Wharf, which is currently the largest in the world. Together with the port at Richards Bay, Durban handles nearly 80% of the country's cargo tonnage.

The Indian culture is a big part of the local culture especially around Durban and the major towns. Many families have their origins in India. Indentured labourers arrived as early as 1870 to work on the sugar cane fields and stayed on in the area. Hindu temples and Muslim mosques are found throughout the province.

The Zulu Kingdom was first established by Shaka, the legendary king of the Zulu (1787-1828), who was known for his aggressive expansionism and brutality. In the 1880s the British annexed the area and broke up the huge kingdom. Traditional kings are still recognised by the state and the Zulu king is the most prominent and powerful king of all the traditional reigning kings in the country.

③ iSimangaliso Wetland Park

Africa's largest estuarine system is renowned for its 220 km of pristine beaches and clear tropical warm waters. Attractions include going on a game drive or seeing the endangered turtles laying their eggs on the beach. Divers may spot the rare coelacanth.

② Hluhluwe

The oldest proclaimed game reserve in Africa, this national park is involved in African rhino conservation programmes to save the animals from vicious poaching.
Experience the Big Five from the comfort of your own car or on a game drive with an experienced guide.

⑦ Battlefields

This is former frontier country with historic battlefields. Historic tours in the battlefields region around Isandlwana and Rorke's Drift take you to sites where the British, Zulu and Boers fought.

① Midlands Meander

This scenic arts and crafts route stretches from Pietermaritzburg to Mooi River. The route meanders through the green hills of the Midlands and passes through picturesque landscape and quaint villages such as Howick and Nottingham Road.

Kingdom
of the *Zulu*

④ The Amphitheatre

The picture-perfect 5 km long and 1 km wide rock edge of the 'Amphitheatre' is the site of the Tugela Falls, the second highest waterfalls in the world. These are only two of the many splendid sights offered in the uKhahlamba-Drakensberg National Park. The four valleys of this world heritage site provide mesmerising scenic views of the rugged mountainscape. Here you can go hiking, mountain biking or horse riding or admire the stunning views from the poolside in one of the resorts. The more adventurous can try tubing down rivers, quad biking or paragliding.

⑧ Sardine Run

The shoals of sardines which migrate up the east coast are accompanied by a big variety of marine life such as dolphins, fish and birds.

⑨ Cape Vidal and Sodwana Bay

These diving sites are two of the world's most famous, with the colourful coral ecosystem of the 12-25 m deep 'Two-mile Reef'. The province's south coast is renowned for excellent deep sea diving as well.

CITIES AND TOWNS

Durban

Durban

Durban is the third largest city in South Africa after Johannesburg and Cape Town and one of the fastest growing metropolitans in the world. The vibrant city is home to the local Zulu population and numerous Indians, as well as expats from all over the world. Durban offers various excellent private and state schools in and around the city and private medical facilities are widely available. There are modern facilities, huge shopping malls and attractions such as the uShaka Marine World, the Moses Mabhida and King's Park Stadiums, the Botanic Gardens, the 'Golden Mile' and the many beaches. Umhlanga and Ballito are popular beach resorts a short drive outside the city. Because of its beachfront promenades lined with holiday accommodation, the city is also referred to as South Africa's Miami. Durban's International Conference Centre offers one of the most advanced conference facilities in the world and has been named 'Africa's Leading Conference Centre' for eight years in a row at the World Travel Awards. The suburbs surrounding the city are bordered by sugar cane farmland.

Pietermaritzburg

The capital and second largest city of KwaZulu-Natal, often dubbed the 'Garden City', is best known for its beautiful settling, its Edwardian and Victoria buildings and nearby nature reserves. Pietermaritzburg is a regional industrial hub for the timber, dairy and aluminium industries. Some excellent educational institutions are located in the city, which is also known for its relaxed lifestyle and well-situated suburbs. The city has many antique and craft shops, markets and restaurants and provides ample attractions for visitors and residents. The city's airport provides daily flights to Johannesburg. The majestic Drakensberg region is within a two-hour drive from the city and nearby Howick Falls, Midmar Dam and Karkloof area are popular for outings.

Richards Bay

Located halfway between Durban and the Mozambique border, the once sleepy fishing town of Richards Bay has one of Africa's biggest harbours and has the world's largest coal export terminal. Today the town still retains a relaxed atmosphere with a small city centre and a waterfront development with a short quay walk. There are modern amenities and educational facilities in the town. Prime housing estates are located near the Waterfront. There are plenty of watersports activities on offer and visits to nearby Shakaland, the Zululand battlefields or the Hluhluwe and Umfolosi game parks are a must visit when staying in the area.

RESOURCES

Province, District and Municipalities

KwaZulu-Natal Province:
www.kwazulunatal.gov.za
Durban/eThekwini Municipality:
www.durban.gov.za
Pietermaritzburg/Msunduzi Municipality:
www.msunduzi.gov.za
uMhlathuze Municipality (incorporating
Richards Bay and Empangeni):
www.umhlathuze.gov.za

Business and Industry

Durban Chamber of Commerce and
Industry: *www.durbanchamber.co.za*
Pietermaritzburg Chamber of Commerce:
www.pcb.org.za
KwaZulu-Natal Business Guide:
www.kwazulunatalbusiness.co.za
KZN Top Business Portfolio:
www.kzntopbusiness.co.za
Trade&Investment: *www.tikzn.co.za*
Richards Bay: *www.rbidz.co.za*
KZN Business: *www.kznbusinessbook.co.za*

National Parks / National Heritage

KZN Wildlife: *www.kznwildlife.com*
Save the Rhino: *www.savetherhino.org*

Tourism and Attractions

KwaZulu-Natal Tourism: *www.zulu.org.za*
Drakensberg Tourism:
www.drakensberg.org.za
Durban Tourism:
www.durbanexperience.co.za
Pietermaritzburg Tourism:
www.pmbtourism.co.za
Midlands Meander:
www.midlandsmeander.co.za

Annual Events

Comrades Marathon in May
Midmar Mile Swim in February
Dusi Canoe Marathon in January

Local Websites

www.durbanlive.com
www.pietermaritzburgevents.co.za
Local magazines such as *Business in
Durban, The Ridge* and *Maritzburg Life*
are available online at
www.famouspublishing.co.za

'Let us Rise and Build'
Provincial motto

Recommended Reading

Derwent, Sue (2010) *KwaZulu-Natal:
Adventures in Culture and Nature*.
Random House Struik

Radford, Dennis (2011) *Guide to
the Architecture of Durban and
Pietermaritzburg*. David Philip Publishers

Stewart, Di (2008) *Durban in a Word*.
Penguin

Golightly, Walton (2012) *Shaka the Great*.
Quercus

MAIN CITIES AND TOWNS

Durban

Municipality: eThekwini
Population: 3.4 million
Elevation: 23 metres
Airport: King Shaka
International 35 km N
of the city

Pietermaritzburg

Municipality: Msunduzi
Population: 1 million
Elevation: 724 metres
Airport: Oribi Airport 5 km
S of the city, King Shaka
International 105 km NE
of the city

Richards Bay

Municipality: uMhlathuze
Population: 908 000
Elevation: 30 metres
Airport: King Shaka
International 150 km S
of the city

LIMPOPO

South Africa's northernmost province borders on Botswana in the west, Zimbabwe in the north and Mozambique in the east and is named after the Limpopo River which forms the border with Zimbabwe. Limpopo means 'waterfalls' in many Nguni languages.

The wild and seemingly untamed landscape is dominated by bushveld and mixed grassland. Majestic mountain ranges and subtropical farmland prevail in the southern highveld. The province is divided into five districts: Mopani, Vhembe, Capricorn, Waterberg and Greater Sekhukhune. Polokwane, located in the Capricorn district, is the provincial capital and main business hub. Limpopo's second biggest town, Tzaneen, is located in a lush valley with fertile soils. The subtropical climate of the area gives rise to tea plantations and many farms. The much smaller towns of Lephalale, Mokopane and Phalaborwa are regional business centres.

The province has a strong agricultural aspect. More than two thirds of all South African mangoes, tomatoes and avocados are grown here and cattle farming and controlled hunting are also major industries. The rich cultural heritage and abundant wildlife ensure a strong tourism sector. Game farms have become lucrative businesses and hunting safaris are a major draw for international visitors. The eco-tourism sector is growing rapidly.

Often referred to being 'the land of myths and legends' it is still home of the 'Rain Queen' and many mystical sites such as the Funduzi lake and Modjadjiskloof are found here. Various world heritage sites such as Makapansgat (Makapan's Cave) and the remains of the ancient kingdom of Mapungubwe are also located in the province.

The climate is in the arid semi-desert, especially hot in summer and mild in winter, in the more subtropical regions in the centre and eastern regions, hot and humid in summer and mild in winter. The eastern parts of the province are a malaria area in the rainy season where the necessary precautions should be taken throughout the year.

 Capital

 Population

 Education

 Languages

Capital	Population	Education	Languages
Polokwane 629 000 inhabitants	5.4 million 43 people per km² Over 60% of people live below the poverty line 90% rural households	Second lowest education levels for adults Over 30% of adults have no schooling Literacy rate of 82%	Sepedi 53% Xitsonga 17% Tshivenda 17% English is main business language

WEEKEND BREAKS

1. **Kruger National Park:** Explore the country's top game viewing attraction

2. **Mapungubwe:** Visit this World Heritage Site where iron-age artefacts were found

3. **Nylsvlei Wetlands:** Enjoy bird watching in pristine nature

4. **Marakele National Park:** Spend time at this wildlife sanctuary in the Waterberg

5. **Bela Bela:** Bathe in the hot springs of this popular health and holiday resort

(See map on next page)

BUSINESS SECTORS

Mining is the primary driver of economic activity in the province. There are over 130 local and international mine operations registered in the province with some large platinum, diamond, copper and coal mines. The De Beers Venetia Diamond Mine is currently South Africa's largest diamond mine. It is still an open-pit mine, but it plans to start mining underground between 2018 and 2021. Platinum is mined extensively, mainly around Burgersfort south of Mokopane. Other reserves include phosphates, gold, vermiculite, silicon, salt and antimony, with Limpopo being the world's largest producer of the resource, which is used in alloys and medicine. Copper and its by-products are mined at the Phalaborwa mine. This is South Africa's only producer of refined copper and also supplies almost 50% of the world's vermiculite. Lephalale's Matimba coal plant was specially constructed for a dry area as the northern region is known for severe droughts and scarce water resources. A new coal-fired Medupi power plant, also in Lephalale, is expected to surpass the output of Matimba power station.

The province produces more than 60% of South Africa's fruit, vegetables, wheat and cotton. Among the produced fruit are mangoes, papaya, avocados and tomatoes. Many international operations such as McCains, Giant Foods and Golden Harvest are located in the province.

The province's biggest employers include Silicon Smelters (silicon smelting), Anglo Platinum (platinum smelting), Eskom (electricity generation), Granor Passi (fruit juices), Bonanza (furniture manufacturing), Mittal Steel (steel), Kanhym (meat processing) and many others.

Limpopo's economy is seen as being closely connected to those of its three neighbouring countries, Zimbabwe, Mozambique and Botswana. The province is in a strategic position as a regional hub for the growing trade with these African countries.

Health	Climate	Infrastructure	Economy
Malaria & bilharzia are prevalent HIV prevalence of 20.7% Lowest doctor to patient ratio	Hot and humid in summer Summer rainfall Mild days and cold nights in winter	Developed highways Polokwane International Airport Smaller airports in Phalaborwa, Musina and Hoedspruit	Mining, agriculture, tourism and manufacturing industries Contributes 7% to the country's GDP

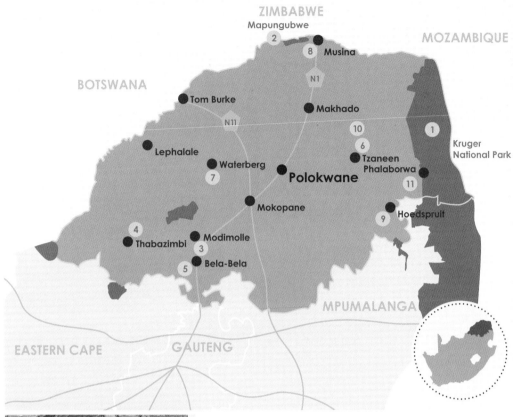

ZIMBABWE

MOZAMBIQUE

Mapungubwe

2

8 Musina

N1

BOTSWANA

Tom Burke

Makhado

N11

10

1

Kruger
National Park

Lephalale

6

Tzaneen
Phalaborwa

Waterberg

7

Polokwane

11

Mokopane

9 Hoedspruit

4

Modimolle

Thabazimbi

3

5 Bela-Bela

MPUMALANGA

EASTERN CAPE

GAUTENG

Mining is carried out extensively in the province, which is rich in mineral resources such as platinum, diamonds, coal, chromium, gold and copper. The open-cast copper mine in Phalaborwa has one of the world's deepest shafts of 898 m and is the world's widest man-made hole of 2 km in diameter.

National parks and conservancies are a major attraction in the province as it has the world's greatest concentration of national parks. Over 80% of the Kruger National Park, where you can view the Big Five and abundant wildlife, lies within the province's borders. There are also many luxurious private game reserves surrounding the Kruger Park.

Archaeological sites such as the World Heritage Sites of Mapungubwe, Thumela and the Makapans Valley offer insights into early history with fossil finds dating back as far as 3 million years. At Makapan's Caves, the 3.3 million year-old fossils of early humankind '*Australopithecus africanus*' were found in 1925.

⑥ Tzaneen

The second biggest town in the province is known for its stunning setting in a fertile valley and its subtropical climate. Surrounded by picturesque farmland used for fruit farming and coffee and tea plantations, the city is convenient for visiting nearby attractions such as Magoesbaskloof with the world's largest baobab trees and the quaint Haenertsburg in the mountains.

⑦ Waterberg Biosphere

The nature reserve offers excellent game viewing and experiences such as the natural hot springs of 53°C thermal waters nearby Bela Bela (formerly Warmbaths). Legends Golf and Safari Resort in the Waterberg offers extreme golfing with a 19th hole that can only be accessed by helicopter and is the highest and longest par 3 in the world.

⑧ Musina (formerly Messina)

Situated on the Limpopo River, the country's northernmost town, formerly known as Messina, connects with the busy Beit Bridge border post.

Land of *Myths* and *Legends*

⑥ African Ivory Route

This eco-tourism route stretches 2 000 km across the province and includes various nature reserves, game parks and private farms and follows the trails of legendary ivory hunters and gold diggers.

⑨ Hoedspruit

Located in the middle of the lowveld between the Blyde River Canyon and the Kruger Park, this small town has an airport that offers daily domestic flights to various destinations and is used by many private game reserves.

⑩ Modjadji Nature Reserve

The unique cycad forest near Modjadjikloof has the world's largest concentration of a cycad species. The area is home to generations of the 'Rain Queen', the hereditary rulers of the area.

③ Nylsvlei Wetlands

The wetlands and floodplains of the nature reserve attract the largest variety of water birds as well as the highest number of birds in the southern hemisphere. It offers refuge to more than 400 bird species.

CITIES AND TOWNS

Waterberg

Polokwane

The capital of Limpopo, often also called 'City of Stars', is referred to in the Sotho language as 'Place of Safety'. The city is located centrally in the Capricorn district of the province on the N1 highway that links Johannesburg with Musina close to the Zimbabwean border. With a wide range of modern amenities and a busy city centre, Polokwane, formerly named Pietersburg, offers the widest range of educational, medical and cultural facilities in the northern part of the country. Polokwane's Mall of the North shopping centre with more than 180 shops and an entertainment centre offers abundant entertainment for the whole family. The city is home to many cultures and the local Art Museum is renowned for its display of traditional Venda, Tsonga and Pedi artifacts. An interesting fact is that there are more public sculptures per capita on display in Polokwane than in any other city in South Africa. The open-air Bakone Malapa cultural village offers insights into Northern Sotho culture and the Arend Dieperink museum in Mokopane deals with the early settlements in the province. Besides the many nearby private game reserves, the lion park at the outskirts of the city is also a main tourist attraction.

Phalaborwa

The town, which is situated in the east of the province, borders the Limpopo Transfrontier Park and is seen as the 'Gateway to Kruger Park'. Palabora Mine on the outskirts of the town is the main economic driver in the area. The centre of town has a shopping mall with modern amenities and many guesthouses cater for tourists in the area. Trips to nearby attractions such as the Tzaneen fruit farms, the Blyde River Canyon and the Three Rondavels are easily managed on day visits from Phalaborwa. The Hans Merensky Golf Course in Phalaborwa is known for its golf experiences in the wild, where a wide range of wildlife can be seen from its greens.

Lephalale

Founded in 1960 as Ellisras and renamed in 2002 to Lephalale, the small town in the far north of the province houses one of the most ambitious mining sites in the country. With nearby Medupi power plant and the projected Matimba plant the town is home to a wide range of foreigners of various nationalities and is expected to double its current population in the next five years. The country's largest open-cast coal mine, Grootgeluk, is also situated here. The town centre has a shopping precinct and mall. A golf club near town offers recreation facilities. The nearest commercial airport is situated in Polokwane, which is 220 km south of the town. The road connections are good.

RESOURCES

Province, District and Municipalities

Limpopo Province: *www.limpopo.gov.za*
Waterberg District: *www.waterberg.gov.za*
Capricorn District: *www.cdm.org.za*
Mopani District: *www.mopani.gov.za*
Vhembe District: *www.vhembe.gov.za*
Sekhukhune District: *www.sekhukhune.gov.za*

Business and Industry

Trade & Invest Limpopo: *www.til.co.za*
Limpopo Department of Economic
Development: *www.lieda.co.za*
Directory: *www.limpopobusiness.co.za*

National Parks / National Heritage

National Parks: *www.sanparks.org*
Kruger National Park: *www.krugerpark.co.za*
Nyslvlei: *www.limpoposouth.co.za*
Waterberg National Park:
www.waterbergbiosphere.org
Marakele National Park: *www.sanparks.org*

Tourism and Attractions

Limpopo Tourism: *www.golimpopo.com*
African Ivory Route:
www.africanivoryroute.co.za
Magoebaskloof Tourism:
www.magoebaskloof.com

Local Websites:

www.lephalale.com
www.lifeinlimpopo.wordpress.com
www.phalaborwa.co.za

Annual Events

Magoebasklof/Haenertsburg Spring
Festival in September
Polokwane Mapungubwe Arts Festival
in September
Northam Oppikoppi Music Festival
in August

'Peace, Unity and Prosperity'
Provincial motto

Recommended Reading

Kipling, Rudyard (2010) *The Elephant's Boy*.
London: Frances Lincoln Publishers

Donve (2001) *Modjadji, the Rain Queen*.
New Africa Books

Huffman, Thomas N. (2005) *Mapungubwe*.
Wits University Press

Haggard, H. Rider (2002) *She. A History of Adventure*. New York: Random House

MAIN CITIES AND TOWNS

Polokwane

Municipality: Polokwane
Population: 300 000
Elevation: 1 200 m
Airport: Polokwane
International Airport
52 km E of the city

Phalaborwa

Municipality: Ba-Phalaborwa
Population: 109 500
Elevation: 420 metres
Airport: Phalaborwa Airport
5 km E of the town

Lephalale

Municipality: Lephalale
Population: 45 000
Elevation: 820 metres
Aiport: Polokwane
International Airport
220 km E of the town

MPUMALANGA

Mpumalanga, the 'place where the sun rises' as the Siswati and Zulu say, is located on the highveld and borders Swaziland to the south-east and the Kruger National Park borders Mozambique to the east. The province is divided into three municipal districts: Ngankala (around eMalahleni), Gert Sibande (around Secunda) and Ehlanzeni District, the latter encompassing the province's capital Mbombela/Nelspruit and the tourist centres of Malelane, Hazyview, White River, Barberton and Sabie. This is the province's 'Panorama Route' and one of the major tourist attractions. The province houses various ethnic groups, the majority among them being the Ndebele, the Zulu, the Siswati and the Tsonga. Although the second smallest province, it has a thriving economy owing to its mining and manufacturing sector and wide range of tourist attractions.

The province is known to have the biggest variety of wildlife in the southern part of its Kruger Park. Numerous private game reserves adjoining the park and tourist facilities in and around the park make it an outstanding experience. The rolling hills in the lowveld and the Panorama Route, with waterfalls and awe-inspiring views from the impressive mountain range at the edge of the escarpment, is a further major drawcard.

The infrastructure in this province is widely developed and eco-tourism has grown constantly in recent years. The Maputo Corridor, the country's first international toll road, links the Gauteng province with neighbouring Mozambique. When travelling the area, take into consideration that in Mpumalanga several towns have undergone name changes and street signage is not yet consistent.

Although most of the province receives summer rainfall, the climate varies considerably between the lowveld and highveld regions. In the lowveld the climate is subtropical whereas in the highveld the winter nights are usually cold and frosty.

Capital	Population	Education	Languages
Mbombela 734 000 inhabitants	4 million people 48 people per km² Over 50% live in rural areas Almost half of the people live below the poverty line	More than 11% are without formal education Literacy level of 76%	siSwati 28% isiZulu 24% Xitsonga 10% isiNdebele 10% English is understood and spoken by most

Blyde River Canyon

WEEKEND BREAKS

1. **Blyde River Canyon:** Admire this green canyon from 'God's Window'

2. **Lake Chrissie:** Go fishing at South Africa's largest freshwater lake

3. **Sabie River:** Enjoy a rafting adventure trip in pristine nature

4. **Kruger Park:** Wildlife viewing is best in the early morning or late afternoon

5. **Pilgrim's Rest:** Experience the gold rush of the 1870s in this picturesque village

(See map on next page)

BUSINESS SECTORS

Mpumalanga is the second smallest province but it has the fourth largest economy in South Africa. The province has some of the country's oldest and biggest mining sites and the three largest power plants in the southern hemisphere. One of them is the coal liquefaction plant in Secunda, which produces liquid fuel from coal. The red ochre mines near Malelane are some of the oldest mining sites in the world.

Extensive gold mining takes place in the province as well as mining operations for platinum, vanadium and chrome. The Barberton Greenstone Belt is still a promising area for gold mining and further mining projects are being considered for the future.

The province's large manufacturing sector also features several internationally operating companies such as Sasol (synthetic fuels and chemicals), Ervaz (steel) and Xstrata (ferrochrome). One tenth of the province is covered by either natural forests or plantations. The agricultural products of the region are used by international food producing companies like McCain, Nestle and PepsiCo. Standerton, in the south, is home to a large dairy industry and Mbombela is the provincial centre for citrus and subtropical fruit as well as sugar production. Ermelo is renowned for its wool production, the biggest of the country. The forests around Mkhondo/Piet Retief as well as those around Sabie and Graskop provide for the country's forestry products. Paper production by Sappi and Mondi is thriving, and the province has the country's largest paper mill.

The tourism sector is strong in the province and the southern Kruger Park and numerous private game reserves make it the most popular tourist destination with domestic travellers after the Western Province.

Health	Climate	Infrastructure	Economy
Malaria is prelavent and precautions are advisable Second highest HIV prevalence of 35.5%	Summer rainfall area Cold frosty winters on the highveld Mild winter with subtropical climate in the lowveld regions	Well-developed roads Kruger Mpumalanga International Airport and several small airports close to industry	Mining, power-generation, manufacturing and service industries Contributes 7% to the country's GDP

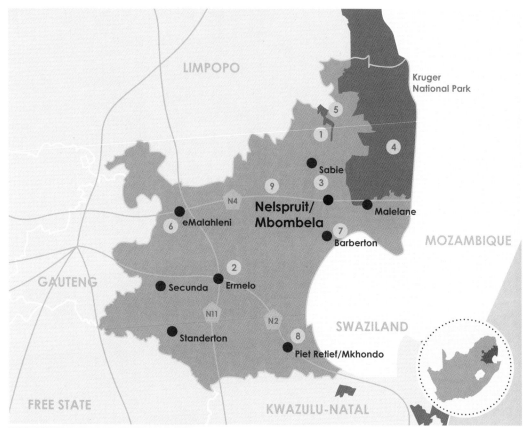

LIMPOPO

Kruger
National Park

5

1

4

Sabie

9

3

N4

Nelspruit/
Mbombela

Malelane

6 eMalahleni

7

MOZAMBIQUE

Barberton

2

GAUTENG

Secunda   Ermelo

N11

N2

SWAZILAND

Standerton

8

Piet Retief/Mkhondo

FREE STATE

KWAZULU-NATAL

Blyde River Canyon, also called Motlatse River Canyon, is the largest green canyon in the world. The 60 km long canyon has a unique lush subtropical vegetation and is also one of the biggest canyons in the world. The panarama route leads past the awe-inspiring views from God's Window and many of the picturesque towns.

Coal mining is extensively done in the highveld surrounding eMalahleni, which is the biggest coal producing region in Africa. Mpumalanga is the third biggest coal producing region in the world: 83% of the country's coal is sourced from the province.

Delicious fruits such as mangoes, papayas, litchis, guavas and avocados thrive in the mild subtropical climate of the region. Another provincial specialty is macadamia nuts, and more than 2 million macadamia trees grow in the province. Approximately 95% of the nuts are exported to the USA and Europe.

⑥ Sudwala Caves

These caves are the world's oldest, formed more than 240 million years ago.
They show unique dripstone formations. The dolomite chamber is used as an amphitheatre for concerts.

⑤ Pilgrim's Rest

This living historic village was established in 1873 during the first gold rush. Mining operations in the area continued until 1971. Today the well-preserved Victorian village is a popular tourist attraction.

② Lake Chrissie

The area around Lake Chrissie is known as 'The Lake District of South Africa'. The pans surrounding the country's largest natural freshwater lake attract many flamingo and water bird species.

④ Kruger Park

Some private concessions with exclusive traversing rights are set in the national park. These and some prestigious private reserves along the park offer a true safari setting.

Place where the Sun rises

⑦ Barberton Rocks

The caves around this historic mining town are renowned for their numerous ancient San rock paintings. The rocks around Barberton are about three billion years old and some of the oldest in the world.

⑧ Mkhondo

The city formerly called Piet Retief is situated halfway between Johannesburg and Durban and is one of the major centres of South Africa's wood-based industry. Surrounding villages are proof of the German settlements from the late 19th century.

Ndebele Artwork

The traditional colourful murals and beadwork of the Ndebele people can be admired at the Kghodwana Cultural Village near eMalahleni and the Botshabelo open-air museum near Middelburg.

⑨ Dullstroom

Often referred to as a mecca for trout fishing, the dam offers a vast variety of nature activities for the whole family.

CITIES AND TOWNS

Graskop Children

Secunda

The highveld town in the middle of the rich coalfields was established when the South African oil company Sasol built their second refinery in the 1970s to produce oil from coal in the area. Since then the town has grown immensely and offers a small shopping centre with modern amenities and various educational facilities. The city also houses 'Graceland', a Disney-style casino and entertainment complex on the outskirts of town. A country club with an 18-hole golf course, which was designed by Gary Player, complements the options. The city is considered especially safe and secure. The dominant language in the town is Afrikaans.

Mbombela/Nelspruit

Established on the banks of the Crocodile River in the 1890s, Nelspruit (Afrikaans: 'Nel's Stream') was renamed Mbombela (siSwati: 'A lot of people together in a small place') in 2009. The capital city of Mpumalanga is the central administrative and commercial hub of the province. The city is located roughly 100 km west of the Mozambican border on the N4, which makes it attractive to Mozambicans who come to the city on the weekends. With numerous modern amenities, the city is home to a multicultural population and attractive to visitors. Mbombela is conveniently placed near the province's attractions such as the Panorama Route or the Kruger Park or even a trip to nearby Swaziland. The city offers various attractions such as the Chimp Eden Santuary, Lowveld Botanical Gardens and a casino. The city's stadium, built for the Soccer World Cup in 2010, boasts seats patterned like zebra skin, giraffe-like roof supports and displays typical Ndebele designs and colours.

eMalahleni/Witbank

Witbank (Afrikaans: 'White Ridge' in reference to the sandstone of the area), was renamed in 2005 as eMalahleni (siZului: 'Place of Coal'). The area around eMalahleni is referred to as the 'cultural heartland' of the province as it is home to mainly the Ndebele, but also the Northern Sotho and many other cultures. In recent years various townships have developed around the city attracting many jobseekers who are looking for employment in the area's mines. The region around the city has a number of ferrochrome smelters, with steel production prominent also in nearby Middelburg. eMalahleni offers modern amenities and a wide variety of activities. Witbank Dam is known to be the largest municipal dam in the southern hemisphere and popular with families and friends getting together for a picnic or braai or enjoying watersports such as waterskiing on weekends.

RESOURCES

Province, District and Municipalities

Mpumalanga Province:
www.mpumalanga.gov.za
Gert Sibande District:
www.gsibande.gov.za
Ehlanzeni District: www.ehlanzeni.gov.za
Nkangala District: www.albertluthuli.gov.za
Mbombela Municipality:
www.mbombela.gov.za
Emalahleni: www.emalahleni.gov.za

Business and Industry

Mpumalanga Business Guide:
www.mpumalangabusiness.co.za
Mpumalanga Companies:
www.mpumalangacompanies.co.za
Mpumalanga Directory:
www.mpumalangahappenings.co.za
Lowveld Chamber: www.lcbt.co.za
Middelburg Chamber:
www.middelburginfo.com
Maputo Corridor: www.mcli.co.za

National Parks/National Heritage

San Parks: www.sanparks.org
Mpumalanga Parks Agency:
www.mtpa.co.za

Tourism and Attractions

www.mbombelastadium.com
www.mpumalanga.com
www.lowveldtourism.com
www.panoramainfo.co.za
www.graceland.co.za

Annual Events

Komatipoort Panorama Cycle Tour in April
Innibos Festival in June
Dullstrom Arts Festival in December

Local Websites

www.graskop.co.za
www.highlandsmeander.co.za
www.infomiddelburg.co.za
www.lowvelder.co.za
www.pilgrimsrest.org.za
www.witbankinfo.co.za

'Work Conquers All'
Provincial motto

Recommended Reading

Fitzpatrick, Percy(2011) *Jock of the Bushveld*. Penguin

Goldblatt, David & Courtney-Clarke, Margaret (2002) *Ndebele*. Thames & Hudson

Ewart-Smith, Cameron (2010) *Kruger National Park*. Getaway Guides

Jacana (2003) *Ntini's Kruger Activity Book*. Jacana Media

Burger et al. (2010) Field Guide to the Animals of the Greater Kruger Park. Jonathan Ball

Hall, John (2008) *Touring Map of Kruger National Park*. Sunbird Publishers

MAIN CITIES AND TOWNS

Mbombela

Municipality: Mbombela
Population: 660 000
Elevation: 677 metres
Airport: Kruger
Mpumalanga 25 km NE
and Nelspruit 11 km SW
of the city

Secunda

Municipality: Govan Bheki
Population: 160 000
Elevation: 1 592 metres
Airport: Johannesburg
OR Tambo International
120 km NW of the city

eMalahleni

Municipality: eMalahleni
Population: 262 000
Elevation: 1 635 metres
Airport: OR Tambo
International 120 km W
of the city

'If you talk to a man in a language he understands,
that goes to his head. If you talk to him in his language,
that goes to his heart.' ~ *Nelson Mandela*

RELOCATION

BEFORE YOU GO

Stereotypes abound in every country, and often it is just too easy to find that the environment lives up to the stereotypes. Allow yourself to embrace the new experience! Always remember that your attitude certainly will make all the difference, so be open to the challenges that every move poses and make sure you enjoy life along the way. Be aware of some of the myths that you may have heard about living in South Africa.

Personal safety is one of the major factors to make or break an expat posting. The perception of personal safety in South Africa is generally ranked higher than might be anticipated. Crime is a fact all over the world and can affect anybody. Petty crime is on the rise everywhere and is also a problem in South Africa. However, if you take reasonable precautions and adhere to common safety rules, your personal safety concerns are no more different than anywhere else in the world. It is true that the number of violent crimes is particularly high in South Africa, but most crimes occur in areas where a foreigner or expat will not visit or reside, and many crimes are of a domestic nature.

While South Africa certainly has a high poverty rate, it is also a highly advanced country. With abundant natural resources, modern infrastructure and well-developed financial, legal, communications, energy and transport sectors it offers an abundance of first-world amenities and facilities. However, there are still areas with high poverty especially in the informal settlements and townships that surround the cities and in the rural areas. There is still inequality between the different population groups but remember that South Africa is still a young democracy. Only with the new constitution in 1994 did South Africans experience a movement to address the massive inequality that was imposed on the country's people during the apartheid years.

The private health standard is world class. The HIV/Aids infection rate is high in South Africa, but you will certainly not be at risk of infection simply because you live in this country. Infection is preventable and depends on your own actions. Blood reserves are screened to international standards and first-class healthcare services are available in the private sector.

The job market in South Africa is very competitive and despite the much publicised skills gap, competition is high for positions requiring special expertise. Work permits are usually only granted to people with special skills and experience, as unemployment is high and preference is given to locals in accordance with BEE compliancy measures.

....

While occupying 4% of Africa's landmass, South Africa boasts more than 50% of the cars, phones, automatic bank tellers and industrial facilities on the continent.

You will need to find a job before you move or, if you plan to open a new business, get networking well in advance. It is also advisable to check your potential salary with various information sources, as local salaries tend to be lower than in many countries overseas.

Johannesburg and Pretoria are huge metropolitan cities and economic hubs with a much faster pace than anywhere else in Africa. Many local businesses are dealing and connecting with customers and clients internationally and thus the pace of business is dictated by their operations.

Most businesses close down from mid-December to mid-January. This is, however, the busiest time for travelling and moving home, so plan as early as possible if you want to move during this time.

Accommodation is available for every budget, but sometimes it takes time to find the right place. Be aware that housing standards might differ from what you are used to at home. Know that an offer to purchase is a legally binding contract!

It is highly advisable to learn about the country and its people and be open to new customs. Do not expect people to come to you; be proactive yourself. Start with learning English and/or Afrikaans and learn some basic local words and slang, and people will welcome you with open arms.

Preparation

Immigration

Apply for your visa as early as possible and be patient when dealing with the Department of Home Affairs. Be prepared and have certified copies of all your personal documents.

Health

Ensure you have health insurance cover prior to arriving. Have your general vaccinations up to date and get refresher immunisations as early as possible so as not to coincide with your move.

Education

Organise transfer documents from your school and apply for a study permit as early as possible. Remember that the school year starts in January.

Driving

Get an international driver's licence. In South Africa they drive on the left-hand side of the road. Get to know the South African driving rules and national traffic signs.

LIVING STANDARDS

South Africa is rated as a 'medium human development' country according to the Human Development Index, which measures the achievements of a country with regard to a long life (health), access to knowledge (education) and standard of living (income). The country ranks 123rd out of 187 countries, Botswana ranks 118th; Namibia ranks 120th; South Africa also ranks 8th out of all African countries and thus higher than all other Sub-Saharan states in the statistics. These statistics refer to the overall standard across the population and there are huge discrepancies in the standard of living between the population groups.

For foreigners in general, South Africa offers a high standard of living. The country ranks high on many indices comparing the liveability of cities and countries for expatriates. The many opportunities for leading an outdoor lifestyle while enjoying a comfortable climate throughout the year and the hospitality of the people influence this quality of life. The quality of living is rated slightly higher in Cape Town (ranked at 88) than in Johannesburg (ranked at 94) out of 214 major cities rated in the Mercer Survey 2012.

The 2012 expat survey by HSBC shows South Africa ranking 9th in overall expat experience and 14th regarding disposable income. With regard to experience and economics, both influencing the perception of quality of lifestyle, South Africa ranks 13th, which is higher than Canada, Australia, Spain or the United Kingdom, which ranks only 29th out of 30 participating countries worldwide. Cape Town and Johannesburg are among the world's top 100 cities to live.

Cost of Living Ranking Ranking out of 214 cities (Where 1 is the most expensive)	
Tokyo	1
Singapore	6
Sydney	11
London	25
New York	33
Paris	37
Auckland	56
Toronto	61
Bangkok	81
New Delhi	113
Buenos Aires	121
Johannesburg	154
Portland/Oregon	178
Cape Town	179
Tunis	209
Karachi	214

(Source: Mercer Survey, 2012)

Neslon Mandela Bridge, Johannesburg

LIVING EXPENSES

For a long time South African cities were classed among the least expensive in the world for expat living. With a weakening rand against the US dollar, living expenses in Johannesburg and Cape Town have risen, but the country is still considered one of the least expensive in the world. In the Mercer Survey 2012, Johannesburg ranks 154th and Cape Town 179th out of 214 major cities in terms of cost of living.

Rising electricity prices, fuel costs and escalating food prices impact on lifestyle. Local purchasing power is considered to be higher in Johannesburg than in Cape Town, and thus when planning a move to Cape Town, expats are advised to take this into account in negotiating contracts.

General living expenses, including groceries, electricity and water, for a family of four will amount to around R10 000 per month in 2013. Food costs alone range from R5 000 and upwards depending on your diet and lifestyle.

Expenses for single expats or young couples will vary as they usually lead a different lifestyle, while general expenses for students are considered to be relatively low. Student expenses will usually amount to around R10 000 per month, including the rent of a room in a shared flat, transport, food, books and general living costs, but excluding course fees.

Families with children might need to budget for school fees. Although education costs for private schools are considered high in South Africa, they are still much lower than fees for equally prestigious schools overseas. You will need to consider fees for private schools from R30 000 per annum upwards. Healthcare costs are reasonable, but you have to make sure that private care is included in your health insurance plan.

Housing costs range widely, depending on locality. Renting a three-bedroom house costs between R10 000 and R20 000 per month. Additional costs for utilities will be around R2 500 for a family of four.

Petrol costs will factor highly in your general expenses as you will use your vehicle for daily commutes, shopping trips and transport for the children. Organised transport by the company or educational institution is rarely offered and public transport is usually not an option. Petrol prices are lower than in Europe but generally higher than in the USA and many other countries.

To calculate your own expenses, the cost of living calculators that are available online, such as *xpatulator*, *expatistan* or *numbeo*, offer various levels of information regarding cost of living for South Africa.

Average Costs

Food Items

1 loaf of toast bread	R10
2 l of milk	R20
250 g ground coffee	R45
500 g salted butter	R35
1 kg free-range chicken	R60
100 g bar of chocolate	R15
1 kg rice	R16
6 cans of Coke	R40

General Household Items

2 kg dog food	R55
2 kg washing powder	R60
9 rolls toilet paper 2-ply	R45
250 ml shower gel	R30
750 ml all-purpose cleaner	R15

Entertainment

Dinner for four with wine	R800
Monthly gym membership	R500
Fast-food meal	R50
Cinema ticket	R50
Theatre ticket	R200

Other Costs

Taxi per km	R12
Broadband Internet monthly	R500
Ladies haircut and blowdry	R200
Manicure	R150
Dry cleaning of trousers	R70

CRIME IN PERSPECTIVE

If you are thinking of moving to South Africa, you must consider the crime rate in the country. South African crime figures are high. However, in 2012 contact crimes, which are defined as violent crimes against a person and comprise the categories murder, rape, house-breaking and hijacking, were reported to have decreased. Crime figures, in general, have decreased significantly in the past ten years. For non-violent crimes South Africa is considered safer than Australia, England or Denmark and ranks below England, France, Australia, Spain and the USA regarding burglaries and robberies.

South Africa does, however, have both a chronic domestic violence problem and, more recently, a growing substance abuse problem. The most concerning factor in South Africa's crime statistics is the level of violent crime. It is worth noting that, according to the crime statistics for 2012, these crimes mostly happen between people who know each other, are from the same family, circle of friends or community. In fact more than 85% of the victims are attacked by a close member of the family, by a friend or somebody of the community. It should also be noted that the highest crime rates occur in townships and areas with poor living conditions.

Be Aware

Corruption

Bribing a South African official is treated as a criminal offence and hefty fines are levied on the offender. People in positions of authority in the public and private sectors can be found guilty of crime if they do not report any corrupt activities that involve bribes above R100 000 to the police.

Drugs

Using and dealing drugs is illegal. The maximum penalty for drug use is 15 years in prison, while dealing in drugs is punished with a prison stay of a maximum of 25 years.

Weapons

Strict gun control regulations apply. Gun owners applying for a new licence have to undergo a competency test. If you want to import a firearm and ammunition you will need a firearm licence and an import licence. The permit will only be issued in special cases, such as for hunting purposes.

You might have heard about xenophobic attacks on foreigners in the media. These attacks were condemned by the vast majority of the South Africans regardless of race and cultural background as racist and unjustifiable. All incidences happened in the townships, in communities with extremely poor living conditions. As elsewhere in the world, racism is higher in areas with high poverty and low education levels. In general, South Africa is seen by refugees as both an economic hub for employment and one of the safe havens on the continent, thus it is not surprising that the number of asylum seekers from other African countries is high. Recent estimates, however, show that only 4.4% of all people in the country are not South African citizens.

Fear of terrorism in South Africa is very low and not considered a deterrent to foreign businesses in the country according to the Global Competitiveness Report 2012. Only 3% of all business owners are worried about the general security of their business ventures and national security is generally considered to be high.

Whilst personal safety cannot be guaranteed, it is easy enough to maintain in South Africa. Living in South Africa's major cities is like living in any other big city and, as is the case anywhere, there are some areas and some habits you should avoid. If you take sensible precautions, there is no need to feel insecure or unsafe. Ensure that you are familiar with the basic precautions mentioned on the next page to feel and stay safe in South Africa.

SAFETY CONSIDERATIONS

Home Invest in a good security system connected to an armed response team.

Liaise with your neighbours and the local neighbourhood watch or security company patrolling the area to be aware of any specific recent criminal activities.

Install outside perimeter control beams, an electric fence and burglar bars to secure your property.

Consider fencing your property instead of having a solid wall. This measure is recommended as a deterrent for break-ins because of improved visibility.

Do not leave your valuables visible through the windows. Store valuables in your well-hidden safety deposit box. The valuables or documents that you will not need every day should be deposited at your bank safety deposit.

Keep your gates, house or apartment door locked and your windows secured.

If someone rings the door bell, check who it is before opening the door. Investing in an effective intercom system is highly recommended.

Driving Plan your route in advance and avoid townships unless accompanied by a local expert.

Carry a cellphone, in case of an emergency or a breakdown of your car.

Keep the car doors locked and close the car windows when stopping at intersections.

Lock valuable items in the boot (trunk) and do not leave handbags, clothing, laptops and CDs visible when driving.

Always park in well-lit areas. When in parking garages, park your car close to the entrance or lifts.

Never pick up strangers. Should you get lost, do not accept help from anyone offering to accompany you to show you the way.

When you have a breakdown, stay in your car and get help with your phone or, if it is a safe area, you could get help by flagging down other motorists.

General Avoid publicly displaying expensive jewelry and other valuables such as cameras, cellphones and laptops.

Never leave your bags, suitcases or rucksacks unattended.

Use safe facilities in hotels, at home or rent a safety deposit box at your bank.

Keep some coins on hand for tipping to avoid having to open your wallet.

Steer clear of isolated areas, building sites and remote beaches both night and day.

ATMs are regular targets for thieves. Limit the use of ATM facilities to daylight hours in busy centres.

Never leave your drink unattended or accept a drink unless it is poured in front of you or from a reliable source.

COMMUNICATION

Leading the communications and information technology sector on the African continent, South Africa's communications structure is highly developed. Fixed lines are 99.9% digital and six mobile phone service providers operate in the local market and have widespread coverage. Broadband is widely available in the major cities, and the larger networks offer countrywide penetration to almost all areas other than very remote locations. Telecommunications is the fastest growing sector in the country's economy. However, many South African still rely on Internet access from their workplace owing to the high costs of the service and the limited access in rural areas. More than a quarter of all South Africans also access the Internet via mobile phones in 2013.

Telkom and Neotel are the only landline telephone providers in South Africa. Telkom offers various packages, which also can include a broadband ADSL line. Neotel offers a limited service but, if you have multiple simultaneous uses for your telephone line, such as Internet, phone calls and alarm system, Telkom is still the best option.

The installation of a landline can take two weeks or longer depending on line availability in your area. If you need to get an engineer to come out to your home and connect it to an outside line, this can take considerably longer. It is a good idea to apply for a line in person and to have a direct contact should you need to follow up on the service delivery.

With your connection you will receive the annual phone directories: the Yellow Pages, which is a business directory, and the Phone Book (White Pages), which is the general telephone directory. These directories are also available online.

While Telkom held a monopoly in landline communications until 2010, the competition in the cellphone sector is very strong. Vodacom, Cell C, MTN, the newcomers 8ta (a daughter of Telkom), Red Bull Mobile and Virgin Mobile are South Africa's six mobile phone operators.

When you purchase a new phone or SIM card, legislation requires you to register with RICA (the Regulation of Interception of Communications and Provision of Communication-Related Information Act), which is free but must be done in person at a local service provider. You will be able to use your new mobile phone number almost immediately. Take along your identity document or passport and proof of physical address (not older than three months) for registration.

Landline and cellphone bills can be paid either at the bigger supermarket stores or online. Airtime for pre-paid services can be paid for via phone banking or automatic teller machines (ATMs) and pre-paid vouchers are obtainable at various outlets.

Public phones operate with coins, phone cards, special discount calling cards (such as Worldcalls, World Traveler or AT&T Global calling cards) or phone cards that you can get at supermarkets, petrol stations and stationery shops.

Internet services via ADSL and broadband are provided by various telecommunications companies. MWeb is the largest Internet service provider (ISP) in South Africa, while WebAfrica and Telkom provide the fastest speed. Wireless options are available from several ISP providers like MTN, Telkom and iBurst.

Access ^{to} Internet

Cellphone
16%

At Home
9%

At Office
5%

(Source: Statistics SA, Census 2011)

Broadcasting tower in Johannesburg

TV AND RADIO SERVICES

There are five local television channels: SABC 1, 2, and 3; M-Net and e.tv. The TV channels show English and Afrikaans programmes and news in all local languages. Most films, movies and sitcoms screened in South Africa originate from England or the USA.

Connections to satellite services are available through various suppliers. To receive satellite television, you will need a satellite dish and receiver with Smartcard and you will have to pay monthly fees to the satellite television provider. The decoder, dish and installation will cost around R2 500 and the monthly fee is about R550 depending on your subscription package. MultiChoice/DStv provide more than 80 television channels and 40 audio channels in different bouquets, such as sports and movie channels, CNN, BBC, SKY as well as Indian and Portuguese bouquets. French, Italian and Spanish channels can be ordered through Multichoice/DStv as well. Deukom is the local provider for German television channels.

Television Standard

In South Africa, television broadcast standard is PAL. Should you intend to bring your TV from the USA which runs on NTSC, it will only work if you have a multi-system TV set. Also consider that voltage is 220V in South Africa and for running any US appliances you will need a voltage converter as well.

There are 18 national SABC radio stations, which broadcast in the official languages, as well as three commercial stations, which are 5fm, Metro FM and Good Hope FM. Some private independent radio stations are granted broadcasting licences. Among these are the very popular Highveld Stereo, KFM 94.5, Cape Talk, Classic FM, Algoa FM, Jacaranda 94.2 and many other community radio stations.

TV and radio licences must be paid annually for each household. You can get licence forms at the South African Post Office or apply online. The television licence costs R265 for a year. When you purchase a new television set in South Africa, you have to show your licence or apply for a new one in store.

Access to Media

TV
84%

Radio
94%

Computer
15%

(Source: Statistics SA, Census 2011)

POSTAL SERVICES

More than 5 000 post offices are located throughout the country and offer a wide range of services. Most of the post offices offer the following facilities: basic mail services, express mail and registered mail, renewal of television and radio licences, fishing licences, philatelic services and stamps, copying services and point-of-sale for special envelopes and parcel boxes.

Post office boxes located near post offices or other amenities are available for rent, but often waiting lists for these are long. However, the post office is not always the most reliable service for sending parcels and letters to or from overseas. Often letters and parcels are lost, especially in high-frequency times around Christmas and the end of the year. You can send items by registered mail and will get a tracking number, but it is advisable not to send money, cheques or valuables via the post office services. Redirection of mail to new addresses can be applied for when moving.

Never send money or cheques via mail. Make use of Internet banking or send postal transfer orders instead. Consider using domestic registered letters with the insurance option for sending important documents to get tracking and tracing facilities.

Post offices are open Monday to Friday from 9h30 to 17h00 and Saturday from 9h00 to 13h00. Mail delivery to post boxes, home and business addresses is usually done once a day Monday to Friday. Registered or oversized letters and parcels will be held at the main post office in your area. You will be sent a notification card and you can fetch the item provided you show the notification card and your identity document, or you can send somebody with your passport or identification number and a written authorisation.

PostNet is South Africa's largest private postal service provider. They offer a wide range of domestic and international courier options. With their Globalmail, your letters, documents or parcels are flown per courier via an international distribution hub overseas to the final destination. This service is more expensive but more reliable than the regular postal service. DHL, Federal Express, UPS South Africa, Berco Express, RAM and many other courier services operate in South Africa as well. From the courier companies you will get a waybill and receive status updates of your delivery service via sms, or you can track the parcel online. Parcels sent from overseas generally attract customs duty and are sometimes inspected at customs.

Remember that sending international letters or parcels by airmail is considerably faster, as items going by surface mail often takes many weeks, if not months, to arrive. When sending mail for the festive season, enquire about deadlines early to avoid disappointment. Generally, you have to send your mail by mid-October at the latest for it to reach its destination overseas in time for Christmas.

At South African post offices, stamps and stamp booklets (containing 10 stamps) as well as packaging products such as boxes, bubble wrap and mailing tubes can be purchased. Remember that customs declarations must be attached to all international mail, except for postcards and standard letters. It is advisable to weigh parcels at home in advance, fill in the customs slip and send your parcels by registered mail.

NEWSPAPERS AND MAGAZINES

Freedom of the press is explicitly mentioned in the South African Bill of Rights. The introduction of a new Protection of Information Act is controversial and currently closely monitored by various organisations.

Reporters without Borders still rank South Africa at 42nd of 179 countries, with a better ranking than the USA (47th), Italy (61st) or Singapore (135th) in their Freedom of Press Index 2011/12.

A wide range of international and national press is available in hotels, airports and stations as well as shops for special immigrants' needs. Local press is generally available at supermarkets, petrol stations and selected bookstores. Various editions of the international press can be ordered and subscribed to online.

In South Africa, there are more than 20 major national and regional newspapers with daily editions, which are read by around one quarter of the population on a daily basis. Most newspapers are printed in English and they contain regional and national news and, to a smaller extent, international news. Sunday editions are available and are especially popular as many have specific advert sections in their editions. *The Sunday Times* is the biggest weekly national newspaper, with a readership of more than 3 million per edition. It is distributed all over South Africa and the neighbouring countries, such as Lesotho, Swaziland and Botswana.

The many local papers often have regular travel, motoring or lifestyle supplements on particular days. Advertising sections and property pages can also be found in weekend editions of the newspapers countrywide. As the local newspapers put emphasis on local events and regional news reports, it is important to read these to know what is going on in your area. Some tabloids, community newspapers and ad magazines are delivered free of charge to your door. Subscription and home delivery is available for most local newspapers. Most major newspapers also offer online editions that you can subscribe to.

Newspapers

National Newspapers

Mail & Guardian
The Star
The Times
The Citizen
News World
Financial Mail
City Press

Sunday Newspapers

Sunday Times
Sunday Independent
Sunday Tribune
Sunday World

Regional Newspapers

Cape Town
Cape Times, Cape Argus

Johannesburg
The Sowetan

Pretoria
Pretoria News

Durban
Daily News, The Mercury,
The Independent on Saturday

Pietermaritzburg
The Witness

Port Elizabeth
The Herald, Port Elizabeth Express

East London
Daily Dispatch

A wide variety of quality South African magazines, with weekly, bi-monthly or monthly editions, are widely available at local supermarkets and bookstores. They cover fields such as home and garden, fashion, motoring and travel. Several magazines are edited and published as South African editions of the most popular international magazines such as *Cosmopolitan*, *Car* or *House & Leisure*. Magazine subscriptions are available and online versions are growing in popularity.

Community magazines are often distributed free of charge to households and carry information about recent news in the suburb or community, notifications about upcoming local events and advertisement sections relating to the local area.

To get a good overview of the area, it is recommended that you ask at the local tourism office, as they usually distribute free comprehensive local event guides, magazines and pamphlets in foreign languages that often also contain information about various attractions and give a good insight into local suburbs and amenities.

Foreign newspapers can be found mainly at the airports and train stations and in some of the bigger hotels. There are some import and foreign delicatessen shops for the expat communities, mainly located in the bigger cities, where you will be able to find print versions of your favourite newspaper from overseas as well.

International magazines, such as *Business Week, Newsweek, Hello, Vogue, Elle, Popular Mechanics or National Geographic*, are widely available at local supermarkets and selected bookstores or can be ordered online. However, you will be able to source most of the news on the Internet in the online editions of major papers.

Expats interested in local and international news and events will find a small selection of expat magazines covering topics that are of special interest to expatriates in South Africa. Also enquire at the nearest tourism office in your area about regional magazines in your language. They might have free glossy magazines with news of interest available.

Several foreign language magazines are published in South Africa, which serve the foreign communities, such as *The Expatriate* or the locally produced *Kapstadt Magazin* or *Echo* in German or the *Gazzetta del Sud Africa* in Italian. You will find more information on them in the clubs and foreign communities section.

RESOURCES

Quality and Cost of Living

Human Development: *www.hdr.undp.org*
Quality of Living: *www.mercer.com*
World Competitiveness:
www.imd.org
HSBC Expat Survey:
www.expatexplorer.hsbc.com
Economist Intelligence Unit Survey:
www.eiu.com
Cost of Living:
www.mercer.com

Cost of Living Calculators

Expatistan: *www.expatistan.com*
Numbeo: *www.numbeo.com*
Xpatulator: *www.xpatulator.com*
Pricecheck: *www.pricecheck.co.za*

Crime and Safety

Crime Statistics: www.statssa.gov.za
Police Service: www.saps.gov.za
Security Studies: www.issafrica.org
Crime Prevention: www.cjcp.org.za
Safety Tips: www.crimeoutloud.co.za
Comparisons: www.nationmaster.com
Crime in SA: www.crimestatssa.com

News

IOL: *www.iol.co.za*
News24: *www.news24.co.za*
Mail&Guardian: *www.mg.co.za*

Postal Services

Post Office: *www.postoffice.co.za*
PostNet: *www.postnet.co.za*

TV and Radio Services

SABC: *www.sabc.co.za*
eTV: *www.etv.co.za*
Multichoice: *www.multichoice.co.za*
DStv: *www.dstv.com*
Deukom: *www.deukom.co.za*
TV Licence: *www.tvlic.co.za*
Go Digital: *www.godigitalsa.co.za*

Internet and Telecommunication

Telkom: *www.telkom.co.za*
Neotel: *www.neotel.co.za*
MyBroadband: *www.mybroadband.co.za*
RICA: *www.gds.co.za*
Cell C: *www.cellc.co.za*
MTN: *www.mtn.co.za*
Vodacom: *www.vodacom.co.za*

Magazines

www.assocmags.co.za
www.magazines.co.za
www.expatriate.co.za
www.lagazzettadelsudafrica.net
www.kapstadtmagazin.de

Recommended Reading

Richman,Tim & Hendricks, Stuart (2013) *Ja Well No Fine. An Alternative Guide to South Africa.* Two Dogs Books

Bristow, David (2011) *Been There, Done That.* Struik

GCIS (2012) *Pocket Guide to South Africa.* Government Communication and Information Systems

George, Richard et al. (2006) *Offbeat South Africa.* Struik

'It is what we make out of what we have, not what we are given, that separates one person from another.'

~ Nelson Mandela

MOVING

Moving to a foreign country is an unsettling experience and presents a variety of challenges. Preparing the move in easy-to-manage steps will make your relocation an enriching and less painful experience. Any moving procedure can be marred by bureaucracy, but the better you prepare your move and the more you know about the culture of your new country, the fewer obstacles you will encounter. You will also need to establish what to expect from your new assignment and what a possible move will mean to you and your family.

Some companies use perks such as comprehensive relocation packages to attract their employees to work abroad but as South Africa is becoming one of the most popular expat destinations worldwide, this is not happening as much nowadays. More and more employers now treat the expat assignment as a cultural enrichment and even a move up the career ladder, and have cut back on the benefits that were granted in the past. With intra-company transfers your compensation and benefits often can be negotiated.

An orientation or familiarisation trip to South Africa before you sign your assignment is highly recommended for expats who have doubts and worries about certain aspects of living in South Africa. It provides an opportunity to explore housing and schooling options and get acquainted with various aspects relating to living conditions, lifestyle and the cost of living.

You will need to make lots of arrangements once your decision to move to South Africa is made. It is very important to start as early as possible. Three months is a minimum suitable timeframe to get your move and, most importantly, your documents sorted out. It is advisable to contact a relocation agency or reputable and experienced moving company to help you. Always remember that your moving experience can make or break your relocation experience.

Leaving a well-known environment where a child feels safe and familiar with the daily routine is challenging for the whole family. Moving abroad and learning about new people and cultures early in life will challenge the feeling of security in children and teenagers, but there are also definite advantages in learning how to fit into a new environment.

Young children, especially, are usually more flexible towards change than adults. The adjustment process for a young child is generally of short duration.

....

'You take a change ... Calculate the odds ... then go for it!'
~ *Sol Kerzner, South African Entrepreneur*

The older children get, the more difficult moving becomes, as friendships might be broken up and the schooling system is different. You should also consider the different types of schooling, learning and teaching styles and compulsory examinations.

Health and safety aspects may be a concern for some parents moving to South Africa. However, as private healthcare standards in South Africa are high and safety is of paramount importance in schools in this country, you should not be any more worried about these aspects when planning to move to South Africa than when considering relocation to any other part of the world.

Remind yourself and your child that moving abroad makes children more culturally open-minded, and they tend to be more accepting of differences, more tolerant and knowledgeable. Different languages will be learned along with new attitudes towards schooling, different cultures and lifestyles.

Even if these advantages are not realised by a young person growing up, certainly later in life these children will greatly appreciate their different upbringing.

Useful life skills, multilingualism and socio-cultural integration abilities are considered the main benefits of parents taking their children on overseas postings.

Moving with Kids

Involve your children

Share the news of the relocation prospects as early as possible and listen to your children's concerns.

Maintain your routine

Maintain regular activities for as long as possible and find out where these are available in South Africa.

Pack up together

Have the kids around when the moving truck gets loaded. Have a trusted friend or a babysitter around for assistance and emotional support for your children – and you.

Time to say goodbye

Empathise with your children's feelings and organise a farewell party. Have a friendship album signed by friends.

Explore together

Book some holiday time so that you can explore your new home and surroundings with your kids when you first arrive in South Africa.

CONSIDERATIONS

Making the best decisions when relocating is often not easy. You will have to take numerous factors into consideration, such as your situation at home, your new job offer and your future job opportunities. For a successful relocation to South Africa you will need to consider the points below.

Family: Focus on your immediate family and research the opportunities for everyone, including children. Remember that if you have frail parents or sick relatives, you should plan for frequent trips back to your home country when they cannot travel or visit. When relocating with children, consider the schooling options carefully.

Immigration: Explore your permit options regarding immigration and enquire with your embassy or the South African Department of Home Affairs about these permits beforehand to avoid disappointment. Research the costs for the permits and the amount of time you need to get the permits sorted out before moving.

Relocating

1. Decide when to move and take holiday periods and school terms into consideration.

2. Arrange your immigration permit and get all your documents in order.

3. Decide what to take along and what to leave behind.

4. Call in the moving experts and request quotes from at least three different relocation companies.

5. Arrange for the moving date and make travel arrangements.

Make extra certified copies of all legal documentation.

6. Arrange for a power of attorney in case there are any issues that require it in your absence.

Language: Prepare for the move by learning one of the widely spoken languages, such as English or Afrikaans, and some local African language basics if you plan to work in rural areas. To ease your children's transition into their South African school, especially if they are at high school, it is highly advisable to send them for English lessons prior to relocating.

Money: You will have to decide whether to take your belongings along or put them in storage for the time of your assignment. Calculate what your expenses will be at home and in South Africa, and include travel back to your home country, which can be costly if done on a frequent basis. Also decide what you want to do with any foreign assets if you consider moving on to another expat assignment after a stay in South Africa.

Property: If you own a home, decide if you want to sell the property or rent it out during your absence. Take into consideration the current housing market in both countries and remember that it is always advisable to take the advice of experts before making any decisions on property investment.

In South Africa you can get copies of important papers certified at your nearest police station or post office without charge. Documents can be translated into English and certified at your consulate or embassy for a fee.

Relocating is always costly. Relocation packages provided by your employer will most likely include general moving costs, such as flights, temporary accommodation and storage or transfer of your personal belongings. In addition, the employer usually pays for immigration assistance for getting the relevant permits as well as some kind of cost-of-living adjustment. With intra-company transfers, repatriation assistance must always be carried by the employer, as repatriation support must be declared in the immigration application you have to submit to the South African Department of Home Affairs.

Annual flights home, a housing allowance and tuition costs will impact on your cost of living. Consider also that household appliances might need to be replaced or converted due to a different voltage. Food costs or general expenses might be much higher in South Africa than what you are currently spending.

Currency changes can impact tremendously on payments made in a currency different from your main income and this should be factored into your package. Make sure you understand all the conditions of your work assignment in South Africa and know your rights and responsibilities. Research the tax implications of the move abroad and know where you have to pay your taxes.

Moving Costs

Insurance costs................................ R

Temporary accommodation.......... R

Private or public transport.............. R

Costs of the immigration process:

Permit fees set by the
Department of Home Affairs......... R

Consultation fees for the
immigration agents........................ R

Translation of documents.............. R

Duplicating legal documents....... R

Medical examination fees
required for Home Affairs.............. R

Language classes, if needed......... R

Acculturation support, if needed.. R

Total costs for your move................ R

INSURANCE

Many moving companies do international relocations but it is best to contact a moving company that is experienced in dealing with customers moving to South Africa. Using an experienced moving company means that the settling-in process will usually proceed much more smoothly. Always insist on references from your moving company and get quotes from at least three different companies.

Professional movers should give you a referral list and comprehensive information about their company, such as the extent and timeframe of their business in the country. A good moving company will also supply information about current import restrictions. Also request confirmation of the moving dates and addresses as soon as possible and insist that the moving company arranges customs clearance for you to avoid getting stuck with the bureaucratic formalities.

Request on-site evaluations, so that you can get a better idea of the moving costs and also get to know the consultant. Remember that many internationally operating companies might not have their own offices in South Africa but partner with South African companies.

It is highly recommended that you take out insurance cover for your goods in transit. Your insurance should cover the complete period from the time of collection of your goods by the moving company to their delivery to your new home. It is also advisable to shop around for insurance quotes, especially if the mover has not offered a third party insurance option. Enquire with your homeowners insurance company whether your belongings will be covered for a move as this may be included if your insurance company is either operating internationally or working in partnership with a local insurance company.

Insurance Cover

Limited Liability Cover

This basic cover is usually given by the moving company for free, but you should always take out full value replacement cover.

Full Value Replacement Cover

This 'all risks replacement cover' protects your goods should they get damaged, destroyed or stolen. The replacement can be in the form of replacement goods or their monetary value, usually at the discretion of the mover.

There are various ways of evaluating the coverage of your goods. Make sure that the insured amount in the contract covers the replacement costs in South Africa. All the items should be listed and insured separately to ensure compensation for items that are of importance to you but which have low monetary value. If you place special value on an item, insure it with the replacement value of an item that will meet your satisfaction.

In the event of an insurance claim, notify your movers immediately. Remember that companies will usually insure only the items that they pack and unpack themselves. If any damages occur during the transport, the items will usually either be repaired or replaced with a similar item that you source at your destination. Some items might be excluded from insurance cover, so you may want to carry them with you under your personal travel insurance. Take note of the excesses when claiming.

You can influence what is packed first, but you might prefer to oversee the whole packing process. Consider staying in temporary accommodation during the packing days. If staying on the premises, remember to put items you still are using, such as toiletries and kitchen supplies, in a separate room and ask the packers to pack them last.

Inventory

Inventory keeping and labelling is very important when packing your belongings. Usually only the goods that are packed by the movers will be insured by the company. Double-check the inventory or packing list. Make sure that you are present and available during the packing process.

Shipment Price

How long you are prepared to wait for your belongings can influence your shipping costs. Shared containers, also called groupage containers, are usually the most cost-effective but are less reliable with schedules as the shipment depends on the other parties sharing your container. Shipping a full exclusive container takes less time, usually four to six weeks, but this option is more costly.

✈ # Tips
for **Moving**

Wrapping

Make sure that glassware, china and ornaments are individually wrapped for protection and labelled as fragile. Clothing can be transported on hangers in upright wardrobe boxes or laid flat in cartons. Pictures, sculptures and lampshades should be protected by special cartons or boxes. Furniture should be wrapped in blankets or bubblewrap. Insist on specially made wooden crates for fragile or very valuable items.

Sea or Air Freight?

Shipping your belongings via sea freight usually costs less than half the air freight costs but involves considerably more time. Air freight is very costly but can speed up any move. To help with settling down faster, consider sending some of your belongings by air and the rest by sea. Enquire if the moving company has its own offices in South Africa. If not, they should use well-known and reliable partner companies in South Africa.

Timeframe

Try to contact moving companies as early as possible. Moving dates on Fridays, over weekends and during the holiday seasons are very popular and get booked up well in advance. In general, shipping to South Africa takes between six to eight weeks depending on your home country. Shipping times vary widely between companies as well. Packing the belongings of a four-bedroom house can take up to three days.

IMMIGRATION

When you move to South Africa you need to have a valid permit. Various kinds of permits are available for foreign citizens who wish to live in the country. Permits need to be applied for at any South African diplomatic representative office or nearby foreign mission. It is also possible to apply for a change of status or to renew a valid permit at any local office of the Department of Home Affairs in South Africa. The following information is meant as a guideline only. Requirements are subject to change and all applications are treated as individual cases. Please enquire with the Department of Home Affairs regarding current legislation.

Together with certified copies of your personal documents, you will need to supply personal details, including information about citizenship, residential addresses of the last ten years and contacts in South Africa. Make sure you have several certified copies of your original documents. Also ensure that relevant identity documentation conforms to the regulations and that your documentation is translated if it is not already in English.

Required Documents

Personal Documents

Birth certificates and marriage or divorce certificates, if applicable, are mandatory. Remember that your passport must still be valid for a minimum of 30 days after the expiry of your intended visit.

Police Clearance Certificates

Applicants older than 18 years need to submit clearance certificates for all the countries they have lived in for longer than 12 months during the last ten years.

Proof of Funds

Written consent of financial support and/or bank statements from the last three months need to be handed in.

Security and Health

A security questionnaire as well as a medical questionnaire accompanied by a medical report and a recent chest x-ray. Get vaccinations up to date.

Health Insurance Cover

Recent proof of medical cover in English must be attached. Make sure the insurance cover is recognised in South Africa.

Police clearance certificates are required from all the countries in which you have lived for longer than 12 months during the last ten years. Residential addresses for these stays have to be submitted by all applicants in the family who are older than 18 years. For police clearance certificates from certain countries you will need to supply finger prints for the documentation. You can arrange to have your fingerprints taken and certified at a police station near you, usually at a charge. Then the certified original prints will need to be sent by you, together with your application for police clearance, to the relevant police commission overseas.

Bank statements from the last three months will need to be supplied to prove that you have sufficient funds for the duration of your stay in South Africa. In the case of study permits for dependents of the main applicant, written consent of financial support is to be included with the bank statements.

Together with a health questionnaire, you will have to submit a recent medical certificate completed on the required form by your doctor or GP. You will also need a recent radiology report filled in by the relevant specialist to confirm that you do not suffer from TB. For this, all applicants over 12 years of age will have to have a chest x-ray done by a hospital or radiology centre overseas. Fees apply. These certificates will not be accepted if they are older than six months when you apply for a permit.

Ask your medical cover provider to supply confirmation of your insurance details in English. Always make sure the insurance is accepted by the Department of Home Affairs.

COMMON TYPES OF PERMITS

Visitor Visa

Travellers from most countries will get a tourist or visitor visa at the border. To get a visa, visitors must show a valid return ticket to the immigration officer at the border. This permit is valid for a maximum of 90 days and can be extended once for another 90 days at the discretion of the Department of Home Affairs. The visitor visa is free of charge on first entry and renewal at the border posts. Renewal at the offices of the Department of Home Affairs is charged a fee of R425*.

Temporary Residency Permit

Most of the permits mentioned fall into this category. Medical treatment permits, exchange permits, retired person's permits and relative's permits also fall into this category. So do permits for foreigners accompanying a spouse, life partner, parent or child with a valid study or work permit, or accompanying a South African national. All these are granted temporary residence under certain circumstances. Temporary residency permits are valid for up to a maximum of three years and can usually be renewed. The duration of the permit is at the discretion of the Department of Home Affairs and the cost for this permit is R425*.

Permanent Residency Permit

Foreigners staying longer than five years in the country on either a valid work permit or as spouses and life partners of South African permanent residents and citizens can apply for this permit. Financially independent foreigners can also apply. It is possible to apply for this category before the five year period has ended but the chances are minimal that you will be granted such a permit. This permit has unlimited validity. Be reminded that permanent residents have to apply for a South African identity document within 12 months of receipt of the permanent residency document, otherwise the permit becomes invalid. Dependent spouses and children or recognised refugees can apply for free, otherwise application costs stand currently at R1 520*.

Study Permit

This permit for pupils and students who wish to apply for a place at a local school, college, university or language institute is granted for taking up studies in South Africa between six months and three years. However this kind of permit can usually be renewed several times. Students with a study permit are allowed to work for a maximum of 20 hours a week. If the school or institute is changed, a new permit has to be applied for. Read more about study permit requirements in the 'Education' subchapter. Cost for a permit is R425*.

General Work Permit

This permit is for persons wishing to take up work in the country. Various forms are available for qualified employees with a job offer. Further details about the different types of working permits are provided in the 'Working' subchapter. Work permits are temporary permits and are granted for up to five years. This permit can be renewed at the discretion of the Department of Home Affairs. Cost currently stands at R425*.

Business Permit

Persons who want to invest in the country and establish or take over a local business can apply for a business permit. Certain requirements and restrictions apply. You will find more information in the 'Working' subchapter. A minimum investment of R2.5 million is required and jobs for at least five South Africans or permanent residents have to be created within the first two years. The permit is linked to the business and thus unlimited. Costs for this kind of permit are currently R1 520*.

Birth, marriage, divorce and death certificates are applied for at your local Department of Home Affairs. The department also deals with adoptions and official changes of name and sex. Remember that registration of changes in personal circumstances is to be done in good time. Your embassy will be able to advise.

Value as at December 2013

CUSTOMS

Personal effects and used household goods for personal use can be imported duty-free when you are in possession of a valid South African residency permit. Among the exceptions are: tobacco, alcohol, motor vehicles, arms and medication. New goods can only be imported duty-free to a value of R3 000 per traveller, while goods are regarded as used if they are older than 12 months.

Make sure you arrive at least two weeks prior to the arrival of your shipment in the country. Otherwise you might incur port storage charges, which are applied to not-cleared goods. The clearance process usually takes ten to fourteen working days and needs to be started before arrival of the goods in the country.

The clearance process usually takes up to two weeks from the date of arrival of your effects in the country. Remember the destination branch of your moving company will require your passport for customs clearance usually at least one week before the ship is due to dock in South Africa. You need to hand in your passport for the clearance process and be available should the customs office have any questions.

Usually the moving company will supply all other necessary documents to customs. These include a detailed inventory of the shipment as well as the Bill of Lading provided by the moving company. The following other documents are needed to be handed in to the customs agent:

- your passport with entry stamp and relevant permit or visa
- if the residency/employment permit is still pending, the application document will suffice
- a letter from your employer confirming your temporary move and work contract
- relevant customs forms, which are to be signed and presented to the Department of Customs
- a packing list, which is usually supplied by your relocation company

In cases where your permit is still pending, you will have to pay a deposit of 50% of the import duty at customs when you or the moving company claim your effects. All personal effects have to be moved during the first six months of your stay, otherwise you will have to declare these goods and apply for special permission from SARS (South African Revenue Services) to import these goods duty-free.

Prohibited Goods

Poisons

Habit-forming drugs

Military weapons

Explosives & fireworks

Counterfeit goods

Cigarettes (more than 2 kg/1 000)

Restricted Goods

Firearms

Animals & products

Plants & products

Certain types of medicine

SA bank notes of more than R25 000

Gold coins, stamps & unprocessed gold

(Source: SARS, 2013)

CAR IMPORTS

Strict rules apply for importing your car or motorbike from overseas. Only one vehicle or motorbike can be imported per family and only vehicles for personal use that have been in your possession for longer than 12 months can be imported with your move.

Temporary residents, intending to import their car for a stay of less than12 months, can apply for a Carnet of Passage from the Automobile Association (AA) and with this they are allowed to import the vehicle duty-free if the car is imported solely for personal use. A Carnet of Passage should be applied for before the move. If you have a Carnet of Passage, you do not need to supply an Import Permit or Letter of Authority to customs. Otherwise an Import Permit has to be submitted to the Directorate of Import and Export Control at ITAC. Furthermore a Letter of Authority (LOA) from the National Regulator for Compulsory Specifications (NRCS) has to be submitted and should be obtained before the move.

Vehicle Import Documentation

- ☐ Carnet of Passage or Import Permit
- ☐ Letter of Authority from the NRCS
- ☐ Motor Vehicle Insurance Certificate
- ☐ Registration papers of the car or motorbike
- ☐ Original invoice (purchase confirmation) or recent valuation of the vehicle
- ☐ Dealer Certificate of Conformity

Although the clearance of the imported motor vehicle can be done by the owner, it is highly recommended that you use expert help to import vehicles. To find reliable customs agents, contact the South African Association of Freight Forwarders for a comprehensive directory of customs agents and international forwarders.

Temporary residents have to pay import duty on motor vehicles if they are imported for more than 12 months even if they are for personal use. In this case a customs duty of up to 65% applies. Remember also that the value of the vehicle will be inflated by 10% and value added tax (VAT) of 14% will be added. If you are not in possession of a Permanent Residency Permit, customs requires a provisional payment of 50% of the value of the car, which will be refunded when the permit is granted.

For South Africans returning to the country after a stay in the UK, full rebates apply on the aforementioned terms, provided they had been granted permanent residency in the UK and now return permanently to South Africa. In general, rebates are available for Permanent Residency Permit holders if the car is for personal use, the car has been in the possession of the permit holder for more than 12 months or if the car will not be sold or leased for a further 24 months. It is highly recommended to check with the International Trade Administration Commission of South Africa for current legislation.

PETS

Pets are subject to strict import and quarantine regulations. There are different regulations for cats, dogs, birds and other small pets. Healthy cats and dogs are only subjected to quarantine when the paperwork is not done completely. If pets come from certain countries they will be subjected to a 14-day quarantine upon arrival.

All pets imported to South Africa need a 15-digit ISO pet microchip and need to travel as manifest cargo. Talk to an experienced pet shipping company if you plan to import your pet. See the box for the documents required by the quarantine officer as well as the pet shipping company.

To file a pet import application form, contact the South African Director of Animal Health. A processing charge must be included with the application. The permits can either be collected in person or by an authorised courier, or posted to you. It usually takes five working days to get the Veterinary Import Permit. A recent blood titer test has to be submitted, which must not be older than 30 days before the arrival in South Africa. This test has to be done by an accredited veterinarian and sent to an approved laboratory. Different rules and regulations apply to other mammals, tropical fishes, reptiles and birds. Find more information on www.nda.agric.za or www.daff.gov.za.

The Independent Pet and Animal Transportation Association International (IPATA) supplies the contact details of its members who are registered with the applicable organisations within their own country and adhere to the rules and regulations of the Live Animals Regulations of the International Air Transport Association (IATA).

Pet Import Documentation

- [ ] Original Veterinary Import Permit
- [ ] Original Veterinary Health Certificate, completed within the ten days before departure
- [ ] Rabies Vaccination Certificate, which must not be older than one year and not newer than 30 days. No certificates are currently needed for animals coming from the UK, Australia and New Zealand
- [ ] Indemnity form, required should your pet need to be quarantined

RESOURCES

Moving Companies

Some of the biggest companies dealing with international relocations:
Biddulphs: www.biddulphs.co.za
Crown Relocations: www.crownrelo.com
Interdean: www.interdean.com
Elliott: www.elliottmobility.co.za
Stuttaford: www.stuttafordvanlines.co.za
Pickfords: www.pickfords.co.za
Anglo Pacific: www.anglopacific.co.uk
Sterling: www.sterlingrelocation.com

Moving with Pets

Global Paws: www.globalpaws.co.za
Animal Travel: www.animal-travel.com
Pet Transport: www.pettransport.co.za
IATA: www.iata.org
ITAC: www.itac.org.za
IPATA: www.ipata.org
Pets2Go: www.pets2gointernational.com

General Moving Tips

www.internationalmoving.uk.com
www.moveinandout.com
www.expats-moving-and-relocation-guide.com

Legal Matters

Law Society: www.lssa.org.za
Legal Resources Centres: www.lrc.org.za
Corruption Watch:
www.corruptionwatch.org.za

Immigration Consultants

Among many others, there are:
Imcosa: www.imcosa.co.za
Ritztrade: www.ritztrade.com
SAMigration: www.samigration.com
Globalvisas: www.globalvisas.com
IBN: www.ibn.co.za

Immigration

Dept of Home Affairs:
www.home-affairs.gov.za
Dept of Foreign Affairs:
www.dfa.gov.za

Relocation Specialists

www.steppingsouth.com
www.intergate-immigration.com
www.relocationafrica.com

Import Matters

Revenue Services: www.sars.gov.za
Freight Forwarders: www.saaff.org.za
Compulsory Specifications:
www.nrcs.org.za
Trade Commission: www.itac.org.za

Self-Storage Solutions

www.stor-age.co.za
www.storagecube.co.za
www.selfstorage.co.za

Recommended Reading

Brayer Hess, Melissa & Lindermann, Patricia (2007) *Expat Expert*. London: Nicholas Brealey Publishing

Davis, Gabriel & Dennen, Sue (2008) *The Moving Book – A Kids' Survival Guide*. Washington: First Books

Burgan, Lori (2007) *Moving with Kids*. Cambridge: Harvard University Press

Shah, Aniket (2005) *Club Expat: A Teenager's Guide to Moving Overseas*. Indianapolis: Dog Ear Publishing

'When you sit under a tree, you benefit from the past, but if you plant a tree, you invest in the future.'

~ Buyelwa Sonjica, African politician

CULTURE SHOCK

Culture shock comes in many guises and is a common phenomenon affecting people moving from one place to another. Whilst this can happen when you move within one country, it will in all probability affect your settling-in process when you move abroad. Every visitor, traveller or expat will experience some feeling of helplessness when encountering other cultural norms or foreign cultural cues. Cross-cultural misunderstandings occur when you are unsure about the meaning of certain gestures or you encounter actions that are not customary in your own culture. For example, time and space have different meanings in different cultures.

In South Africa you may experience that the locals stand unusually close to one another; you may find people talking loudly to each other across the street and that people tend to act differently because they are not from the same cultural background as yours. Feeling unsure about how to react in certain situations may leave you feeling insecure. It takes time to accept the way things are done in South Africa. It helps to prepare yourself so that you have a better idea of what to expect and why things are done differently.

Anthropologist Oberg describes the experience of culture shock as follows: Like a fish, you have been surrounded by familiar waters. The cultural norms and traditions of your immediate environment come naturally to you and you do not have to reflect on the culture you are living in. You live like a fish who doesn't think about what water it is swimming in. When relocating, you have to remember that your identity is shaped by your cultural upbringing. Because you do not know all of the values and cues that are common in your new environment, you will 'feel like a fish out of water'.

When confronted with a new set of cultural values or cues, you must know that verbal communication (tone of voice, dialects and slang) and non-verbal signals (body language, facial expressions and gestures) are different in different cultures. This is why learning about the country's customs and etiquette when preparing for a move are of utmost importance to any newcomer.

Culture shock varies between individuals. Being aware of the symptoms and different stages of culture shock is a good start to dealing with the adjustment process. Culture shock is experienced by everyone moving abroad, regardless of their knowledge of the new country, the individual's maturity, social position or former exposure to other cultures.

....

'After a great hill, one only finds that there are many more hills to climb.'
~ Nelson Mandela

There are both positive and negative signs of culture shock that may suggest that you are experiencing that feeling of transition. Various common physical and psychological symptoms can be experienced by adults and children. Always remember that culture shock is a normal reaction during the acculturation process. The effects and degree of the feeling of not belonging varies depending on the individual. Knowing the signs of culture shock and how to handle them, you will already be a step closer to dealing with them. However, if you experience severe symptoms it is advisable to consult a doctor.

Cultural adjustment is a process that can be eased by taking certain actions to ensure a smoother settling-in process. Do not expect, however, that an awareness of differences in cultural standards and norms will completely eliminate the experience of culture shock. The effects might only be reduced. Nevertheless, you will most certainly find yourself more open to anticipating problems and solving them successfully.

The more you know and understand about your own cultural identity as well as about your new home country's customs, values and attitudes, the more confident in everyday life you will feel and the easier it will be to master the daily challenges.

Culture Shock Symptoms

Physical Signs

Headache	Sleep disorders
Backache	Allergies
Stomach ache	Dizziness
Eating disorders	Mood swings

Psychological Signs

Feelings of being alone or an outsider, not trusting anyone.

Isolating yourself and making excuses to stay indoors.

Being afraid to make contact with the locals and withdrawing from contact with others.

An increased self-awareness and fear of losing your own identity.

Being preoccupied with your home country and culture.

Denying that there is any good in the new country or criticising the new culture.

Feeling misunderstood and being easily irritated.

Continually complaining and fighting against anything new.

CHILDREN

Culture Shock in Children

1 Changes in activity levels ranging from withdrawal to hyperactivity

2 Emotional withdrawal and regression

3 Immature behaviour and hypersensitivity

4 Increased clinginess and separation anxiety

Although children tend to adapt more easily, they also experience culture shock. Insecurities can manifest in many ways, especially in young children. If you feel that your child needs special help, approach a general practitioner or a psychologist for help during the adjustment process.

Should your child display signs of culture shock, listen to your child's worries and try to spend some extra time with him or her and offer extra physical closeness. Overreactions in children are often exaggerated if parents also display insecurities, so try to be as calm as possible and keep to important family rules. Establishing a new routine as early as possible and trying to have a predictable schedule will make settling in easier for the whole family.

Children who are raised in a different culture from their parents will encounter various challenges that are not common in the acculturation process of adults. These children, also called 'Third Culture Kids' or TCKs, will grow up with cultural cues and traditions different to their peers. They often assimilate with all the cultures they come in contact with, but do not define themselves as being part of one particular culture.

The term 'Third Culture Kids' was coined first by American anthropologist Dr Ruth Hill Useem in the early 1950s. Ted Ward later called the TCKs 'prototype citizens of the future' as they hold a unique and special worldview, identifying and adapting to more than one culture. The third culture is considered a shared culture and often more similarities are shared with other Third Culture Kids than with kids from the cultural background of the parents (first culture) or that of the environment where the expat child is temporarily living (second culture).

Common TCK characteristics include fluently speaking at least one additional language outside the mother tongue and maintaining social contact with peers from different social, cultural, religious and linguistic backgrounds. This gives them advantages later in life when they are highly sought after by globally-minded organisations and international businesses due to their high ability to adapt to new circumstances, their open-mindedness and multicultural orientation.

Expat kids are considered high achievers later in life. Of former expat kids, 81% obtain a bachelor's degree.

Explore Learn about the new culture. Find out as much as possible about South Africa and differentiate between myths and reality. The more you know about what to expect and why things are done differently, the easier your transition will be. Read and learn about the different cultures and customs.

Know Your Roots

Know your individual values, assumptions and beliefs and keep in touch with family and friends back home. Whilst they might not encounter the same problems, talking and listening to their feedback may put your thoughts into perspective. Continue with traditions from home and join an expat club if you feel the need for support from fellow expatriates.

Meet Fellow Expats Social interaction with people who can recall their own experiences is often helpful in the settling-in process. Meeting people from 'back home' often helps to adjust more easily to life in the new environment and the impact of culture shock is then less noticeable for the newcomer. Join expat groups both online and in your community.

Build Skills Identify the standards and values in your own culture through reading and watching movies set in other cultures. Meet up with people from different cultural backgrounds to find out what shapes your own identity. Cross-cultural training seminars might be a good option to start with. Internationally operating relocation companies and local immigration consultancies will help find trainers in your area.

Get Networking

Build up a network of support of old and new friends. Take the initiative to meet and get to know new people and do not wait for invitations. Take up a new hobby or share your skills or interests in a social club. It always helps to listen to the locals and ask, ask, ask lots of questions.

Tips for Adjusting

Expect Misunderstandings

Expect people to act differently and to have other reactions to those you learned during your own upbringing. Be aware of your own reactions of anger or frustration when encountering cultural misunderstandings and accept that you will be making mistakes due to cross-cultural misunderstandings. Remember, time and space have different meanings in different cultures.

Stay Positive

Settling in a new country takes time. Be patient – mainly with yourself. Familiarise yourself with positive South African news. See the beauty in simple achievements and realise that every day you grow stronger and know more about your new home. Try to smile a lot and try even harder to enjoy the journey.

CULTURE SHOCK STAGES

Common theories describe the adjustment to living in a new culture as a natural process with different stages. Anthropologist Oberg in 1958 was one of the first to describe the effects of moving to other cultures in five distinct stages. Subsequent theories often use more stages. Common to all is that the stages can be described as a learning curve that shows the degrees of being at ease with a different culture. They can also be seen as being part of a cycle that repeats every time a person moves to a new country or is confronted with adjusting to a different culture.

Honeymoon Stage

Fascination. When you arrive in your new environment, everything seems to be exotic and interesting. You are curious to explore your new surroundings. You mainly see the positive side of your relocation and are in a state of euphoria. You are seeing everything with keen interest and you embrace everything new as exciting. This state usually lasts for a couple of weeks.

Anger Stage

Irritation. After some weeks you realise how different everything is to what you know from home. You feel like you have lost the ground and begin to miss home. It may seem that everything you know is turned upside down. You feel you do not understand the locals and that you are misunderstood.

Regression Stage

Rejection. At the lowest point, the process manifests itself through the common culture shock symptoms. You feel you are in the wrong place and start avoiding people and places. The experience might be short but can sometimes last up to several months before you understand the new cultural cues.

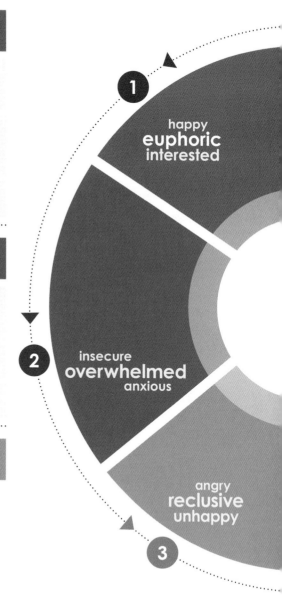

1 happy **euphoric** interested

2 insecure **overwhelmed** anxious

angry **reclusive** unhappy **3**

Reverse Stage

Repatriation. Once your relocation period ends, you feel anxious about leaving your newfound friends and lifestyle. But the dominant feeling will be of great anticipation about going home again to the familiar people and the things you missed. You then find that people and things in your original culture have also changed and evolved whilst you were away. This stage then leads into phase one of the relocation cycle and the process begins again.

Assimilation Stage

Integration. You begin to feel safer and more content with your life and become more proactive again. You start to go out, meet new people and find new ways to live and enjoy your new lifestyle. You learn the local language, customs and way of living. Life becomes easier and you understand more of what is happening around you. You adjust slowly without losing your own cultural identity. You still compare the advantages or disadvantages of your new home with your country. But in a more realistic way. Things normalise; you know your new routine and feel comfortable with your new surroundings. You feel less anxious and more content. You begin to live and enjoy a lifestyle with your new friends that you never thought possible.

curious
excited
anxious

5

content
comfortable
settled

4

'Honest differences
are often a
healthy sign of progress.'

~ Mahatma Gandhi

GREETINGS AND GESTURES

There are various greeting styles depending on the ethnic heritage. In many cultures, respect is paid to the elders by greeting them first. It is common in African cultures to remain seated when being introduced or greeted, while Western people will stand and make eye contact. Traditional Africans do not make eye contact with elders or superiors as a mark of respect and this should not be considered discourteous. Greetings between strangers are reserved but polite. A handshake and a smile are generally an accepted greeting.

Western Handshake

In South Africa there are two kinds of handshakes, the standard Western-style handshake with various grades of strength for the grip, and the African handshake.

Fist Handshake

Some traditional African cultures also share a fingertip handshake as a friendly gesture when meeting. Younger people also have a different 'fist handshake' when only their fists touch. It is similar to a 'high five' gesture.

High Five

African Handshake

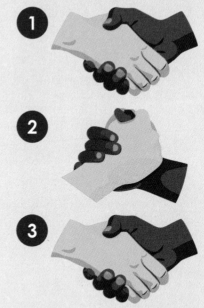

The African cultures acknowledge and greet each other with a longer handhold consisting of three movements. The first part of the movement is by shaking hands in the standard Western style, then gripping the hand around the thumb and then once again the traditional Western handshake in one extended shaking gesture.

Kissing

Kissing on the cheeks or hugs instead of shaking hands is common between friends and close acquaintances and amongst the younger populations of all cultures. Older Afrikaners still greet each other with kisses on the lips if they know each other well. In general, greetings often include time for exchanging pleasantries and some small talk.

Indian handshakes are usually not very firm and often involve only the fingertips.

Placing hands together with palms touching in front of the chest while bowing slightly and nodding the head is a gesture used as a greeting by Indian women. Placing both hands together similar to the Indian greeting gesture means 'Thank you'.

Muslims never use the left hand when greeting, as the left hand is commonly regarded as unclean. Muslim women sometimes initiate greetings with a handshake but men never touch a woman first. Women do not always shake hands but sometimes only nod their head in recognition.

Silent Language

In any communication, only about 10% of the meaning is understood through the message's content, while 30% of the meaning is understood from the pitch and tone of voice of the speaker. However, 60% is understood through non-verbal cues such as gestures, facial expressions and body language.

Raised Fist

The raised fist is used as a sign of greeting comrades and for victory and resilience.

Thumbs Up

A thumbs up is generally understood as a positive gesture or a sign of agreement.

 ## DO

When yawning, sneezing or coughing, cover your mouth with your hand. When someone sneezes, it is polite to say 'Bless you'. It is customary not to respond to a statement if you disagree with it and to ignore a question that is deemed to be rude or inappropriate.

 ## DON'T

The following behaviour is considered rude and unacceptable: pointing a finger at people, gesticulating wildly, cursing, snorting or sniffng loudly and spitting.

CUSTOMS AND ETIQUETTE

In South Africa you will encounter many different cultural cues owing to the many different cultures living together. Black South Africans certainly have very different customs and traditions compared to the Coloureds, Indians or Afrikaners. You will have to study your environment well to learn the different customs and etiquette in the respective ethnic groups. On these two pages you will find some insights into cultural traditions that are acknowledged and accepted by all South Africans regardless of cultural upbringing.

The main business customs in South Africa relate to the major Western cultural traditions. However, knowing some basics about local business etiquette is imperative for establishing a successful business in a foreign country. Your cultural knowledge paired with a tolerant attitude will be welcomed by the locals and help in avoiding a cultural faux pas.

Time

In the cities, Western standards of being punctual are commonly practised. In rural areas you will encounter more laissez-faire and easy-going attitudes relating to time. In African cultures, not being punctual is not only more acceptable than in other cultures but is also to be expected, while leaving a gathering early is often a sign of disrespect. South Africans often use expressions of time in a more relaxed manner and 'now' is not usually followed by immediate action, whereas an emphasised 'now now' is acted upon with more urgency.

Gratuities

Workers in the service industry are heavily reliant on tips for good service. Assistants usually earn a minimum wage and most of their income is made up from the tips received.

Personal Space

Personal space is often much closer than many Westerners find comfortable. Noise in restricted spaces is usually not considered a nuisance and talking loudly is more common than in many Western countries. Muslims have restrictions regarding personal space between men and women, and thus showing affection like hugging and kissing in public is not encouraged.

Socialising

People like to socialise with friends and family after work or on the weekends. Having a braai on Saturdays, being invited to watch a sports match or going out to a local restaurant to view matches on big screens is a popular way of socialising for many South Africans. After a party or meeting, it is polite to send a short thank you note. Sending an email or SMS with a thank you message is common practice. In some businesses, it is customary to go for a drink together with your colleagues after work. Even if you do not like this sort of gathering, put some effort into going out with your colleagues now and then. Official company dinners and year-end celebrations are usually dinner events that are organised long in advance and should be attended. Often partners are asked to come along to these festivities.

Invitations

If you receive a written invitation to a party or event, it is customary to reply early. Usually an invitation to dinner includes your spouse or partner. Oral invitations should be followed up by a call to confirm a suitable date and time. If you are invited to a braai, it is polite to ask if you can bring some food to share. Bring-and-braai invitations are common, so enquire what kind of dish or drink you could

Tipping for Service

Petrol Attendants
R5 – R10

Car Guards
R5 – R10

Hair Salon Assistants
R10 – R20

bring along, such as a salad or dessert. It is customary to bring along some beers or a bottle of wine to share. Men can be quite forward when asking for a date. It is not impolite to decline or take friends along for a double date.

Gifts

When visiting somebody at home, take along a small gift as a token of appreciation. This can be flowers or chocolates for the hostess or a bottle of wine for the host. As Muslims do not drink alcohol, enquire about preferences beforehand. Exchanging small gifts is customary on Christian holidays, such as Easter and Christmas, with families, friends, school teachers and good colleagues. Gifts are usually opened while the visitors are still there. According to the Zulu custom, gifts are handed over using only the right hand. The left hand supports the right elbow. This is a gesture to show there is nothing hidden in the left hand. The Xhosa people, however, tend to give with both hands simultaneously outstretched and with a slight bow of respect.

Dress Code

There is no standard dress Code for everyday life. Some Africans like dressing in 'bling' style and are proud to show their modern sense of dressing. Muslim and Indian women can be seen wearing traditional dress in some areas, but most people dress rather casually. For special occasions be sure to have appropriate dress. Companies renting formal suits and evening gowns can be found in the major cities.

The dress code in big companies, banks and consultancies is quite conservative. A suit and tie is always a safe option, but a collared shirt is usually adequate. In smaller companies, the dress code is more casual. In summer,

Business Etiquette

Greetings

It is common to shake hands with a firm handshake when meeting. Always address the older person first.

Meetings

Meetings are usually held only after having arranged an appointment. Make it your routine task to confirm meetings beforehand. Being punctual and keeping appointments is standard in business environments.

Negotiations

When negotiating contracts, realistic discounts and proposals are considered. After negotiating, be sure to obtain a detailed contract including set dates, agreed prices and payment regulations. A contract is signed by both parties. Price deductions are usually offered for timely payment.

Secretary's Day

Mark the first Wednesday in September in your diary as this is 'Secretary's Day' and treat your secretary or personal assistant to something special, such as a bouquet of flowers or some chocolates.

men may wear short-sleeved shirts under a sports jacket and they may take the jacket off. Contrary to some beliefs, shorts and knee-high socks are not common business attire. Long trousers are a must for men in any office.

Waitrons

10 – 15% of bill

Porters

R5 – R10 per bag

Hotel Maids

R20 per day

Movers

R20 per helper

EXPAT PARTNERS

Expat spouses or life partners accompanying work permit holders might experience adjustment difficulties due to the restrictions in the residency permits. While in other expat destinations expat partners are usually allowed to contribute their own skills to the new communities and are allowed to take up work, in South Africa spouses and partners are only classified as accompanying the main work permit holder. If you are a spouse or partner in this situation, this will inevitably restrict much of your freedom, as you will not be able to conduct any business or even help out at a charitable organisation without the relevant permit. Thus culture shock often hits partners who stay at home harder than those who are involved at work. Loneliness might be felt at an exaggerated level and regular contacts with colleagues and friends will be missed. There are various possibilities for the one staying at home to keep occupied.

Stay in Touch

In South Africa, expats mix and mingle with the locals, but sometimes you might feel the need to meet your co-nationals too. The most active expat communities are located in the major cities. You will get information about meeting venues of associations and clubs in your area from your embassy or the international schools and cultural organisations. Regular meetings and get-togethers for wine tastings, concerts or film screenings are also usually organised or supported by the foreign embassies, consulates and cultural organisations of your home country. Foreign national day celebrations are also a great way to meet new friends from the same home country or share some experiences.

Settling-in for Spouses

1 Get involved with a local charity. But remember that you need to get a volunteer visa even if helping without payment.

2 Get in touch with cultural organisations or commercial tour operators and explore the new area and local culture.

3 Join a book club. Enquire at your local library for meeting times.

4 Become member of a sports club or fitness centre. Staying fit helps ease or combat many symptoms of culture shock.

5 Learn the local language or take part in a language course.

6 Join your community church and get involved with their activities.

7 Get involved in activities at your children's schools and volunteer to help at school events.

Get Involved

International charitable organisations, church communities, national outreach associations, non-governmental organisations (NGOs) as well as locally operating welfare organisations will gladly welcome newcomers to South Africa. You do not necessarily need to be a member to take part in outings or initiatives. You can enquire about sharing your interests, knowledge or experience or about becoming part of a social group. Specific club activities range from book clubs, bridge meetings to sports clubs for golf, bowls or tennis.

RESOURCES

General Information

www.culturecrossing.net
www.kwintessential.co.uk
www.internations.org
www.diversityabroad.com
www.inspiringwomen.co.za
www.etiquettescholar.com
www.everyculture.com

Intercultural Training

www.communicaid.com
www.deanfosterassociates.com
www.expatica.com
www.opportunityindiversity.com
www.rtcultures.com

Orientation

www.expatsa.meetup.com
www.jobourg-accueil.org

Expat Specific Sites

www.easyexpat.com
www.expat-blog.com
www.expatfocus.com
www.expatarrivals.com
www.expatforum.com
www.expatica.com
www.expatwomen.com
www.ixpat.com
www.expatcapetown.com
www.joburgexpat.com
www.expatexchange.com
www.femmexpat.com
www.expatfinder.com

Charitable Organisations/NGOs

www.charitysa.co.za
www.ngopulse.org
www.nacosa.org.za

News and Magazines

SA Good News: *www.sagoodnews.co.za*
The SouthAfrican:
www.thesouthafrican.com
SA Times: *www.southafricantimes.co.uk*
Sabona: *www.sabona.com.au*
The Expatriate: *www.expatriate.co.za*

Third Culture Kids

www.tckworld.com
www.tckid.com

Recommended Reading

Axtell, Roger E (2005) *Gestures: The Do's and Taboos of Body Language Around the World*. New Jersey: Wiley

Logogog (2010) *Rainbow Nation Navigation*. Cape Town: Logogog Press

McLeod, Guy (2002) *Cultural Considerations in South African Business*. New Africa Books

Pascoe, Robin (2009) *A Broad Abroad*. Vancouver: Expatriate Press

Pollok, David (2009) *Third Culture Kids*. London: Nicholas Brealey Publishers

Rabe, Monica (2009) *Culture Shock – Living and Working Abroad*. Eugene: Wipf & Stock

Rissik, Dee (2011) *Culture Shock South Africa. A Survival Guide to Customs and Etiquette*. New York: Marshall Cavendish

'Differences are not intended to separate, to alienate. We are different precisely in order to realise our need of one another.'

~ Desmond Tutu

'We have a vision of South Africa in which black and
white shall live and work together as equals in conditions
of peace and prosperity.' ~ *Oliver Tambo*

DAY-TO-DAY LIVING

HOUSING

In South Africa there is a wide variety of housing options, from apartment complexes in the metropolitan areas to houses in the suburbs and to remote farms in the countryside. Finding a home in South Africa is as time and energy consuming as anywhere else in the world. It is important to get to know a potential new neighbourhood, and this takes time and effort. To make the best choices and take some of the pressure off moving, consider renting a fully furnished and serviced apartment or house when you first arrive in South Africa.

For several years, South African property has proven to be popular with international investors. This is due to the stable economy and positive economic outlook as well as the overall high return on investment (ROI). Investments in the real estate sector are considered safe and there is a wide range of investment properties available. House prices have experienced constant growth in South Africa, albeit at a slower rate in the recent years. For a global perspective, see the box on the next page, which compares the global house price growth over the last decade (2001–2011).

Among the main reasons to invest in South Africa, the high growth potential due to a property shortage and a favourable exchange rate is seen as the dominant factors. The potential prime rental price in South Africa still stands at US$5 500/R 50 000 for a four-bedroom house in a prime location, with yields ranging at 5% according to Knight Frank's *Africa Report, 2013*.

South Africa is a top holiday destination with a high demand for luxury property. Foreign investors also enjoy tax breaks on property development in designated areas and there is no VAT or stamp duty payable on property purchases, although a capital gains tax applies in certain conditions. The number of foreign property buyers has thus risen over the last few years. In 2012, 4% of the total residential property in South Africa was bought by foreigners. This amounts to the same share as South African expats invested in the property market overseas.

Many foreign pensioners make South Africa their new home, as the restrictions that apply to immigration by pensioners in many other countries are not applicable in South Africa. There are neither age restrictions nor any financial obligations to transfer your assets from abroad, as long as you meet the basic requirements regarding your financial status and needs to support your retirement in the country. Pensioners moving to South Africa frequently invest in local property. A popular option is to live in one of the many private retirement villages, which cater for the

. . . .

South Africa was rated the best performing housing market in the world over the long term.
The Economist, 2011

Muizenberg Beach, Western Cape

needs of persons within a specified age bracket. These luxury complexes or estates often offer a wide range of accommodation options and amenities, and foreigners who meet the age requirements may choose to rent or purchase property in these estates.

The country offers a wide variety of lifestyle options and for those who are financially independent it is easy to enjoy your retirement.

The types of housing and amenities you can expect are:

- North facing homes offer more natural light and are more sunny during the colder months. Most houses are not insulated, so you will feel the cold during the winter months when the room temperature rarely exceeds 15 °C. You will need either electric radiators, heat panels or gas heaters. Many houses have built-in fireplaces or gas or electric heaters. Some luxury homes have air-conditioning or under-floor heating.

- Kitchens are always fitted with cupboards and are frequently equipped with stoves and possibly even fridges and microwaves.

House Price Index	
South Africa	+114%
France	+75%
Australia	+74%
Britain	+56%
Spain	+25%
USA	-7%

(Source: The Economist, 2012)

- Bedrooms usually have built-in wardrobes and are usually carpeted. In modern and upmarket homes, the bedrooms often have tiles, laminated or solid-wood flooring.

- Swimming pools are common in the gardens of upmarket homes. Cluster homes and apartment complexes often have a communal pool on the premises. In many gated and golf estates you will find an amenities complex with swimming pool and gym facilities.

- Older houses usually have outside rooms and ablutions for live-in domestic workers.

- Almost all homes are surrounded by a wall or fence with electronic gates, and they have a security system linked to a private security company.

Camps Bay, Cape Town

LOCATION

A wide range of housing options is available in South Africa. Many foreigners choose to live in a gated estate. Although this gives a sense of security, living in a gated estate is not necessary in many places. The factors below should be considered when choosing a new home in South Africa.

Investigate the infrastructure and the transport options in the area. Bear in mind that in most suburban areas public transport is seldom an option and commuting might be challenging because of congestion during peak traffic volumes. You might want to choose your home close to your work place to reduce long commutes.

Check the proximity of your prospective home to reputable schools and pre-school facilities, and scout the amenities in the area. Living close to the school will help your kids settle in more easily and provide better networking opportunities for your family. Investigate the proximity of shops, restaurants, parks, sports facilities, healthcare centres and hospitals in the area. Nearby shopping malls and attractions will not only make life more comfortable but will influence your daily commute and routine as well.

Observe the way in which surrounding houses, gardens and public spaces are maintained. Municipal services are usually better if there is an active community forum and if the ratepayers association has a good base of interested and involved community members. Enquire about the municipal rates of the suburb, as rates differ from area to area. All complexes have monthly maintenance levies over and above the rates. Get advice and ask around about the crime rate in the suburb or surrounding area.

RENTAL AND ESTATE AGENCIES

Rental agents are the link between tenant and landlord and facilitate the negotiations of a suitable rental agreement, whereas estate agents are the link between the buyer and the seller. Good agents will give you comparisons of houses in your price category, point out the reasons an owner is either selling or renting out the property and tell you about any defects and restrictions of use.

The easiest way to find the right agent is to browse the Internet or check the property pages of the local weekend newspapers. Try to get referrals for good local agents, if possible. Bear in mind that individual agents' portfolios are usually limited to particular suburbs.

Consult agents from different areas and agencies to widen your options. The bigger agencies have good networks and often refer clients or offer shared mandates should you decide to consider a different suburb.

Many estate agencies operate nationwide in South Africa. Some of the major agencies even offer support through overseas branches. The big estate agency companies in South Africa include RE/MAX, Seeff Properties, Pam Golding Properties and Wakefields. There are also many smaller regional companies operating in South Africa.

House Hunting

Target

Choose a location according to your lifestyle. You may have the option of living by the sea, mountain, in the centre of town, in a suburb or rural area or gated estate.

Research

Get acquainted with the different suburbs in your target area and investigate the area in which you would like to live and which is most suitable for your lifestyle.

View

The time to go house hunting in South Africa is on Sunday afternoons. Most estate agents advertise houses that are on show in the weekend papers and on agent signboards in the area.

Always check if your agent is registered with the Estate Agencies Affairs Board (EAAB) or the Institute of Estate Agents in South Africa (IEASA). Registered estate agents are governed by the code of conduct of the EAAB and have to adhere to strict rules and regulations regarding the buying and selling process.

When moving into a rental home, always arrange for an inspection of the property. Complete the inventory together with the landlord or the agent in the first two days and check that all appliances and built-in cupboards are in good working order and any defects are documented.

As a non-resident, you can also consider working with a buyer's agent. A buyer's agent acts as a consultant to provide independent advice in situations where you feel the need for additional support.

Agent Commission

In South Africa, tenants or buyers do not pay the agent fees, the landlord or seller is responsible for paying the commission to the agency. You should be aware that allowances for these are included in the rental or purchase price. Also be advised that when buying or renting a home it is important to negotiate the price and lease terms. If a tenant or buyer breaches the terms of an agreement, however, they may become liable for payment of commission.

RENTING A HOME

Renting is a good option if you want to be flexible and enjoy life in South Africa without worrying about the maintenance of your own property. Reasonably priced rental accommodation is available for both short and long stays. However, rental costs vary widely depending on rental terms, location, furniture, appliances and facilities, such as a swimming pool or gym. Take the opportunity to connect with locals to get their views on the different housing options in the area.

Rentals

Short Term

Short-term rental is available throughout the year but during the summer holiday months of December and January it is advisable to book your short-term stay in advance. During high season periods prices increase and rental is often charged daily or weekly. Electricity, water and gas are usually included in the rental price.

Long Term

Long-term rental is paid monthly in advance. The tenant is usually responsible for electricity, water, sewage and gas and the landlord pays for the rates, taxes and complex levies, if applicable. Satellite TV, if provided, is often also included in your monthly rental payments.

All residential leases are regulated by the Rental Housing Act, which states the tenant's and landlord's rights and provides an overview of clauses common to South African leases. Rental periods are usually negotiable. One year leases are the most common, although short-term leases are available. Extensions are negotiable.

If disputes arise with the lease, you can get in touch with the Rental Housing Tribunal. Failure to repair faults, exorbitant rent increases or failure to refund deposits are the main issues arising when dealing with landlords.

Remember that when you sign a lease, a deposit is payable into an interest-bearing account belonging to the property owner. There is no restriction on the amount of the deposit but it needs to be stated in the contract. For long-term leases, the deposit is usually an amount equivalent to one or two months' rental, depending on the size and location of the property. Deposits will be refunded, with interest, within one month after the end of the lease, subject to the conditions of the lease. A utilities deposit may also be required.

The rental is dependent on the number of bedrooms in the house. The number of bedrooms refers to the number of rooms in which people sleep and does not include the living room(s), bathroom(s) and kitchen. For accommodation in gated golf estates, add at least R5 000 on top of the average rental. Popular areas charge much higher rates, particularly during the high season.

Average Rental Costs

Shared flat
R4 000 – R7 000

2-bedroom
R7 000 – R15 000

3-bedroom
R15 000 – R20 000

BUYING A HOME

Non-residents and temporary residents can buy property in South Africa. However, foreign buyers can only obtain a mortgage bond for a maximum of 50% of the purchase price. If a foreign buyer is living in South Africa with a temporary residency permit and valid work permit, higher bonds can be negotiated.

Property prices vary widely between regions and suburbs. In suburbs popular with expats, two-bedroom apartments in modern and well-maintained complexes will usually cost from R1.5 million, while large homes with three to four bedrooms on an average-sized stand with swimming pool will cost from R2.5 million upwards.

When you put in an offer for a house it is possible to sign the offer to purchase, according to the Consumer Protection Act, with a 'subject to' clause. This provides for a five-day cooling-off period that effectively allows a buyer to cancel the Offer to Purchase within the specified period.

The extra costs of buying a home, such as deeds office fees or transfer duty, usually amount to up to 6% of the property's purchase price, as detailed below. These costs are over and above the purchase price and you should budget accordingly.

Bank mortgage initiation fees: These costs usually range between R3 500 and R5 700 depending on the lender.

Deeds office levies and fees: These costs vary depending on the purchase price and the value of the mortgage bond. These fees range between R900 for registering a bond of R1 million and R1 500 for a bond over R5 million.

Conveyancing fees: The conveyancing fees, legal fees and the bond registration costs are paid to the transferring attorney and the bond attorney. Although the conveyancer is usually appointed by the seller, the purchaser is responsible for the conveyancing legal fees. The conveyancing and bond registration fees are usually equivalent to approximately 1–2% of the value of property.

Value added tax (VAT): This is not usually payable on property transactions unless the seller is a registered VAT vendor and the property is sold in the course of the seller's business. If the property is sold for business purposes as a going concern, application can be made for the VAT to be zero rated. If VAT is payable then the transfer duty described below will not be applicable.

Transfer duty: The transfer duty is a government tax equivalent to stamp duty in the UK or USA and is levied on any property sale. This duty is payable by all persons, including companies and trusts and payable prior to sending the documents for registration.

Buying Property

1. Evaluate your finances and lifestyle. Websites offer various calculation tools.

2. Compare interest rates between lending institutions and obtain a pre-approved loan.

3. Find the home you want to buy and view it at least twice at different times of the day.

4. Sign an offer to purchase only after a thorough inspection of the property.

5. Arrange for the mortgage bond and/or transfer of the money from overseas.

6. Sign the documents with the conveyancing attorney, who will submit the documents for registration at the deeds office.

UTILITIES

Municipal Services

In urban areas the local municipality provides electricity, water, sewage and refuse removal. You will need to register with the municipality and pay a refundable deposit for these services. Water and electricity meters are read regularly and services are charged for on monthly accounts. You are also sent a monthly account for the property rates. Should you default on payment, the service will be suspended and a reconnection fee will be levied.

Sewage

In metropolitan areas, most sewage systems are waterborne and are billed with your municipal rates but rural and older areas may still utilise septic tanks. If your home has a septic tank, find out which company is commonly used for sewage removal in the area.

Water

The quality of South Africa's water supply is good and tap water is usually drinkable. Water is scarce in many regions, and in some areas water restrictions are imposed during the dry season. All South Africans are encouraged to save water, and most municipalities ask that you refrain from hosing down pavements or vehicles or watering the garden with potable water between the hours of 10h00 and 17h00. Some properties have borehole water for the garden irrigation system.

Waste and Garbage Removal

In all suburban areas your municipality will do household garbage collection at least once a week. Garden refuse is usually collected separately or done privately by a garden service company, or it can be disposed of at various refuse collection sites or communal tips. There are also free drop-off facilities for glass, plastics, cans and other recyclable goods in many communities. Recycling containers are also often located at petrol stations and in the parking areas of some shopping centres or schools. Enquire in your community about facilities in your area. More recently, many regions have started collecting recyclable waste together with garbage collection. Be careful not to encourage vagrants and brigades of usually harmless 'trolley pushers' to the area on bin days. Only put your rubbish out just before collection, if possible.

Electricity

Electricity is generated by Eskom, mostly through coal-fired power stations, and supplied directly or as a municipal service. Some newer houses and apartments have pre-paid meters. If you have such a meter in your new home, you will require documentation with the number of the meter to get connected. You can pay for your electricity electronically or buy vouchers at certain Eskom or City Power outlets and from the petrol stations in your area. You may have to pay cash at the paypoints for the top-up as debit or credit cards are usually not accepted. Check that your name and address are correct on the slip immediately, as the voucher will not be returned or refunded thereafter.

The Power Supply

The power supply in South Africa is 220/240 V, single phase, 50-cycle alternating current. You will need plugs with three round pins. In bathrooms, you may find a socket for a two-pin round European-type plug.

Gas

In some households, gas is used for cooking and heating. All gas installations should be certified when you move into a new home. You can purchase gas cylinders in various sizes at petrol stations, DIY stores, gas depots or any other gas dealer. You can also get gas cylinders delivered to your home. It is advisable to get some gas heaters for winter, as electricity for heating can be very costly. It is also advisable to have stand-by gas cooking facilities in case there are power cuts.

Security Companies

Most householders install security and alarm systems supplied by private security companies. Also, in many suburbs there are neighbourhood watches that patrol the area. Before taking out a security contract, check whether your local neighbourhood watch or ratepayer's association has negotiated a community rate with a security company in your area or if they recommend a specific reputable armed response company. Alarm systems usually work via telecom and radio lines. Should there be a power cut, the alarm system will still work on a battery for up to eight hours. Wireless systems are available. If you feel you need someone to guard your property and your belongings while moving, arrangements can be made with reputable armed response companies.

Television and Radio

All television owners must pay a television licence fee, which can be purchased at the local post office or online. There are four public television channels in South Africa, which you can get with an ordinary television antenna. For the DStv subscriber channel you need a decoder. More channels are available when you get connected to South Africa's satellite programme provider MultiChoice. For this, you will need a decoder and a satellite dish to be installed. You then register your key card at the offices of MultiChoice.

Telecommunications

Telkom is the main telephone and Internet provider in South Africa. Phone bills and pre-paid recharge vouchers can be paid online, at the bigger supermarkets or via postal cheque. To apply for a new connection either visit one of the Telkom shops in major shopping centres or apply online.

Postal Services

Mail is delivered to street addresses every weekday. You can also apply for a post office box address. Post boxes are located at post offices, shopping centres and petrol stations. You have to register at the South African Post Office for this chargeable service. You can also set up a mailbox with PostNet, which is a private mail courier company offering a variety of postal services and post boxes at their stores. Be advised that there are often waiting lists for post boxes at both service providers.

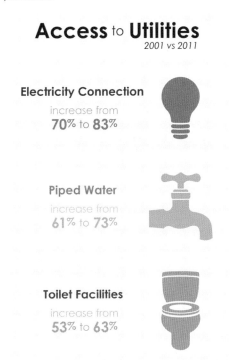

Access to Utilities
2001 vs 2011

Electricity Connection
increase from
70% to **83%**

Piped Water
increase from
61% to **73%**

Toilet Facilities
increase from
53% to **63%**

(Source: Statistics SA, Census 2011)

Conveyancing

It is not customary to have a property survey done but this can be arranged with the assistance of the estate agent or a property lawyer. You will require a transferring attorney, to address the transfer of the property, who is usually appointed by the seller. The bank may appoint a different bond attorney to attend to the registration of the mortgage bond. Registration of transfer usually takes around 8–12 weeks.

Tips
for **Purchasing**
a House

Capital Gains Tax

Capital gains tax, which applies to both South Africans and non-residents, is a tax on the profit made when property that is not considered a primary residence is sold. Excluded, in most cases, are gains from the sale of your primary residence, if the property is smaller than two hectares and if the profit is less than R2.5 million. It is calculated at 25% of the profit to be added to the income of the taxpayer and is paid in the year the sale is made.

Resale

Remember that in order to recoup your initial outlay you will need to factor into the resale price the agent's commission and the initial transfer duty that was paid at the time of purchase. The proceeds of the sale of property in South Africa can be freely transferred out of South Africa by temporary residents. Foreign nationals with temporary residency are allowed to expatriate earnings accumulated during the stay or any capital introduced without limitations apart from the capital gains tax that may be due.

Compliance

The seller will be required to supply beetle (entomologist), plumbing, electrical and a rates clearance certificate. In some instances a gas certificate or a homeowners' association letter are also required.

Occupational Rental

The Offer to Purchase agreement allows for a clause regarding occupational rental, which should be checked thoroughly. This clause details the payment of rent to the seller if the buyer takes occupation of the house prior to the transfer date or to the buyer if occupation takes place after the transfer date.

Interest Rates

Mortgage interest rates in South Africa are higher than in many other countries. Nevertheless, in 2012 the South African interest rates were at a 30-year all time low! Fixed interest rates can be negotiated but expect the rate to be higher.

Offer to Purchase

An Offer to Purchase is legally binding in South Africa. It is however, possible to sign an Offer to Purchase with a 'subject to'clause. A five-day cooling-off period that allows any buyer to effectively cancel an Offer to Purchase was introduced in 2011 with the new Consumer Protection Act. At a later stage, an offer can be withdrawn within 90 days only if the buyer is not able to get the finances sorted out during this time. Gazumping, done in many parts of the world, is illegal.

Land Restitution Act

The Land Restitution Act of 1994 is a land reform programme, which was started after 1994 to redress injustice and inequality in land ownership. The former apartheid legislation expropriated land from the black and coloured population, affecting 87% of the previously disadvantaged population. The land reform programme is based on a 'willing buyer, willing seller' concept, whereby the government buys land from land-owners to redistribute to the people who were displaced through the Natives Land Act of 1913. The programme is progressing slower than anticipated. This reform process, however, applies to rural development and farmland, and is unlikely to affect your property investment. The conveyancing attorney will assist in providing the necessary assurances in this regard.

Consumer Protection Act (CPA)

The Consumer Protection Act of 2011 states that any material defects that are not disclosed in a purchase agreement can be used to either cancel the mandate or Offer to Purchase or to be used to claim for damages in the form of a refund for repairs. This recently revised act increases the rights of the consumer with several new regulations. These include: a cooling-off period, improved rights for receiving quality service from any service providers, disclosure of the price of goods and services, protection against false, misleading or deceptive representations. The new act also limits lease agreements to a maximum of 24 months, and the tenant is required to give 40 to 80 days advance notice if he does not intend to renew the lease. The CPA does not apply in certain instances like when you purchase a property from a private seller as opposed to an agent.

Green Buildings

As is common practice all over the world, awareness around green living is growing in South Africa and green building practices are increasingly being adopted. Consciousness about the environment is increasing in local households with various recycling initiatives, and alternative power generation is gaining support. Several initiatives are already funded by the government to introduce energy efficient and energy conserving methods to homeowners. Subsidised electric solar panels on low income housing and incentives on solar water heating systems are being taken up by more and more South Africans. Sustainable living projects are taking place but are still in the early development stages. Commercial wind farms produce 'green electricity', which is available to householders in some regions. Users have to register to purchase Green Electricity Certificates.

Electricity Blackouts

In the recent years, Eskom has been criticised for rationing, or so-called load shedding, of the power supply during high demand periods for electricity. These outages have occasionally occurred during scheduled maintenance works and peak usage periods. Blackouts are not a frequent event, and can be usually be managed by the private household. Shopping centres and companies often have back-up generators that start up during power cuts. South Africans are regularly reminded by alert messages on radio and television during high usage times to conserve electricity.

Mortgage Base Rate

 South Africa **9%**

 Australia **6%**

 USA **3.5%**

(Source: Various Central Bank Rates, 2014)

155

HOUSING TERMS

Boma: Barbeque facilities in an enclosed area, sometimes with a thatched roof.

Cluster home: A smaller house in a complex, with a small garden and communal facilities.

Cottage: A small house with a garden.

Duet house or semi-detached: One of two attached houses on one stand.

Erf: A small piece of land, plot or stand demarcated for building purposes. Building plans always refer to the erf numbers.

Gated estate: An upmarket residential housing complex with controlled entrance facilities, perimeter fencing or possibly even guards who regularly patrol the estate.

Rondavel: A circular traditional house with a thatched roof. Older farmhouses may have a rondavel that is used as a garden cottage, or for staff accommodation.

Serviced apartment: A furnished apartment that is cleaned on a daily or weekly basis and is sometimes part of a housing complex, hotel or guesthouse accommodation.

Stoep or patio: A veranda for outdoor living frequently with a built-in fireplace.

Townhouse: A house in a complex, usually with small garden. A monthly levy to cover maintenance fees applies. The house may be freestanding or semi-detached. A single storey townhouse is called a simplex and a double storey townhouse is a duplex.

Cape Dutch Architecture

Traditional Rondavel

Voetstoots

This term means 'sold as is' and is usually included in contracts. It means that the buyer accepts the property as it stands, with all its defects, whether obvious or latent. The Customer Protection Act excludes developers, speculators, and investors with property portfolios who sell property in their ordinary course of business from this clause. They cannot exclude their liability for defects as is still possible for private sales.

Modern Home with Pool

RESOURCES

Property Search Engines

www.property24.com
www.propertygenie.co.za
www.propertyjunction.co.za
www.privateproperty.co.za

Property Agents

www.seeff.com
www.pamgolding.co.za
www.remax.co.za
www.rawson.co.za
www.engelvoelkers.com
www.sotherbysrealty.co.za
www.harcourts.co.za
www.chaseveritt.co.za
www.soukop.co.za
www.jawitz.co.za
www.acutts.co.za
www.maxprop.co.za

Property Advice and Information

Estate Agencies Affairs Board (EAAB):
www.eaab.org.za
Institute of Estate Agents in South Africa
(IEASA): www.ieasa.co.za
www.propertyfactor.co.za
www.sahomeloans.com
www.housecheck.co.za
www.anthonywhatmore.co.za
www.deeds.gov.za

Investing in Property

Knight Frank: www.knightfrank.co.za
ABSA House Price Index: www.absa.co.za
FNB Property Barometer: www.fnb.co.za
www.economist.com
www.thepropertymag.co.za
www.globalpropertyguide.com
www.realestateinvestormag.co.za
www.realestatemagazine.co.za

Home Building Help

www.nhbrc.org.za
www.mbsa.org.za
www.buildingregulations.co.za

Utilities and Services

Electricity: www.eskom.co.za
Post Office: www.postoffice.co.za
PostNet: www.postnet.co.za
Telkom: www.telkom.co.za
Neotel: www.neotel.co.za
Satellite TV: www.multichoice.co.za
Green Building Council of South Africa:
www.gbcsa.org.za

Home Security Companies

Chubb: www.chubb.co.za
ADT: www.adt.co.za
For more security companies:
www.sasecurity.co.za

Recommended Reading

Duncan, Paul (2011) *Style Icons: Top South African Designers and their interiors*. Struik

Fish, Jill (2005) *A Guide to Buying or Selling a House in South Africa*. Spearhead Press

Various South African banks provide detailed homebuyer's guides free of charge. These can be also be accessed via the banks' websites.

Magazines such as *South African Garden and Home, House and Leisure* or *The Property Magazine*, can give an overview of the South African housing market and information on property trends.

'Houses are built on foundations with walls and a roof. Homes are built with things much deeper and less concrete.'

~ Sandile Dikeni, poet

HEALTH

The South African health system is split into two sectors: a strong private sector and an ailing public health sector. The private healthcare sector offers excellent facilities and health care whereas the facilities in the public sector, being under-staffed and under-funded, are generally considered to be poor and less reliable.

The distribution of health and health services in South Africa still varies widely within the provinces and the population groups. Although 80% of all South Africans use public health facilities, most of them still do not get the healthcare that they need because of the lack of funds, specialists or facilities. However, the public health care system is currently undergoing a huge transformation and substantial changes are expected in the near future owing to the introduction of a new National Health Insurance Scheme (NHI).

Three-quarters of all general practitioners and medical specialists work in the private sector. South Africa currently has a shortage of certain health professionals, including physiotherapists, dieticians and radiographers.

You will mostly find excellent general practitioners and medical assistance in private medical care. This should always be your first choice when seeking treatment. Well-trained medical personnel and first-class facilities can be found at various hospitals, medical centres and private clinics. The private hospitals often have adjoining medical centres where the specialists have their private practices. You will find a directory of medical practitioners in your area on the websites of hospitals or enquire at your local pharmacy.

Most private hospitals charge the current private care medical aid rates, which are higher than the rates charged in the public sector. However, considering the high rates for medical care abroad, these rates are usually much lower than the fees charged for the same services overseas. Depending on the terms of your insurance contract, some international medical schemes will reimburse medical bills from accredited private health providers.

South Africa's private hospitals offer modern facilities and are well equipped. They have motivated and well-trained healthcare practitioners, nurses and doctors and access to the newest state-of-the-art equipment. Treatment is usually very good and you will find all the relevant medical disciplines from audiology and cardiology to ENT, paediatrics and urology. The private hospitals have in-house ambulance services and well-trained emergency staff.

The world's first successful human heart transplant was performed by Dr Christiaan Barnard at Cape Town's Groote Schuur hospital in 1967.

Brookdale Health Hydro, KwaZulu-Natal

The three largest private hospital groups in South Africa are Netcare, Mediclinic and Life Healthcare, which operate private hospitals in all the provinces. Patients will usually only be admitted for non-emergency treatment or overnight stays after prior payment of a deposit. For hospital admissions, you will require an identity document or passport and you will either have to pay a deposit in cash or with a credit card, or you will have to get authorisation in writing from your insurance company to confirm that they will carry the costs. Sometimes the hospital will assist you in getting the required authorisation from your insurance company.

To receive private treatment in South Africa it is virtually essential to have private medical insurance. A hospital plan and primary healthcare cover are compulsory for non-residents. You also need proof of medical insurance for a work or study permit. If you want to use your private foreign insurance scheme, make sure that it covers the costs of healthcare in South Africa, as there are only a few bilateral agreements for healthcare between South Africa and other countries.

If you do not have international cover from your home country, you should take it out in

Private vs Public
Healthcare

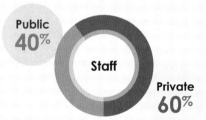

Public **40%** — Staff — Private **60%**

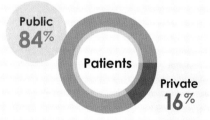

Public **84%** — Patients — Private **16%**

(Source: Statistics SA, Census 2011)

South Africa. Some of the biggest insurance companies offering health policies are Liberty Health, Discovery, Bonitas, Momentum Health, and Selfmed. There are also international providers, such as BUPA or Prudential. A reputable medical insurance broker can advise you on the most appropriate insurance. Many companies have their own in-house health insurance schemes or subsidise the contributions to a preferred medical scheme. Check if your employer uses a specific provider.

GENERAL CARE

For minor ailments, go to the nearest pharmacy. Independent pharmacies and pharmacy chains, such as Durbell, Dis-Chem or Clicks, offer a wide variety of over-the-counter medicines and pharmacy services. Painkillers can also be bought at supermarkets. Scheduled medicines, such as antibiotics, require a doctor's prescription. Chemist counters with qualified personnel are often even found in the bigger supermarket chain stores. Remember to get a detailed receipt for reimbursement from your insurance company.

There are numerous day clinics at the hospitals or medical centres in and around the major cities and towns. The bigger medical centres are also affiliated with the private hospitals. In general, the treatment at these centres is excellent and most times you can choose your doctor.

Should you be looking for a general practitioner, dentist or specialist who speaks your language, enquire at your consulate or embassy for a list of affiliated doctors. Homeopathic practitioners are found all over South Africa and offer a wide range of treatments as well.

As a private patient, you will be required to pay for your visits to the doctor or dentist when you have your consultation, so you should make sure that your insurance will cover the fees. In the big medical centres you can pay either with cash or with a debit or credit card but rarely with cheques. The costs in private practice are generally higher than usual medical aid rates of the National Health Reference Price List.

Health Clubs and Fitness Centres

Chains of health clubs are located in most towns and cities throughout the country. Specialist equipment for pilates, yoga, spinning and other fitness and wellness programmes is available in most fitness centres. Personal trainers are gaining in popularity and can be booked for individual classes even in more remote areas.

Virgin Active and Planet Fitness are South Africa's biggest health club chains with a wide variety of classes for the whole family. Curves gyms offer fitness, weight-loss programmes and circuit training for women only.

General Health Tips

Heat, Humidity, Sun Exposure

To avoid exhaustion or heat stroke, drink plenty of fluids. Avoid over-exposure to the sun as this can cause sunburn, sunstroke or skin cancer. Apply sunscreen with a minimum of SPF30 and wear a hat, even when it is overcast.

Food

Wash it, peel it or cook it! Avoid diarrhoea and vomiting by taking basic precautions when preparing food. Tap water is of a good standard in South Africa but choose bottled water if the source seems unsafe.

Outdoor Activities

Do not hike, climb, surf or swim in the ocean alone. Dress adequately and wear proper shoes when hiking or kloofing. Swim at beaches with lifeguards on duty. The Atlantic Ocean's Benguela current is very cold, so wear appropriate wetsuits when surfing or diving.

Medical ID Bracelets

If you suffer from allergies or any medical condition, such as diabetes or asthma, you should wear a medical ID bracelet, which in South Africa is called a 'medic alert bracelet' obtainable from MedicAlert.

Practice Safe Sex

Know the HIV status of your sexual partner. Using a condom will reduce the risk of transmission of HIV and other sexually transmitted diseases.

Many bigger fitness centres also have an indoor swimming pool and wellness facilities such as saunas and steam rooms. Smaller individual gyms, studios and sports clubs offer fitness classes and supervised training as well as wellness facilities. The equipment and standard of the programmes and training sessions vary widely so it is advisable to check the state of the fitness centre before you submit your membership application and get tied into a contract for a prolonged period. Always read the membership policies carefully, especially the cancellation procedures, before committing to a contract.

South Africa's major health insurance schemes, such as Discovery Health or Momentum, support preventative measures to stay healthy with their wellness programmes which offer access to local fitness centres at a much discounted rate to its members. Fitness facilities in major or upmarket hotels often have day passes for non-guests. Check your local community newspapers for specials or find a listing of most clubs in your local *Yellow Pages* telephone book.

Living with Special Needs

In South Africa, about 6% of the population is recognised as living with a disability, mostly a sight or hearing disability. Disability grants are paid to physically or mentally disabled South Africans on certain conditions. Awareness of special needs is growing. The special media coverage of the extraordinary sports achievement of South African Paralympic champion, such as Natalie du Toit, tremendously helped the advancement of disabled persons.

There are various organisations that support people with special needs. The head organisation, Disabled People South Africa (DPSA), is a national organisation supporting many smaller community-based organisations, while the Disabled Children's Action Group (DICAG) is an action group that has the largest membership base in the country and is the main support structure for parents looking for advice. The Living Link supports the inclusion of people with intellectual impairments into society and offers a wide range of information for employers on its website. Dial-a-ride services are available in the major cities. This public transport service is provided by the cities to disabled person who need transport for daily commutes. Enquire at your municipality about available transport options and support groups. Primary education for disabled children is usually provided in special schools. However some private schools offer inclusive education with facilities for kids with special needs.

Medical Tourism

Due to the world class services and comparably low prices, healthcare tourism is booming and South Africa is considered a prime destination for foreigners who have certain medical needs. More than 400 000 tourists visit every year to have their medical procedures performed by highly skilled and qualified South African specialists. These procedures include laser eye surgery, dental work, cosmetic surgery and other major surgeries. There are many practices and clinics that offer special packages for healthcare tourism to visitors from overseas.

Costs of
Healthcare

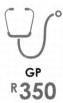

GP
R**350**

Dentist
R**400**

Optometrist
R**300**

DISEASES

Hepatitis A and B. Hepatitis A is a self-limiting viral disease contracted through direct person-to-person contact or through exposure to contaminated water or food. Hepatitis B, however, is mostly spread by very close contact with the blood of an infected person or by sexual contact. Symptoms include fever, nausea and vomiting. Vaccinations again hepatitis A and B are safe and effective and they have been part of the routine childhood immunisation programme since 1995.

Influenza. Regular vaccination drives are offered in winter. These are offered for free to persons with a compromised immune system.

Bilharzia is an infection that infects the bladder or intestines and is contracted through open sores on the skin when swimming or bathing in contaminated fresh water. The disease is prevalent in KwaZulu-Natal, the Northern Cape and the North West province. It is advisable to seek medical attention if you experience fatigue or signs of blood in your urine or stools. The infection can be treated.

Cholera outbreaks have been known to occur in rural areas. Water purification is imperative if clean water is not available. Do not bath in standing water or drink unpurified water if it does not come from a reliable source. Seek immediate medical attention if severe diarrhoea is experienced.

Rabies outbreaks occur sporadically in isolated areas. The disease poses a particular risk in less developed areas. Pets in suburban areas are required to be vaccinated. If you are bitten by a stray or unimmunised dog, it is advisable to seek immediate medical attention. A rabies vaccination is highly recommended if you plan to live or work in an area with a significant risk of exposure.

Polio poses no risk. The last reported case of polio in South Africa was in 1989. However a vaccination is recommended.

Tick bite fever can result from a bite from a tick which is the carrier of the infection. A tick bite can pass unnoticed, but you should consult a doctor if you develop a possible bite lesion or high fever and headache after being outdoors in an endemic area. When walking in the bush wear long pants or boots and check for ticks on your skin afterwards.

Vaccinations

Before you arrive in South Africa it is advisable to get your vaccinations up to date. The vaccine recommendations below may change at any time and you should visit a travel clinic as early as possible for the latest information regarding your vaccination requirements.

Compulsory

A yellow fever vaccination is mandatory for people older than one year whose journey to South Africa starts or passes through the risk areas of Africa and South America.

Advisable

Diphtheria	Measles
Tetanus	Mumps
Pertussis	Rubella
Polio	Tuberculosis
Hepatitis A	Hepatitis B
For Rural Areas:	
Typhoid	Rabies

Measles is a self-limiting disease but it can lead to serious complications. Outbreaks are known to occur and vaccinations are recommended, particularly in children and persons with compromised immune systems.

Typhoid fever is a risk, particularly in smaller towns or rural areas. Prevention is possible by ensuring food is thoroughly cooked and drinking purified water if water from a reliable source is not available. Vaccination is highly recommended if you will be working or living in rural areas.

Yellow fever poses no risk of infection in South Africa. The disease is, however, endemic to other parts of Africa and hence vaccination for entering travellers is required. You will not be able to get a visa to South Africa without a yellow fever vaccination certificate. People who arrive from areas where yellow fever is prevalent without a certificate will be refused entry or quarantined for six days at their own expense.

MALARIA

Although the biggest killer disease worldwide, malaria is under control in South Africa and limited to specific endemic areas. South Africa has made steady progress in controlling malaria between the year 2000 and 2011, when the number of malaria cases in South Africa decreased by 85% (from 64 622 cases to 9 866) and the number of malaria deaths decreased by 81% (from 458 to 89). Ninety per cent of all South Africans live in malaria-free areas.

Some areas in the North West, Limpopo, KwaZulu-Natal and Mpumalanga provinces as well as the Kruger Park area are malaria-risk areas. Because the infection is carried by mosquitoes and transmitted by their bites, the risk of contracting malaria is higher during the warm rainy summer months with the main transmission season falling between October and April. Mosquitoes are most active from dusk and at night.

If you travel into high-risk regions, malaria prophylaxis is highly recommended. Depending on which anti-malarial treatment you take, the course will need to start a week before entering the malaria area and continue for up to a month after leaving the area. Symptoms only develop after 2–4 weeks hence it is imperative to complete the course of anti-malarial medication. Anti-malarial treatments are obtainable from general practitioners and pharmacies countrywide. It is strongly advisable that pregnant women and children under five do not travel to malaria areas.

Malaria Prevention

1. Dress in light colours.

2. Wear long sleeves and trousers after sunset.

3. Use insect repellents. Lotions and sprays are widely available. Traditional mosquito coils and electrical operated mosquito repellents also offer protection.

4. Sleep in air-conditioned rooms or under a mosquito net.

5. Take malaria prophylactics when entering a malaria area.

6. Check with a doctor immediately should you develop flu-like symptoms after visiting a malaria-risk area.

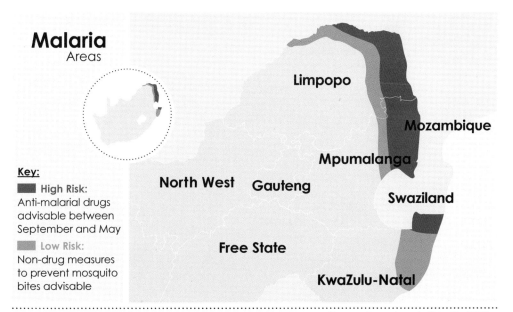

Malaria Areas

Limpopo

Mozambique

Mpumalanga

North West **Gauteng**

Swaziland

Free State

KwaZulu-Natal

Key:

■ High Risk:
Anti-malarial drugs advisable between September and May

■ Low Risk:
Non-drug measures to prevent mosquito bites advisable

(Source: Department of Health, 2013)

HIV AIDS

Aids stands for Acute Immunodeficiency Syndrome and describes the deficiency of the immune system resulting from an infection with the Human Immunodeficiency Virus (HIV). People who are infected with HIV are considered to be HIV positive. About half of the people who are infected with the virus and who do not receive any treatment with antiretrovirals will develop Aids. However, if people with the HIV infection receive medical treatment and antiretroviral therapy, have a balanced diet and lead a healthy life, they can lead productive lives for many years. Unfortunately there is currently no cure for Aids although there are some exciting breakthroughs in the development of an Aids vaccine.

South Africa has an estimated 5.6 million HIV-infected people, the largest population with HIV in the world and the fourth highest infection rate, after Swaziland, Botswana and Lesotho. About 3 million South Africans with HIV receive antiretrovirals. There are 1.9 million Aids orphans in South Africa.

South Africa has the largest antiretroviral therapy programme in the world. Currently 1.4 million South Africans receive this life-prolonging treatment, although this intervention is not yet available to everyone in need. Due to Aids awareness and prevention campaigns by the government and numerous NGOs in recent years, the HIV prevalence has dropped significantly.

HIV prevalence is highest in women of child-bearing age. Almost 75% of all new infections affect women between the ages of 15 and 24 years. The HIV infection rate for young women aged 21–24 years is three times greater than for men in the same age group. The prevalence of HIV in South Africa's nine provinces ranges widely from 39.1% in KwaZulu-Natal to 15.1% in the Western Cape.

Prevention

1. Never have unprotected sex and always using a condom.
2. Never re-use needles or syringes.
3. Ensure that the instruments are sterile for tattoos or piercings.
4. Know your own status and insist that new partners get tested.
5. Never share razor blades.

In Cape Town more than 40% of actively homosexual adult men are living with HIV.

HIV can only be contracted through contact with infected bodily fluids, such as blood, semen, vaginal fluids or breast milk, via unprotected sex, sharing contaminated needles or sharp instruments, an infected mother giving birth to her baby or blood transfusions. Contrary to popular belief, you cannot get infected with HIV through shaking hands, hugging, kissing or through mosquito bites.

The only way to know you or your partner's HIV status is to have an HIV test. Testing is available at medical centres, clinics and hospitals, is strictly confidential and is usually free of charge. Should you have been exposed to the virus, see a doctor immediately as medical intervention is required to decrease the risk of an HIV infection. It is imperative to start post-exposure prophylaxis for HIV (PEP) within 72 hours of a possible infection.

A weakened immune system due to HIV is often the underlying cause of death from pneumonia, influenza and tuberculosis.

Rate of **HIV**
Infection
2002 vs 2008

	from		to
Children 2–14 years	5.6%	DOWN	2.5%
Teens and Young Adults	10.3%	DOWN	8.6%

(Source: Avert, 2012)

TUBERCULOSIS

Tuberculosis (TB) is widespread. It is the biggest killer disease in South Africa, and mainly affects people living under poor socioeconomic conditions or those with a compromised immune system. Prevalence is highest in the Western Cape due to the population density and poor living conditions in townships and informal settlements. Because HIV compromises the immune system, tuberculosis and HIV are often linked, and persons with HIV infections are highly susceptible to TB.

Tuberculosis is a contagious disease, which is spread through the air and affects the lungs and other organs of the body. The bacteria are spread by coughing, sneezing or spitting and, if left untreated, an infected person can infect many others. Almost one third of the world's population has been exposed to the TB mycobacterium. Many people carry the infection but show no signs of the disease. The disease breaks out in 5–10% of infected people, especially when the immune system is compromised. TB can be cured but requires rigorous unbroken treatment that lasts for up to six months. Treatment for tuberculosis is widely available in South Africa, and chemotherapy is generally used for curing drug-resistant TB.

The main symptoms include coughing, chest pain, weakness, chills and fever. Testing for TB is done via a chest x-ray, sputum test or skin test. Testing is recommended if you have been in close contact with a person infected with the disease. Medication given to people with TB will within a few weeks usually stop them from spreading the TB bacteria, after which they can resume school or work.

Chris Hani Baragwanath Hospital in Soweto, near Johannesburg,
is the largest hospital in the world.

Emergencies

If you require immediate medical assistance and transport to a nearby hospital call the emergency services number. Patients will receive treatment in life-threatening circumstances even if admission requirements, such as an identity document for identification or the payment of a deposit, are not met.

Medical Centres

Arrange an appointment with a local GP, dentist or specialist. Find directories for doctors from your embassy or at a local private hospital's website. Take a passport for identification and a credit card for payment.

After Hours

Outside of regular GP practice hours you can find urgent medical help at the private hospitals. The emergency rooms deal with patients according to a medical triage system. You will be allocated a sister, doctor or specialist by the triage nurse. Special emergency unit fees will apply.

Minor Ailments

Most large towns have 24-hour pharmacies, where a trained pharmacist will be available for advice and over-the-counter medicines.

Personal Support

There are many support groups for people with special needs, such as cancer, diabetes, autism, depression and anxiety disorders. There are also free helplines for many support needs.

In Case of Emergency

Save a contact number of a family member or close friend on your cellphone contacts under 'ICE' to enable emergency services to contact your next of kin.

Where
to get **Help**

Emergency
numbers

10111	Emergency (landline)
107	Emergency Cape Town only (landline)
112	Emergency (cellphone)
084 124	ER24 Private ambulance
082 911	Netcare Private ambulance

24-Hour
helplines

0800 055 555	Childline
0800 150 150	Lifeline
0800 246 432	Contraception
0800 012 322	Aids Helpline
021 689 5227	Poison Hotline
0800 567 567	Suicide Helpline

RESOURCES

Health and Diseases

General Health: www.health24.com
Dept of Health: www.health.gov.za
World Health Organization: www.who.org
Communicable Diseases: www.nicd.ac.za
Disease Control & Prevention: www.cdc.gov
Health Professionals: www.samedical.org
Tuberculosis Coalition: www.stoptb.org
Averting HIV & Aids: www.avert.org
Malaria: www.malaria.org.za
National Aids Council: www.sanac.org.za
Vaccinations: www.immunize.org
MedicAlert: www.medicalert.co.za
Health News: www.health-e.org.za

Private Hospitals

Life Healthcare: www.lifehealthcare.co.za
Mediclinic: www.mediclinic.co.za
Netcare: www.netcare.co.za

Special Needs

Accessibility Portal: www.napsa.org.za
Physical Disabilities: www.ncppdsa.org.za
Disabled People SA: www.dpsa.org.za
Mental Health: www.safmh.org.za
Quadpara Association: www.qasa.co.za
www.independentliving.org
www.rollinginspiration.co.za
www.disabledtravel.co.za
www.thelivinglink.co.za

Directories

www.medpages.co.za
www.sadoctors.co.za
www.whatclinic.com
www.emergencymedicine.co.za
www.dentists4u.co.za

Support Groups

Autism: www.aut2know.co.za
Cancer: www.cansa.org.za
Cerebral Palsy: www.napcp.org.za
Depression and Anxiety: www.sadag.org
Down Syndrome: www.downsyndrome.org.za
Epilepsy: www.epilepsy.org.za
Family Crises: www.famsa.org.za
Lifeline: www.lifelinejhb.org.za
Rape Crisis: www.rapecrisis.org.za

Fitness Centres

www.virginactive.co.za
www.planetfitness.co.za
www.curvesafrica.com

Recommended Reading

Van Wyk, Ben-Erik (2009) *Medicinal Plants of Southern Africa*. Briza Publications

Uys, Herman (2004) *God's Pharmacy*. Red Pepper Books

Centres for Disease Control and Prevention (2014) Health Information for International Travel. New York: Oxford University Press

Wells, Kate, Dewhurst, Kurt et al. (2012) *Siyazama – Art, AIDS and Education in South Africa*. University of KZN Press

Various South African Health, Fitness and Lifestyle magazines such as *Longevity, Health Intelligence, Natural Medicine, Men & Health* or *Men's Fitness* are available in shops and online.

'It's all right to hug me and play with me. It doesn't hurt you and it helps me deal with this.'

~ Nkosi Johnson, child Aids activist

TRANSPORT

South Africa's air and rail networks are the most extensive on the African continent. The country's rail infrastructure provides more than 80% of all rail services in Africa, and the South African ports are strategic hubs for the whole region. The transport infrastructure is currently undergoing massive reconstruction and development in many parts of the country.

The road infrastructure in the cities and most towns is modern and well developed. Highways, motorways and regional roads in and around the major towns are also fairly well maintained and comparable with major cities around the globe. For regular motoring and daily commutes, you will not need a 4x4 or sports utility vehicle (SUV). However, rural roads in remote areas are often underdeveloped and/or in need of maintenance and there are mainly gravel roads or roads with rough surfaces, potholes or steep inclines.

Reliable and sophisticated public transport systems are limited to the main cosmopolitan centres. As the majority of South African's do not own a car, they either walk or rely on minibus taxis and bus services for their daily commute to work and school. Dedicated bicycle lanes are under construction in many cities, but riding a bicycle in heavy urban traffic is not recommended. In the suburbs it is easier and safer to navigate the area on a bicycle.

New bus commuter routes and transport systems have been successfully implemented in some provinces and are currently being developed in others. The recently introduced Integrated Rapid Transit system (IRT) in Cape Town and the Rea Vaya system in Johannesburg are considered a major improvement to the transport situations in these areas. These bus services and the related upgraded public train services are safer and more reliable methods of commuter travel for everybody. Commuting along the new routes is considered a safe and convenient way to avoid the bumper-to-bumper traffic during the rush hours.

Africa's only high speed train, the Gautrain, links Pretoria with Johannesburg, the main business hub of the country. This intercity 160 km/h train link includes a station at OR Tambo International Airport, and is the newest addition to the transport network of South Africa. It currently connects ten suburban stations along the 80 km track and is integrated with a metro train service and the Rea Vaya Bus Rapid Transit (BRT) system in Gauteng.

South Africa is home to Africa's largest air carrier, the largest port and has the largest and the most developed road and rail networks on the continent.

In Cape Town, the Metrorail service links various suburbs to the city centre. These train services as well as their bus feeder services are considered safe in most areas during the day but special caution should be taken when travelling very early or late at night. Travel by Metrorail and bus services is paid for with rechargeable cards, which are purchased and loaded in advance. There are various tariffs and options for regular commuters available.

Regular metered taxi and chauffeured transport, which are also referred to as shuttle services, are widely available. Although these services cost more, it is recommended that only reputable companies are used for taxi or shuttle transport. The taxi companies are generally reliable. They can be found in local telephone directories and taxis should be booked in advance.

In South Africa, there is an informal public transport system in the form of minibus taxis. Minibus taxis serve mainly the rural and township communities. This method of public transport is not a recommended option for those not familiar with the system and the local areas.

Minibus transport is regulated and each minibus taxi has a dedicated route, which is displayed on a sign at the back of the taxi. Drivers attract the attention of potential passengers by hooting. A unique taxi sign language specific to each route is used to indicate the required destination.

DRIVING

Getting your own transport is highly recommended as reliable public transport is not widely available in many areas.

In South Africa, vehicles drive on the left-hand side of the road, as is common in British Commonwealth countries. If you are not from the Commonwealth countries or Japan, you will have to get used to driving on the left side of the road and in a 'right-hand drive vehicle'.

You also need to adhere to certain local driving rules and driving styles. However, the traffic on roads outside of the urban areas is usually not as heavy and a lot less congested than many overseas roads, which makes driving easy and enjoyable.

Road signage is usually good and road safety signs are compliant with international practice. You will, however, come across signs that are not commonly used in other parts of the world.

Almost 20% of the national roads are maintained via toll collection. These toll roads are well signposted. Tolls for roads or tunnels can be paid with cash and usually by credit card but not with American Express or Diners Club cards. It is advisable to always have money available within easy reach in your car for toll fees, as well as loose change to tip a car guard or petrol attendant for good service.

Police speed checks and road blocks for checking driving licences, vehicle roadworthiness and driver alcohol levels are common. Safe driving awareness campaigns are increasingly implemented on the roads, especially on weekends and during holiday periods when police presence is augmented.

Having your own vehicle is certainly the most convenient and recommended option for getting around. The costs of driving your own vehicle are, however, high as are car prices, which are significantly higher in South Africa compared to Western countries. South Africans pay more for a new car and the country ranks second for operating costs. The average operating costs per month in South Africa are 60% higher than in the USA.

Although buying a new car in South Africa is expensive, the cost of importing a vehicle is more. Importing cars is subject to high customs duties. Furthermore, you should consider that in South Africa you drive on the left and the local cars are, therefore, more suitable.

Petrol or Diesel?

In South Africa, you get leaded and unleaded petrol as well as diesel. At petrol stations, helpful attendants will fill your tank and offer various services, such as cleaning windows and checking oil, water and tyre pressures. It is customary to reward the friendly service with a tip in the region of R5 to R10. The fuel price in South Africa is regulated by the government and fluctuates depending on the price of crude oil. Prices are changed countrywide on the first Wednesday of each month. Several levies, including a fuel tax and a contribution to the road accident fund, are included in the petrol and diesel prices.

DRIVING LICENCES

If you want to drive in South Africa, you will need a valid driver's licence. Visitors and holders of a Temporary Residency Permit are allowed to drive with a valid international driver's license or a valid foreign national driver's permit, provided it is translated into English and has a photograph of the holder. Official translations that are validated by your embassy or a local sworn-in translator are usually accepted.

Permanent residency permit holders need to convert their foreign driver's licence within five years of being issued a permanent residency permit, otherwise a local driving examination will have to be taken. Enquire about the documents needed for a conversion of your licence at the Department of Transport.

Foreign learner licences are not recognised and a South Africa learner's licence will have to be obtained.

Temporary residents with a foreign licence that has to be renewed regularly are advised to either apply for renewal timeously abroad or to register for a South African licence. Remember that even an unlimited foreign driving license is only valid until permanent residency is granted. The transfer period has been extended to five years. Persons with a foreign licence are not allowed to drive vehicles for which a professional driving permit is required, such as vehicles transporting more than 12 persons or when payment for driving services is received. International licences are only recognised in combination with a valid foreign licence. They are valid only for a maximum of one year and only if the driver is not an ordinary or permanent citizen in South Africa.

Obtaining a local South African driver's licence is a three step process that involves obtaining a learner's licence, writing a theory exam and doing a practical test. The whole process can be lengthy and frustrating. A learner's licence is obtained after passing a written test. Someone with a learner's certificate can only drive if accompanied by a licensed driver. Learner drivers must drive with a red L-sign displayed on the car's rear window. To get a regular driver's licence, the driver must pass a further written exam and a practical driving test. You will also have to have an eye examination, which can be done at any optometrist or at the municipal transport department at the time of booking the licence test. The current driving test is called the 'K53 Test' and is a copy of the United Kingdom standard driving test from the 1980s. You can register and book for the test at the local municipal office of the Department of Transport. The test manual can be bought online or at selected bookstores.

Driving lessons are not mandatory but they are recommended in preparation for the practical driving test. You may do the practical test in your own car or that of your driving instructor. It is not uncommon to fail the practical test, in which case you can redo the test. A South African driver's licence is valid for five years after which it must be renewed at the offices of the Traffic Department after passing a new eye exam and paying a renewal fee.

For advanced driving skills and learning how to manage the South African traffic as well as for driving lessons with a 4x4, contact a local driving school. The Automobile Association of South Africa can advise on reputable companies.

Driving lessons are not mandatory but they are recommended
in preparation for the practical driving test.

DRIVING A VEHICLE

Renting a Car

Renting a car is a good option for the first weeks after your arrival. A more robust vehicle such as an SUV is advisable if you plan to go on holiday off road. The major international car rental companies, such as Avis, Budget, Europcar, Thrifty and Hertz, as well as many other national and international companies service the South African market. Rental offices are located at the airports and in the city centres, with smaller depots in many suburbs. Consider carefully the insurance and excess options associated with the rental contract. Long-term rentals and leasing options are available and are often offered through your employer. Be aware that various terms, conditions and taxes may apply if your personal car is used as a company car as well. If you use a company car for personal use after working hours, it is best to get advice from your company's accountant or a tax consultant about the tax implications.

Buying a Car

Buying your own transport is certainly cheaper than renting a car for an extended period but you need to consider the relatively high prices for both new and used cars. If you are purchasing a second-hand car, ensure that you select a reputable dealer. Competitive car dealerships are usually located in or near the main business districts or along major arteries into the towns and cities. It is always advisable to have a car checked thoroughly by an independent, experienced and qualified advisor. You must register a car in your name within 21 days of purchase.

Cost of New Cars

Small Car
ᴿ90 000–ᴿ200 000

Sedan
ᴿ250 000–ᴿ500 000

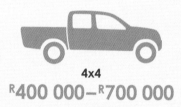

4x4
ᴿ400 000–ᴿ700 000

Roadworthy Certificate

The Automobile Association (AA) offers roadworthy checks and car inspections for its members. Although a vehicle safety test is mandatory at regular intervals for licensing a car in many countries, in South Africa it is only mandatory when changing ownership. The onus for obtaining the Roadworthy Certificate is on the buyer. This certificate is issued by registered testing stations. The cost for this certificate ranges between R200 and R380, depending on the testing station and province.

Global Prices of Entry Level Cars

China
ᴿ100 000

USA
ᴿ105 000

UK
ᴿ120 000

Germany
ᴿ130 000

South Africa
ᴿ150 000

(Source: Wesbank, 2012)

The scenic Chapman's Peak Drive is a 9 km toll road between Hout Bay and Noordhoek. The drive winds its way around 114 curves and offers spectacular views of the Atlantic coastline.

Car Registration

To register your car you will need the original registration papers of the car, proof of purchase or the sales contract, the Roadworthy Certificate and proof of your local address (in the form of a municipal water or electricity bill in your name or a bank statement). Your car dealer will usually assist with the registration process. Vehicle registration fees vary in the different provinces. Personalised number plates are available for a fee at the registering authority.

The car registration licence is valid for one year and has to be renewed annually at your local traffic department. Vehicle licence fees differ, depending on province, vehicle make, size and tare (weight). A renewal notification is sent out by the Department of Transport prior to the expiry date and should be produced when you renew your licence. If your renewal form has not arrived before the licence runs out, it can be renewed at your traffic department when you bring your registration papers. The renewal fee has to be paid up to 21 days after your licence expires otherwise you will be fined. The licence can be paid either in cash or by cheque at selected post offices or the local office of the Department of Transport. Some offices now also offer an EFT payment option.

Car Insurance

Although car insurance is not mandatory and only about one third of all vehicles are insured, it is highly advisable that you take out comprehensive car insurance. Always take out insurance with a reputable insurance company. When you rent a car, the rental companies provide insurance for a fee and you will be offered various insurance waiver options. If you are paying with a credit card, check whether your bank includes car rental insurance as a value added service. As in other countries, the insurance premium largely depends on the make and model of the car. The majority of cars in South Africa are white or silver in colour. Insurance premiums for cars with other colours or with metallic paint are higher than for those with white or silver paint! Your premiums will be affected by the area in which you live and whether or not your car is locked in a garage overnight. In general, the higher the excess, the lower the annual premium you have to pay. Insurance premiums are lower if a car is fitted with anti-theft features such as tracking devices, immobilisers and alarms. Sophisticated vehicle tracking systems cover the entire country and are highly recommended, especially for newer or more expensive cars. Companies offering satellite car tracking devices include Tracker, Netstar, Matrix and Ctrack.

Know the road signs

There are some prohibition and warning signs that you may not be familiar with. Look at *www.arrivealive.co.za* for more details.

Buckle up!

Wearing a seatbelt is mandatory for all occupants of the vehicle if it has seatbelts or child restraints in the car.

Do not drink and drive!

The blood alcohol limit is 0.05 g per 100ml blood. Use one of the many chauffeur services available to drive you home after a night out.

In South Africa a **traffic light** is called a *robot*. If traffic lights are out of order, treat the crossing as a four-way-stop.

Keep to the **speed limit**
Speed Limits in South Africa

60 — 60 km/h **Urban areas**

100 — 100 km/h **State roads**

120 — 120 km/h **Motor-/highways**

No cellphone

Only use cellphones while driving when you have a hands-free car kit. If you are caught talking or messaging without this device you will be fined and your cellphone will be confiscated for 24 hours.

Be alert for animals,

such as antelopes, cows, goats or donkeys, which can be found grazing on the side of many roads and highways. It is extremely dangerous when they roam across the road, especially at dusk and dawn.

Think pedestrian

Always be aware of pedestrians, either at the side of the road or randomly crossing it, even on the multi-lane highways and at any time of night or day. Nearly 40% of all road deaths in South Africa are pedestrians.

Minibus taxis are known for dangerous driving practices. Drivers are often accused of overloading, speeding and reckless driving. They often change lanes erratically, drive on the shoulder of the road and stop unexpectedly.

Motorbikes Keep an eye out for approaching motorbikes from behind when changing lanes as motorcyclists may weave dangerously in and out of traffic.

Keep left – Pass right

Slower vehicles will often pull over into the shoulder of the road to let faster cars pass. This gesture is usually acknowledged with a flick of the emergency hazard lights.

Plan your route

in advance and enquire about safe routes. Invest in the most recent edition of a road map, which are available at petrol stations, bookshops and many supermarkets. Do not rely solely on a navigation system. Use the road map to familiarise yourself, in advance, with the route suggested by your navigation system.

Name changes

Towns, cities and streets are constantly being renamed in South Africa, which causes confusion when the new name does not match the name on the map or navigation systems. You will find a list of renamed towns in the annexure.

Check your tyres

regularly and keep a spare tyre in your car. Rough surfaces and debris on the roads are the main threats to your tyres.

OR Tambo International Airport earned the distinction of being Africa's leading airport.
World Travel Awards, 2012

Air Travel

Nowadays most people travel to South Africa by airplane. With more than 200 000 aircraft landings annually, South Africa is the African continent's major hub for air travel.

More than 70 national and international airlines offer regular flights to the country. There are non-stop flights to and from destinations all over the world, with OR Tambo International Airport offering most international flight connections. Direct flights to Europe, the UK and Northern America take around nine to twelve hours, while flights to Asia and Oceania take considerably longer.

Domestic air travel is affordable and well developed. Travelling by air is usually the most comfortable and time-effective way to travel between provinces. Seven major domestic airlines service the major airports, while several smaller airlines offer private flight services using smaller airports and private landing strips. The state-owned South African Airlines (SAA) belongs to the Star Alliance group and is thus part of various code-sharing schemes with domestic and international partner airlines. SAA and its domestic carriers, SA Airlink and SA Express, as well as British Airways (operated by Comair) operate the domestic flight sector with services to many locations and regular daily flights.

The low-cost airlines, Kulula and Mango, service the local domestic market with their no-frills flights. They are considered safe, convenient and cost-effective and offer regular online promotions. There are numerous private charter options available for executive charter travel.

The airports in Johannesburg and Cape Town are linked with modern Rapid Transport Systems to the city centres. Independent shuttle services, private chauffeur services or metered taxis are on standby at all the major airports or they can be pre-booked to pick you up at either the airport or at your private address. It is advisable to use only recommended and registered services. The major car hire companies also offer daily chauffeur services.

Short and long-term parking options are available at the airports. Information about parking is available on the airport websites, which also give live information about flight and arrival times, a parking fee calculator and seasonal flight schedules.

Major Airports
Map

Bloemfontein
Bram Fisher International

Cape Town
Cape Town International

Durban
King Shaka International

Johannesburg
Lanseria
OR Tambo International

Mbombela/Nelspruit
Kruger Mpumalanga International

✈ Polokwane — LP

MP ✈ Nelspruit

GP
NW 🛫 Johannesburg

✈ Upington   FS ✈ Bloemfontein
✈ Kimberley

NC   KZN   🛫 Durban

EC

✈ East London

Cape Town 🛫   WC   ✈ George ✈ Port Elizabeth

Bus Travel

Intercity bus services link the major cities and many smaller towns. Long-distance travel by bus is considered more secure than train travel, although it is often only marginally less expensive than air travel. Translux, Greyhound, City to City, SA Roadlink and Intercape are the main bus operators that service many towns and cities. Bus drivers are required to adhere to strict road transport regulations. If you have any complaints, you can report them to the relevant companies and transgressions are taken very seriously. Bus stations are conveniently located in the town centres. Caution should be taken to avoid becoming a victim of petty crime. Use common sense, as you would in any station around the world.

Train Travel

South Africa's rail infrastructure is the biggest on the African continent, providing more than 80% of all the rail services in Africa. Most of the extensive rail network is utilised for cargo and generally not considered safe for commuting. The exceptions being the Gautrain in Gauteng, which offers first-class airport transfers and is highly recommended, and the Cape Metrorail services linking the northern and southern suburbs with Cape Town's city centre.

Best Scenic Train Travel

Blue Train: The world's leading luxury train runs between Pretoria and Cape Town. *www.bluetrain.co.za*

Rovos Rail: This luxury steam train offers excursions from Johannesburg, Port Elizabeth and Cape Town. *www.rovos.com*

Shongololo Express: Advertised as a safari adventure. These trains offer luxury cabins on four routes. *www.shongololo.com*

Vehicle Recovery

Tow truck operators recover vehicles if you have a breakdown or an accident. Be aware that the tow trucks that you see at the more dangerous traffic crossings can be very insistent with their 'kind' offers of help but often charge much more than any affiliated road assistance company would charge. It is a good idea to use only operators registered with either the South African Towing and Recovery Association (SATRA) or the United Towing Association of South Africa (UTASA).

Accidents

Should you be involved in a collision, you must report the accident at the nearest police station within 24 hours. If there are persons injured or major damage to the car, then you must always call the police to the scene. If the incident is minor, and there are no injuries, the vehicles may be moved if they are blocking other traffic.

Road Accident Fund

It is estimated that around 35% of road users in South Africa are uninsured. The Road Accident Fund (RAF) pays compensation to those who have been injured in road accidents. Compensation is also paid to support the dependants of people injured or killed in road accidents arising from negligent driving. If you are involved in an accident and the other party is not insured, you should seek legal advice.

Road Assistance

Join a road assistance scheme that will provide help in the event of a breakdown. If you are a member an Automobile Club (AA), you can get a discount when you register with the local AA (bring your membership details). Check whether your insurance includes road assistance.

Driving Considerations

Traffic Fines

Speed cameras, speed traps and regular speed checks occur on most roads, especially at dangerous intersections or accident-prone stretches of road. If you are caught speeding, you will be fined. Fines can be paid online, via the post office or at the local traffic department. If you do not pay the fine by the due date you will be required to appear in court. The introduction of a points system similar to those in the UK and the USA is currently under discussion.

Emergency
numbers

112	Emergency (cellphone)
083 843 22	Roadside assistance by the AA
086 1072 872	SATRA advice
084 124	ER 24 private ambulance
082 911	Netcare private ambulance

Remember to save the telephone numbers for emergencies, car insurance and road assistance on your cellphone.

RESOURCES

Getting Around by Car

Dept of Transport: www.transport.gov.za
Road Safety: www.arrivealive.co.za
Ombudsman: www.miosa.co.za
Driving Tips: www.drivesouthafrica.co.za
Automobile Association: www.aa.co.za
Traffic Info System: www.enatis.co.za
National Roads Agency: www.nra.co.za
Mapstudio: www.mapstudio.co.za
SADD: www.sadd.org.za

When Things go Wrong

Road Accident Fund: www.raf.co.za
Road Conditions: www.i-traffic.co.za
Police Services: www.saps.gov.za
Towing and Recovery Associations:
www.satra.co.za
www.utasa.co.za

Vehicle Tracking

Tracker: www.tracker.co.za
Ctrack: www.ctrack.co.za
Matrix: www.matrix.co.za
Altech Netstar: www.netstar.co.za

Air Travel

Airports Company: www.acsa.co.za
South African Airlines : www.flysaa.com
Mango Airline: www.flymango.com
Kulula Airline: www.kulula.com
Airlink: www.flyairlink.com
SA Express: www.flysax.com

Public Transport

Metro Rail: www.capemetrorail.co.za
Gautrain: www.gautrain.co.za
My City IRT: www.capetown.gov.za
Rea Vaya BRT: www.reavaya.org.za

Chauffeur Services

Road Trip: www.roadtrip.co.za
Elite Chauffeur: www.elitechauffeur.co.za
Good Fellas: www.gfellas.co.za
Smartguyz: www.smartguyz.co.za

Intercity Buses

City to City: www.citytocity.co.za
Greyhound: www.greyhound.co.za
Translux: www.translux.co.za
Intercape: www.intercape.co.za
SA Roadlink: www.saroadlink.co.za

Car Rental

www.alamo.co.za
www.avis.co.za
www.budget.co.za
www.tempestcarhire.co.za
www.europcar.co.za
www.firstcarrental.co.za
www.hertz.co.za
www.sixt.co.za
www.tempestcarhire.co.za
www.thrifty.co.za
www.woodford.co.za

Recommended Reading

Visagie, Justus (2009) *What Your Driving Instructor Didn't Tell You*. Metz

Gibson, Clive & Hoole, Gavin (2012) *The New Official K53 Manual for the Learner's and Driving Tests*. Metz

Car magazines such as *Auto Trader, Top Car and Wheels24* are available in supermarkets and online.

'There is nothing like returning to a place that remains unchanged to find the ways in which you yourself have altered.'

~ Nelson Mandela

'If we have intelligence, imagination, and the ability to dream, things can happen.' ~ *Graça Machel*

WORK AND STUDY

ECONOMY

With an abundant supply of natural resources, a well-established financial sector and well-developed infrastructure, the country is both the leading business region in Africa and one of the leading emerging markets in the world. As a result of the forward-looking macroeconomic policy decisions made by the government, the country experienced a more moderate economic recession than many other countries in recent years. The country does, however, rely heavily on commodity exports and hence a global decline in demand for export products and a fall in commodity prices mean that it is vulnerable to the influences of the foreign exchange rate and changes in the world's markets. Measures, such as the establishment of a sound fiscal position and flexible inflation target as well as the creation of a broader skills base, have been taken to minimise the impacts of further global recessions.

South Africa's economy is considered the foremost emerging market in Africa due to its well-developed finance, communication, energy and transport sectors. Johannesburg, Cape Town, Durban and, to a lesser extent, Port Elizabeth are the main economic centres in South Africa. Although the infrastructure is considered to be well advanced in most regions, the massive influx of rural people into the big metropolitan cities presents a constant challenge. A massive overhaul of the rail and road infrastructure, with the aim of providing efficient and safe public transport systems, is currently being undertaken in many cities.

Various challenges, such as the high unemployment figures, especially in rural areas, high crime and corruption rates and low education levels of the population, are addressed by government initiatives such as the National Growth Path and the National Policy Action Plan. Major incentives (like B-BBEE) are thus provided for reducing the skills shortage in many employment sectors, for job creation to counteract high unemployment rates and also for finding energy-efficient solutions to combat the worldwide energy crisis.

The primary sector (agriculture, fishing and mining) and the secondary sector (manufacturing, construction and utilities) add to a healthy mix. South Africa is self-sufficient in most agricultural products and its agricultural output is in the top 20 of the world's economies. The country's major products are corn, wheat, sugar, fruit, vegetables, beef, poultry, mutton, wool and dairy products. Almost half of the products harvested in South Africa are exported. South Africa is the second largest exporter of fruit in the world.

South Africa is ranked eight out of the world's 60 top economies for overall steadiness of its banking system and 19th for financial stability.
World Economic Forum, 2011

Johannesburg skyline

Due to abundant mineral resources, the country is one of the world leaders in the mining and refining industrial sectors and is the largest producer and exporter of many minerals and base metals. Sixty per cent of South Africa's exports originate from this sector.

The manufacturing sector employs 13% of the population. Major industries include automobile assembly, metalworking, machinery, textiles, iron and steel, chemicals, fertiliser, foodstuffs, and commercial ship repair. South Africa's automotive industry and the chemical industry are both the largest on the continent. Major multinationals invest heavily in this sector in return for using the country's resources and manpower.

Since the 1990s, the service industry has played a dominant role in the economy, with growing retail and wholesale sectors as well as strong tourism and communication sectors. In recent years the country has established itself as a knowledge-based economy, with a strong focus on the financial services, information technology, renewable energy and technology sectors.

Natural Resources

Platinum

World's number one producer of platinum, holding 88% of all platinum reserves.

Manganese

World's number one producer of manganese, holding 75% of all reserves.

Ferrochrome

World's number one producer of ferrochrome, holding 70% of all reserves.

Gold

Third largest producer after China and Australia, holding 35% of all gold reserves. About 40% of all gold ever produced is from South Africa.

South Africa is the information technology hub of the continent and is especially strong in the electronic banking segment. Communications is one of the key growth sectors for investment, and South Africa boasts the fourth fastest-growing cellphone market in the world and the largest Internet market in Africa with more than 14 million Internet users. Tourism is another key growth sector in the economy and employs more than 1.2 million people. Growing at three times the world average, tourism has become one of the most important sectors in South Africa and is overtaking gold exports as the main earner of foreign currency. Tourism accounted for more than 9 million visitors coming to the country in 2012.

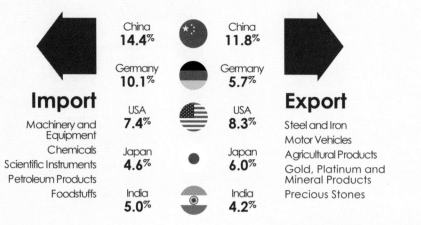

Import

China **14.4%**

Germany **10.1%**

USA **7.4%**

Japan **4.6%**

India **5.0%**

Machinery and Equipment
Chemicals
Scientific Instruments
Petroleum Products
Foodstuffs

Export

China **11.8%**

Germany **5.7%**

USA **8.3%**

Japan **6.0%**

India **4.2%**

Steel and Iron
Motor Vehicles
Agricultural Products
Gold, Platinum and Mineral Products
Precious Stones

(Source: CIA World Fact Book, 2014)

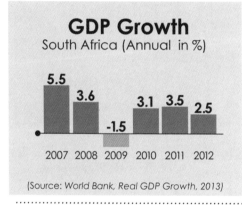

GDP Growth
South Africa (Annual in %)

5.5   3.6   -1.5   3.1   3.5   2.5

2007 2008 2009 2010 2011 2012

(Source: World Bank, Real GDP Growth, 2013)

GDP
Per Capita (in US$)

USA	49 965
EU	36 551
Brazil	11 340
▶ World Average	10 171 ◀
South Africa	7 508
China	6 091
India	1 489

(Source: World Bank, 2013)

Largest Industries

22.4% Finance

16.8% General Government Services

16% Wholesale

12.6% Manufacturing Industry

(Source: Statistics SA, 2013)

Central Bank Rates

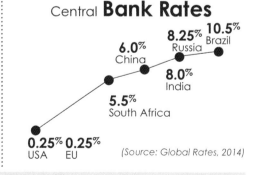

10.5% Brazil

8.25% Russia

6.0% China

8.0% India

5.5% South Africa

0.25% USA   **0.25%** EU

(Source: Global Rates, 2014)

BRICS

In 2010, South Africa joined BRICS, the alliance of emerging economies: Brazil, Russia, India, China and South Africa. These countries, home to 40% of the world's population, are considered to be in a similar state of economic development. According to the International Monetary Fund (IMF), the BRICS countries will account for 61% of global growth within the next three years.

Economic Gap

While the major cities are hubs of economic activity, the rural areas lag behind in growth and development. A high poverty rate and lack of economic empowerment are the main issues to be dealt with by the government. A wide economic gap is evident between the population groups, with one third of the population still living below the poverty line. Almost half of the country's disposable household income is shared by 10% of the population.

Youth Unemployment

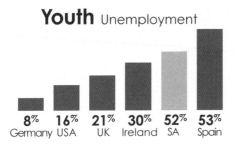

8%	16%	21%	30%	52%	53%
Germany	USA	UK	Ireland	SA	Spain

(Source: World Bank, 2014)

Social **Grants**

The government provides social grants to roughly one third of the population. The government also provides free public health facilities, schooling, housing, water and electricity in poor communities. Child support grants are paid for 10.7 million people and the old age pension is paid to 2.7 million pensioners. Disability grants are provided to 1.2 million South Africans.

Distribution of **National Income**

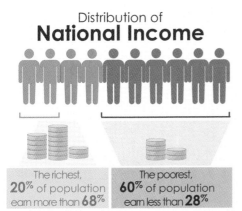

The richest, **20%** of population earn more than **68%**

The poorest, **60%** of population earn less than **28%**

(Source: Statistics SA, 2009)

Inflation

The inflation rate in the last three years has fluctuated between 4% and 6%, which is in line with the average inflation rate for the emerging market countries. Inflation has come down significantly since the end of apartheid where it ranged between 10% and 20% between 1974 and 1992.

Global Inflation Comparison

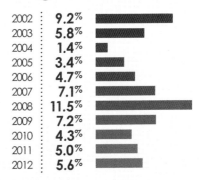

USA	1.5%
UK	2.0%
China	2.5%
South Africa	5.3%
Brazil	5.9%
Russia	6.5%
India	11.5%

(Source: Global Rates, 2013)

Average Annual Inflation

2002	9.2%
2003	5.8%
2004	1.4%
2005	3.4%
2006	4.7%
2007	7.1%
2008	11.5%
2009	7.2%
2010	4.3%
2011	5.0%
2012	5.6%

(Source: Statistics SA, 2013)

THE FINANCIAL MARKET

The stable financial market is supported by the policies of the South African central bank and the South African government. South Africa's financial policies are highly respected by its foreign counterparts due to a massive reconstruction in recent years to curb inefficiencies.

South Africa is considered the top country for the regulation of securities exchange in the world and the country's financial system is rated as one of the most efficient and stable worldwide.

Stock Exchange

The Johannesburg Stock Exchange (JSE), which was established during the Gold Rush in 1887, is today one of the largest in the world. The IMF ranked South Africa 8th out of the 20 countries belonging to the G20 nations in 2011. The country even outperformed the G7 nations, which include France, Germany, Italy, Japan, UK, USA and Canada.

There are no restrictions on foreign nationals who want to invest foreign funds in the country, but approval by the South African Reserve Bank in terms of the international regulations of the Financial Intelligence Centre Act (FICA) is needed for every transfer. Repatriation of funds is also available without restrictions, provided that exchange control approval was granted for any initial investment.

The purpose of FICA, implemented in 2001, is to counteract money laundering and prevent organised criminal activities. Banks must register the personal details of anybody opening an account or dealing with the financial institutions. As a result, when transferring money into South Africa or opening a bank account, you will be asked to produce your passport, proof of residential address and your personal details.

Foreign Exchange Control

Exchange control is administered by the South African Reserve Bank (SARB), which delegates powers to banks licensed to deal in foreign exchange. Over the last decade, South Africa's exchange control regulations were liberalised through increased foreign exposure limits for institutional investors as well as increased foreign asset limits for individuals.

Non-residents of South Africa are not subjected to exchange control. Foreign nationals from outside the common monetary area are allowed to transfer and repatriate money that was introduced into the country as well as all monies received from regular salaries and earnings, provided there is proof of the money's origin. Banks assist with the endorsement of regulatory forms for the repatriation of funds.

Foreign exchange control applies to all transfers by South African permanent residents and transfers between foreigners and South Africans. Therefore if you transfer money to invest in property, you will have to declare your permit status. A 'resident' is either a natural person or legal entity who has taken up residence or is domiciled or registered in South Africa, independent of nationality.

The rand is one of only 17 currencies worldwide where forex transactions are immediately exchanged at the current rate across all time zones.

CURRENCY

The South African rand has been the official currency since 1961 when the South African pound was abolished. This currency is the most actively traded currency in the emerging markets. The name 'rand' comes from Witwatersrand, the region around Johannesburg where gold was found in the 1880s. The international code for the South African currency is ZAR, which stands for *Zuid Afrikaanse Rand* and means 'South African Rand' in Dutch.

One rand equals 100 South African cents. There are coins with a value of 5c, 10c, 20c, 50c, R1, R2 and the bi-metal R5 coin. Banknotes are available in denominations of 10, 20, 50, 100 and 200 rands.

South African banknotes are colourful and the latest design has a portrait of Nelson Mandela on the front and one of the 'Big Five' animals on the back. In accordance with internationally practised safety measures, banknotes are changed at regular intervals. This happened in South Africa at the end of 2012. The new banknotes are in circulation, but the old notes will remain legal tender for a certain time and then be slowly be replaced.

South Africa, Swaziland and Lesotho form a Common Monetary Area (CMA) in which the rand is legal tender. Namibia withdrew from the CMA with the introduction of the Namibian dollar. The South African rand is accepted in Namibia for payment, but payments with Namibian dollars are not accepted in South Africa. The rand is on a par with the Namibian dollar.

BANKING

Getting your finances in order is one of the more challenging tasks for expats. You might opt to keep your bank account in your home country to pay for any insurance, pension fund, mortgage and other payments that you may still have to make. A South African bank account will be needed for day-to-day banking, such as paying rent and receiving your salary. You should try to make banking arrangements that are flexible and secure. Expats often transfer money between countries and new safe banking arrangements with reputable banks have to be found.

Banking in South Africa is as easily done as in many developed countries overseas. Local banks offer financial services ranging from current and savings accounts to investment funds and loans. Major financial institutions in South Africa offer branch services as well as automated teller machine (ATM) services countrywide. Online banking and telephone or cellphone banking are standard methods of banking.

The biggest banking institutions that offer a vast array of financial services in South Africa are: ABSA, Standard Bank, Nedbank and First National Bank. Some major banks also offer 'Islamic Banking' for their Muslim customers. Banks are usually open on weekdays between 9h00 and 15h00 and on Saturday mornings but are closed on Sundays and public holidays.

Only permanent residence permit holders are allowed to open an account with a bank. Tourists and people with temporary visas without their own work permits will not be allowed to open a cheque account but can open a simple transaction account. Credit facilities are not provided for non-residents.

All new accounts need to be approved in terms of the FICA regulations. Banking specialists and financial advisors can assist expats with their banking needs. Special expat banking is available through many South African banks and financial institutions, which often employ specialist private bankers to provide support and expertise in dealing with international transactions or offshore banking. Most major local banks also offer highly flexible expatriate savings and moneymarket accounts, where a minimum balance is required but interest is calculated on a daily basis and higher lump sums can be withdrawn, even without prior notice. Bank accounts are also available in pounds, dollars and euros. It is recommended that you shop around for the best support and advice.

Krugerrands

The prestigious Krugerrand gold coins are available at the various weights and denominations. First minted in 1967, the 22-carat gold coin is still popular with collectors and investors as it contains exactly one ounce of fine gold. The South African Mint also offers other special uncirculated coins at its own offices and through various official dealers, such as SCOIN shops, which you will find in many bigger shopping centres, airports and through a network of international coin dealers abroad.

Cards (Cheque, Credit and Cash)

In South Africa, the most common forms of payment are cash and bank cards ('plastic'). Most overseas bank cards will allow you to draw money from an ATMs (automated teller machine) or from your overseas account at the counter of the local banks. Credit and debit cards are accepted for payment in most shops and restaurants. Many stores also offer customer cards that are linked to a credit account. You can choose to use these store credit cards for debits or as proper credit cards. South Africans refer to their cheque cards as debit cards.

Common Methods of **Payment**

Cheques

Many small businesses accept personal cheques for deliveries or services. However cheques are often not accepted in stores. Make sure that you carry a picture ID as proof of your identity when intending to pay by cheque and ask about this facility ahead of receiving any service. Traveller's cheques are not accepted in stores.

Online Banking

Common financial transactions are increasingly done through online banking. In South Africa you need to apply for online banking, and you will be given a user-ID and a pin code and a password. Online banking frequently uses transaction numbers that you receive via cellphone when making payments online.

Garage Cards

When you open a cheque account in South Africa, you will be offered a garage card, which is used at filling stations for payments for petrol, diesel and oil as well as other services offered by garages and carwash outlets. These cards can only be used to pay at the petrol stations. This service was started to counter crime related to credit card fraud.

Bank Cards

Cirrus and Maestro cards are widely accepted as well as debit and credit cards of various local banks. Credit cards from overseas banks are usually accepted as long as they are supported by VISA or MasterCard, American Express, Diners, VISA-Electron or Maestro.

Cash

Cash is often the preferred way of payment in smaller stores or as payment for services. You can draw money from your account during banking hours or draw cash from an ATM at any time. Most of the ATMs in South Africa are linked to an international network of major credit card systems, which enables you to draw money from your foreign bank accounts with credit cards. Most ATMs are conveniently located in shopping centres and petrol stations as well as outside the banks' branch offices. Often these ATMs offer various simple banking facilities besides drawing money. You can make online transfers, print mini statements and buy recharge vouchers for your cellphone. Always be aware of your surroundings when using a cash machine and never accept help from strangers when drawing money or making transactions with your card.

PAYMENT ACROSS BORDERS

Foreign Exchange Bureaus

American Express, Travelex and Rennies are the biggest companies that do currency exchange. You will find exchange bureaus in major shopping centres and foreign exchange (forex) offices in most cities. Some of the bigger hotels offer currency exchange facilities for their guests at any time of the day but will usually charge quite a hefty fee for this service. All the major South African banks also offer exchange facilities. Foreign exchange services are also offered by a number of authorised dealers, who may, however, only offer limited forex services as their trading permits allow only the facilitating of travel-related currency exchange. Some of these forex service companies, such as Travelex, Forex World Limited or Imali Express, also offer a round-the-clock service, including delivery. A full list of authorised dealers is available through the South African Reserve Bank.

Online Transfers

Once-off and on-going international money transfers require expertise and efficient handling by specialists in foreign exchange to avoid poor exchange rates or high transaction fees and commissions. Various specialists offer online money transfer services. Among the most reputable online foreign exchange specialists are: Travelex, FXFirm, Moneycorp, Worldfirst, International Foreign Exchange, Smart Currency Exchange and Venstar Exchange. The online site *mycurrencytransfer.com* helps with comparisons and links to major companies.

Traveller's Cheques

Traveller's cheques always give you a safety net when travelling or for the first days of settling in the country before you have opened a local bank account. Missing and stolen cheques can always be reported and replaced, as traveller cheques generally carry an inherent insurance. Traveller's cheques have to be cashed at local banks, exchange bureaus or major hotels as they are not usually accepted for payments in stores. So take note of the opening times of the exchange bureau and remember to always take your passport along when intending to exchange the cheques. Foreign exchange cheques can be purchased in South Africa for your foreign travel needs. For exchanging or buying traveller's cheques you need the following documents: a valid passport, proof of travel arrangements, a green bar-coded identity document or temporary resident permit and proof of residential address that must not be older than three months. In South Africa, banks also offer currency cards that can be loaded with foreign currency in preparation for travel abroad. These cards are linked to a local cheque account.

MoneyGram

MoneyGram provides a convenient money transfer option if you do not have an account. With MoneyGram it is possible to send up to US$10 000, or the equivalent in any currency, to or from more than 194 countries worldwide with the help of an authorised agent. In South Africa, you can send and receive money during banking hours through Standard Bank or Bidvest Bank without needing a bank account. You will have to pay the relevant service fees.

Telegraphic Account Transfers

These types of transfer are another possibility when you have already opened a South African bank account and intend to transfer money from your bank account abroad. Transfer methods like CHAPS and SWIFT - or by quoting your International Bank Account Number (IBAN) - are only available to account holders. You will need to note the SWIFT, CHAPS or IBAN numbers of your foreign and local banks to make transfers. Fees and commissions from both banks apply.

PayPal

PayPal is an internationally operating money transfer service that can be used to transfer money overseas for making online purchases. This service does not reveal your financial information publicly nor does it provide the other party with your bank details. PayPal accounts can be set up with either an existing bank account or a credit card. There are three different account types available. Bear in mind that personal accounts can only be used for incoming transfers of up to $500 per month. You will have to pay PayPal transaction fees. PayPal accounts are compliant with South African Reserve Bank (SARB) exchange controls, and funds received must be deposited into a regular bank account within 30 days.

Specialist Brokers

For expats, finding a reliable and cost-effective international money transfer method is an important consideration. Your main aim is to get an exchange rate as close to the interbank rate as possible. Specialist brokers usually achieve better deals than the banks, whose rates are as close to the live rates as possible but are usually not as flexible as those of brokers. Shop around to get the best service for your requirements and to secure the best rate available for your fund transfers. Always remember to check if a currency broker or financial service provider is registered with the Financial Services Authority (FSA) and check their Federal Registration Number (FRN) before transferring any money.

Offshore Banking

This process is legally undertaken by many expat and international workers who receive earnings in countries other than their home country and invest the funds legally through different taxation structures in the various countries. Holding assets offshore may bring some tax advantages for expats, and it is advisable to speak to an experienced financial advisor for guidance. Offshore banking is to be considered especially if, for tax purposes, you are neither a resident in your home country nor in South Africa. This is usually achieved if you reside in your home country for less than 183 days in the tax year, then become a resident in another country and also live there for less than 183 days in their official tax year. Take into consideration that different dates apply for the tax year in different countries. Eighty-five per cent of the expats in South Africa hold an offshore account, as many of them have already worked in other countries and are experienced when it comes to offshore banking and its tax advantages. Interest on offshore accounts is usually paid out without tax being deducted.

INVESTING

Global Competitiveness
Ranking out of 142 countries
(Where 1 is the best rating)

South Africa (Overall Ranking)	52
Auditing & Reporting Standards	1
Efficacy of Corporate Boards	1
Soundness of Banks	2
Financial Market Development	3
Quality of Management Schools	15
Property Rights	26
Judicial Independence	27
Local Supplier Quality	34
Transparency of Government Policy	35
Business Sophistication	38
Availability of Latest Technologies	39
Innovation	42
Availability of Research & Training	51
Infrastructure	63
Higher Education & Training	84
Health & Primary Education	132

(Source: World Economic Forum, 2013)

South Africa continues to be an important destination for investment on the continent. According to the World Bank's *Connecting to Compete* survey in 2012, South Africa not only outperformed the rest of Africa and the BRICS nations but also all the upper middle-income nations. The most recent *Global Competitiveness Survey* and the *Doing Business Survey* show that South Africa compares well with other countries.

With almost no restrictions on the form or extent of financial investment and a financial sector that is rated as one of the most efficient and stable worldwide, South Africa attracts investors from all over the world. And with a world-class and progressive legal framework in the areas of labour, commerce and maritime issues, South Africa is considered a healthy environment for investment.

Foreign direct investment (FDI) in Africa is considered to be very attractive, especially with investors from the emerging markets. Attractive long-term growth potential is expected from investors due to improving prospects in the whole region. In general, the growth rate on the African continent has impressed investors even in times of global economic crisis. Three quarters of all FDI were effected in ten African countries and reflect high confidence in the region. South Africa is perceived as the most attractive country for FDI in Africa (59%) and is regarded as a stepping-stone into Africa by many investors.

The top sectors for FDI projects in the last decade were software and IT services, followed by financial and business services and major projects in the automotive and metals sectors. There are no restrictions on foreign investors acquiring companies or businesses and investing in South Africa.

Unlimited inward capital transfers and the acquisition of shares are available to foreign investors. Loans, however, require approval by the South African Reserve Bank. Investing in property is one of the most favoured forms of investment for foreigners living in the country, particularly for expats who experience a higher disposable income in South Africa than expats living in other countries.

A wide range of world-class expertise is available in the country to guide an investor through the process of opening a business and investing in an existing business or registering a new entity in South Africa. Various incentive schemes exist to attract international investors. These incentives are available for investment either in creation, design and improvement of new ventures or for investment to acquire and upgrade existing businesses.

Investment in specific sectors that facilitate the enhancement of competitive advantages and economic growth and development is supported as well. Foreign investment grants are given to participants in the Manufacturing Investment Programme. Incentives are given especially for the upgrade of assets to establish or expand infrastructure and support the textile and automotive industry.

There are numerous international, regional and local chambers of commerce that will guide and advise international investors throughout South Africa.

Doing Business
Ranking out of 185 countries
(Where 1 is the best rating)

South Africa (Overall Ranking)	39
Getting Credit	1
Protecting Investors	10
Paying Taxes	32
Starting a Business	53
Registering Property	79
Enforcing Contracts	82
Trading Across Borders	115
Getting Electricity	150

(Source: World Bank, 2013)

Estate Planning

Even if you have a valid will in your own country, you are advised to set up a will as soon as possible after making any investment in the country. It is normal practice to set up a will in South Africa and the local laws are the same for both foreigners and residents. You should consider doing this with the help of a lawyer or your bank. Many banks and even attorneys will help to write a basic will for free. Contact the law society in your region to get contact details of an attorney in your area. Banks usually charge a small fee for providing safe custody of a will and other documents.

Wills made outside South Africa in respect of property or investments in South Africa are considered valid as long as they comply with South African law. The Wills Act does not require wills made by foreigners outside South Africa to be validated by the South African authorities before they can be implemented in South Africa. If, however, a resident dies intestate, the estate will be divided according to the terms of the rules of intestate succession, depending on your marital status and the number of children. Therefore it is advisable to list all assets and all potential heirs in the will, which must be signed by two witnesses of sound mind and over 14 years of age. Estate duty is levied at 20% of the dutiable amount of estates over R3.5 million. If the estate is given to the surviving spouse, then the estate is exempt from duty until the spouse dies. The disposal of a deceased's estate under South African law usually takes between six months and two years.

INSURANCE

When moving abroad, you should take out expat insurance to protect your family in case of an emergency. Among the biggest insurance companies in South Africa are Santam, Sanlam, Momentum, Outsurance, Mutual & Federal and DialDirect. Alternatively, consider an insurance brokerage firm, such as Lyall Morgan & Associates or Hollard, who will be able to help you make the right decisions.

There are several types of insurance that will be really useful when living abroad as an expatriate. Remember that you can make significant savings if you combine various insurances by the same insurer. For example, your vehicle insurance is combined with your household contents insurance on the same policy. Besides health insurance and car insurance, which are covered elsewhere in this book, you should consider the following insurances:

SASRIA

South African Special Risks Insurance Association (SASRIA) covers damage caused by politically motivated riots, non-political riots, public disorder (including labour disturbances, civil unrest, strikes and lockouts) and terrorism. The cost is usually a small percentage of the premium and is included in every insurance policy if not removed at the request of the policy holder.

Annual Travel Insurance

This insurance will provide cover for trips abroad to countries that are not covered by your expat health insurance. However, if you have a general international health insurance you should not worry about any holiday trips abroad. Be advised, however, that you might have to take out additional cover for any longer trips back to your home country if you have an expat health insurance for only one specific country. Usually only a short period in your home country is still covered, so be sure to know about any time limits for trips abroad. Annual travel insurance is often also offered by your bank or credit card provider, as well as your travel company. Check the basic insurance that is included in any gold or platinum credit card membership before committing to another insurance premium. Depending on the cover, you might not need to take out extra cover for your travels.

Expat Life Insurance

Life insurance is also considered to be an important cover for expatriates. Living in a foreign environment often brings different kinds of dangers, and you should take out life insurance to protect your family in case of an emergency. There is usually an age limit for term life insurances, which you should enquire about with the insurance companies.

Other Insurance Options

Critical illness cover, personal accident insurance and home contents insurance should be considered as well. It is advisable to get familiar with these insurances. Get advice on which insurance is most cost-effective to keep in your home country and which will be better, or even cheaper, to take out in South Africa.

Remember always to take your previous insurance or expat insurance details along when moving, as you will often be able to negotiate rebates for non-claim status when you can prove this with a letter from your previous insurance company.

RESOURCES

General Information

Dept of Trade and Industry:
www.thedti.gov.za
National Treasury: *www.treasury.gov.za*
BRICS: *www.brics5.co.za*
Statistics SA: *www.statssa.gov.za*
Revenue Services: *www.sars.gov.za*
Law Society (LSSA): *www.lssa.org.za*
Financial Services Board: *www.fsb.co.za*
Credit Reports: *www.experian.co.za*
Credit Alerts: *www.mytransunion.co.za*
Chamber of Commerce: *www.sacci.org.za*

Banks

Reserve Bank: *www.resbank.co.za*
Ombudsman: *www.obssa.co.za*
Credit Regulator: *www.ncr.org.za*
Absa: *www.absa.co.za*
Bidvest: *www.bidvestbank.co.za*
First National Bank: *www.fnb.co.za*
First Rand: *www.firstrand.co.za*
Grindrod Bank: *www.grindrodbank.co.za*
Investec: *www.investec.co.za*
Nedbank: *www.nedbank.co.za*
Rand Merchant Bank: *www.rmb.co.za*
Standard Bank: *www.standardbank.co.za*
Wesbank: *www.wesbank.co.za*

Foreign Exchange

www.mcy.co.za
www.americanexpressforex.co.za
www.mycurrencytransfer.com
www.travelex.co.za

Credit Cards

www.americanexpress.co.za
www.dinersclub.co.za
www.mastercard.co.za
www.visa.co.za

Investment

Trade Leads: *www.tradeinvestsa.co.za*
Investment Analysts: *www.iassa.co.za*
Chartered Accountants: *www.saica.co.za*
South African Mint: *www.samint.co.za*
www.investmentincentives.co.za

Insurance

www.saia.co.za
www.insurance-guide.co.za
www.hollard.co.za
www.momentum.co.za
www.oldmutual.co.za
www.outsurance.co.za
www.sanlam.co.za

Surveys

Africa Attractiveness: *www.ey.com*
Global Competitiveness:
www.weforum.org
HSBC: www.expatexplorer.hsbc.com
Mercer: *www.mercer.com*
Open Budget:
www.internationalbudget.org
World Bank: *www.doingbusiness.org*

Recommended Reading

Botha, Ziets et al. (2012) *Understanding South African Financial Markets*. Van Schaik

Roux, André (2014) *Everyone's Guide to the South African Economy*. Zebra Press

South Africa's Oil and Gas Alliance (2011) *Investor's Handbook 2011/2012*.
www.saoga.org.za

> 'South Africa is admired for its wealth and skills, feared for its power, resented for its brashness and despised for its youthfulness.'
>
> ~ Moeletsi Mbeki, businessman

WORKING

South Africa attracts people from all over the world who come to work in the country, as the largest economy on the African continent offers many business opportunities for investors. People with sought-after professional skills are also encouraged to create new jobs in the country.

Vacancies abound for scarce or critical skills in South Africa and highly skilled expats from around the world are welcome to fill these posts to create economic growth. However, if you do not have these critical skills, finding a job in South Africa can be difficult owing to the high competition in the local job market as applicants from previously disadvantaged backgrounds will be preferred.

Affirmative action measures, referred to as Black Economic Empowerment (BEE), are in place to create more awareness of the discrepancies in employment between the races and to ensure better opportunities for formerly underprivileged South Africans. The number of local unskilled and semi-skilled workers who are looking for work far outnumbers the jobs available and thus there are only limited opportunities for the employment of foreigners if they are not highly skilled and experienced in their chosen field of work. The official unemployment rate stands at 25%, but many adults work in the informal sector. In some parts of the country the unemployment figure rises to as high as 80%.

You will only be allowed to work in South Africa if you have a valid work permit. Every foreigner who does not have a permanent residence permit must have a work permit of some sort to work in South Africa. A temporary residence permit only allows you to stay in South Africa but not to take up work, not even voluntary or charitable work. Unlike in many other countries, expats accompanying their spouses or partners who have either a permanent residence permit or a work permit are not automatically granted a work permit. Spouses and partners need to apply for their own work permit if they want to take up work.

Employment
in South Africa
Age 20+ years

25%
Officially
Unemployed

52%
Economically
Active

(Source: Statistics SA, 2012)

Volkswagen factory , Eastern Cape

When looking for a job in South Africa, it is usually imperative to have some expertise in your specialist field or work experience abroad. Many companies are more inclined to support your application for a work permit if you know several foreign languages and have work experience in their sector, especially if it is impossible to find these qualifications in the local job market.

In South Africa, there are no work-seekers permits available. Entering the country on a visitor permit with the purpose of finding a job is illegal and you can get into serious trouble for staying in the country without the correct permit.

Job Market

The scarce skills in South Africa are:

Artisans • Engineers
Social Workers • Pharmacy Assistants
Nurses • Medical Doctors
Technical and Business Managers
Teachers and Educators
Accountants • IT Specialists

International head-hunting companies and local recruitment companies will be able to support you in your job search before you come to the country, targeting companies in your special field of expertise and helping you to find placement. Head hunters usually approach employees to move from one company to another, while recruitment agencies get paid for their work by the employer who factors the commission into the employee's salary. Pre-screening and interviews are usually done by the recruiter. Among the most prominent local recruitment companies are Mindcor, DAV, ISC World and Drake. Browsing the Internet and starting to network within expat forums and various professional social networks, such as *za.linkedin.com,* are recommended.

Highly skilled and experienced professionals such as engineers, teachers, medical staff and IT consultants will find great job opportunities in South Africa and so will skilled foreign workers with scarce professional skills. Several professions have been identified as being in great demand but in short supply.

South Africa ranks 35th out of 183 countries regarding the Ease of Doing Business.
World Economic Forum, 2012

PERMITS

It is imperative to have a work permit before starting work and it is illegal to enter the country on a visitors permit for the purposes of looking for work. Given the high unemployment rate in the country, a work permit is only granted to a foreigner who possesses special skills, such as foreign languages, or suitable qualifications that are in limited supply on the local labour market. Thus, a letter of motivation from the employer as to why a South African citizen or permanent resident could not fill the position needs to be submitted to the Department of Home Affairs. Efforts made to fill the vacancy from the local workforce, such as advertisements in local newspapers, have to be documented.

Getting your documents in order and applying for the relevant work permit usually takes a lot of preparation and requires time and, above all, patience. Be advised that a work permit application or renewal usually takes at least six to eight weeks and involves a substantial amount of paperwork. Make sure you bring all your professional diplomas when you move. When you apply for a work permit, it is mandatory to have your overseas diplomas, degrees and certificates recognised by the South African Qualifications Authority (SAQA). SAQA evaluate national and international educational certificates and compare overseas degrees, diplomas and certificates with the South African equivalent.

As the requirements for the various work permits vary, it is advisable to contact an immigration practitioner to help you with the application. The Department of Home Affairs treats each application as an individual case.

Work Permit Documentation

☐ A completed and signed application form

☐ A passport that is valid for no less than 30 days after the expiry of the intended stay

☐ Payment of the application fee

☐ A vaccination certificate, if you are coming from or travelling via a yellow fever region

☐ Medical and radiology reports on the prescribed forms

☐ A police clearance certificate from each country in which the applicant has resided for longer than 12 months since the age of 18

☐ A cash deposit, return ticket or an undertaking of repatriation by the employer

☐ Proof of financial means to support your living expenses

☐ A contract of employment or proof of exceptional skills

☐ Proof of qualifications and an evaluation by SAQA

Always investigate the current legislation with the Department of Home Affairs. The documents mentioned in the table are considered essential, regardless of the type of permit. New regulations will be introduced in 2014 which will require an application for work permits to be effected from the relevant South African missions abroad.

Documents can be certified a true copy by a commissioner of oaths at the local post office and/or police station. In certain instances, a document may need to be certified as true by a public notary. You will find a public notary at most attorney offices.

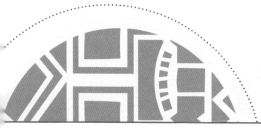

TYPES OF PERMITS

General Work Permits

General work permits fall into the category of temporary permits. Spouses or partners and children usually get temporary residency permits to be able to accompany the work permit holder. A work permit is granted for a period of up to five years and can be renewed. Note that accompanying family members are granted permits for a maximum of three years only, so expiry and renewal dates of the permits might differ.

Intra-company Permits

International or multi-national companies who send their employees abroad via intra-company transfers or secondments can obtain visas for these employees via the South African High Commissions abroad. Contact the embassy in your home country at least six weeks before your departure to South Africa and hand in your firm job offer and all the other necessary documents relating to a work permit there. Intra-company permits are usually granted for a maximum of two years only.

Quota Work Permits

The Department of Home Affairs offers special work permits, called 'quota permits', for foreigners who have scarce skills. Quota permit holders can change employer during the stay but need to stay in the same occupational category. This listing currently includes 53 categories for roughly 35 000 jobs and is updated once a year. For any quota work permit, you need at least five years of work experience. Furthermore, proof of registration with a statutory body, professional board or council is necessary. Once a permit is granted, you have 90 days to prove that you have secured employment in the country. This permit category needs to be applied for before coming into South Africa and cannot be obtained when already in the country on a tourist visa. It is anticipated that the new regulations which are to be introduced in 2014 might impact on the Quota Work Permits.

Exceptional Skills Permit

This special work permit applies only to persons with extraordinary skills and who are not bound to a particular job. This category is only available to foreigners with skills that are deemed critical for the advancement of South Africa's economy. Applicants need to supply a comprehensive curriculum vitae stating trade and peer references and important publications, and are usually seconded by state organs (such as major international cultural bodies or business associations) to highlight the applicant's exceptional skills and status amongst peers worldwide.

Visas for Voluntary or Charitable Work

Working for a local non-profit, religious or other charities requires a specific visa allowing volunteer work experiences. Getting a visa under the category of voluntary or charitable activities is necessary and this applies for both paid and unpaid charitable work. Charitable or volunteer work can also be undertaken with a study permit with a specific endorsement.

Work Endorsement for a Study Permit

If a student wants to study at a South African college or university and is in possession of a valid study permit, it is possible to work for a maximum of 20 hours a week as part of practical job experience or an internship. An endorsement to your study permit must be applied for at the Department of Home Affairs.

Work Endorsement to Visitor Visa

An authorisation to work can be applied for with seasonal or other short-term project work and unpaid internships. This endorsement is linked to the visitor's visa and is less difficult to obtain than a work permit.

Corporate Worker Visa

This visa can be applied for by a company that has an ongoing need for foreign specialist workers. This permit is issued to the employer and not the individual.

DOING BUSINESS

B-BBEE Scorecard

1. *Ownership*: the effective ownership of the enterprise by black people (25 points).

2. *Management Control* and *Employment Equity*: the effective control of the enterprise by black people and initiatives intended to achieve equity in the workplace (15 points).

3. *Skills Development*: the extent to which employers carry out initiatives designed to develop the competencies of black employees (20+5 bonus points).

4. *Enterprise and Supplier Development*: the extent to which the enterprise carries out initiatives intended to assist and accelerate the development and sustainability of black entrepreneurs or enterprises and the extent to which the enterprise has initiatives that contribute towards development that promotes access to the economy for black people (40+4 bonus points).

5. *Socio-economic Development*: the extent to which the enterprise has initiatives that contribute towards development which promotes access to the economy for black people (5 points).

The South African government supports international investors if they want to establish a new business or if they want to invest in an existing business venture. South Africa has well-developed and well-regulated company laws and regulations, which are based on English company law. All companies are regulated by the Companies Act. The body monitoring the requirements of the act is the Companies and Intellectual Properties Commission (CIPC). Major distinctions lie between profit and non-profit companies, but no distinction is made between South African-owned or foreign-owned companies in the Companies Act.

If a business is 100% owned by a foreigner, no special government approval is required beyond a business permit. Several types of business can be established by an investor. Your choice will depend on various factors, such as taxation and limited liability, which need to be considered. A popular way of doing business in South Africa is to establish a franchise operation, and 13% of franchises are foreign-owned. Foreign investors should consider the option of buying a business as a going concern. This will mean a significant saving, as the VAT and property transfer duty are not applicable. It is advisable to consult an attorney to assist with the formation of companies, business structures and assets.

Black Economic Empowerment (BEE) measures were first implemented in 2003 and Broad-Based Black Economic Empowerment (B-BBEE) measures introduced in 2007 to create equal work opportunities for the black population. This group is defined as African, Coloured, Indians or South African Chinese who were resident in South Africa prior to the inception of the new constitution in 1993 or were out of the country by virtue of seeking asylum or born post 1993. According to these affirmative action measures, companies are scored on criteria such as black participation in ownership, the percentage of black employees and the number of black employees in management (see the scorecard above).

The B-BBEE measures involve an economic transformation process that is meant to broaden the employment base and stimulate economic growth. Considering the low education levels and high numbers of unskilled workers, this is a massive undertaking. It will take many more years to create equality in the job market. Although compliance with BEE standards is voluntary, it is essential for companies involved in public procurement or interested in supplying goods or services to the public sector. Public entities are required to adhere to these affirmative action measures. Companies are rated on their BEE commitment according to a point scale, which is set out in the BEE Codes of Good Practice. Enterprises that do not meet the specified minimum annual turnover are exempt from these regulations.

STARTING YOUR OWN BUSINESS

There are various business structures available to start your own business, depending on the size of the venture and the number of partners or shareholders. National and international business associations will help you source specific information about your business sector and are a good starting point for investing or opening a business in the country. Take into consideration that the registration of any business venture takes about four weeks to get a business permit, while it may take up to three months if you apply for a business or an import/export licence. It is advisable to contact an attorney specialising in company and taxation laws.

Depending on the business structure, the business venture will need to be registered with various bodies. The South African Revenue Services (SARS) requires businesses to register for company income tax, 'pay-as-you-earn' (PAYE) tax deductions for employees and for VAT (value added tax) if the business exceeds the stipulated turnover bracket. You will also need to register with the Department of Labour for unemployment insurance (UIF) and 'Compensation for occupational injuries and diseases' (COID). Industry-specific licences are required in certain industries such as the health, food and entertainment or hospitality sectors. Employers in certain sectors pay a Skills Development Levy equivalent to 1% of their total wage bill, which is used to upskill the workforce. This amount is payable to their registered SETA and employers can then claim between 20–45% of the levy back if their approved training plan has been implemented.

All foreign business ventures need to be financed with the investment of a prescribed minimum capital contribution and will also need to create new jobs for at least five people. The prescribed minimum financial capital contribution stands currently at 2.5 million rand, but the capital requirements may be reduced or waived for investments in the information and communication technology, clothing and textile manufacturing, biotechnology or tourism sectors.

To apply for a business permit, in addition to the financial and employment requirements stipulated above, you will require a business plan and an undertaking to register with SARS. Proof of registration with the relevant trade body, board or council might also be necessary. Furthermore, you will have to pay a repatriation deposit equivalent to the value of a return ticket to your country of origin/permanent residence. This deposit is refundable and you will be reimbursed after having acquired a permanent residence permit. Other non-business permit specific requirements, such as police certificates or medical reports, apply. Enquire with the Department of Home Affairs regarding the most recent regulations.

Business Structures

Sole Proprietor

This business entity is owned and run by one owner, also called a 'sole trader'. All transactions are entered into in personal capacity and the owner is fully responsible for all debts. No formal documents are required.

Partnership

Business with a minimum of two and a maximum of 20 partners. A partnership agreement is essential. Rights, duties and liablities are shared and bind the partners individually.

Private Company

This entity, also known as Pty Ltd may have up to 50 shareholders. The company must be registered with CIPC. Conduct of the company and duties such as audits are strictly governed by law. Debts are limited to the shareholders' investments.

Trust

Although not regulated by statute, a trust can be viewed as a separate entity similar to a private company. A trust can offer benefits such as protection of assets and a savings on certain duties.

Labour Laws
in South Africa

All employees, including foreign employees, are protected by South Africa's employment laws. The basic conditions are regulated in the Basic Conditions of Employment Act (BCEA), the Labour Relations Act (LRA) and the Employment Equity Act (EEA). The EEA specifically regulates equality at the workplace for companies with more than 50 employees or a certain turnover and for employees working under tariff conditions. The following basic work conditions apply:

Unions

South Africa has active trade unions in most industries, including the public service. Minimum wages are set for most business sectors. The Labour Relations Act is the framework for both unions and employers regulating the right to strike and promoting collective bargaining between employers and the trade unions. Unions engage employers over issues affecting the workforce. The most prominent trade union federations articulating workers' interests are the Congress of South African Trade Unions (COSATU), the Federation of Unions in South Africa (FEDUSA) and the National Council of Trade Unions (NACTU). These are independent and compete for members, but they join forces in campaigns, such as demonstrations against amendments to the Labour Relations Act.

Maternity Leave

Women are entitled to four months unpaid maternity leave and the position must be kept open for her return during this time. Unemployment benefit is payable at 45% of the monthly remuneration up to the maximum limit. This applies to persons who have been contributing to the fund for at least two years, have been employed by the company for a minimum of 13 previous weeks and whose weekly working hours exceed 24 hours.

Minimum Age

Strict regulations apply to the minimum age for workers. Children under 15 years of age are not allowed to work in South Africa.

CCMA

The Commission for Conciliation, Mediation and Arbitration (CCMA) is an independent body that is aimed at promoting fair practices in the work environment. It is charged with resolving labour disputes and provides advice and training on labour relations. Both employees and employers in dispute (disputes can also be referred by unions or employer organisations) can access the CCMA over matters including dismissal, wages, working conditions, workplace changes or discrimination. The actual processes are run by commissioners and cases follow a process of conciliation, mediation and arbitration. The CCMA is run by the Governing Body comprising of representatives of the three social partners: workers, business and government. The commissioners are appointed by the Governing Body. Senior commissioners monitor the process and assist in the allocation of cases. Once a commissioner is vested with a matter, no other party or person may interfere with the discretion of that commissioner, except for a higher court of law, such as the Labour Court.

Probation Period

Usually, the probation period is between one and three months, depending on the job. Probation time can, however, not easily be ended. Poor work performance needs to be addressed during the probation period. Efforts to remedy shortcomings are expected to be made by the employer as well as the employee.

Sick Leave

An employee is entitled to 30 days fully paid sick leave in a three year cycle. Sick leave can rightfully be taken in accordance with the company's policy. If an illness lasts longer than two days or for more than two days in an eight week period, a doctor's certificate may be required. Up to three days leave a year are granted for family responsibility leave or compassionate leave.

Work Hours

According to the law, work hours are limited to a maximum of 45 hours per week, with not more than ten hours overtime per week. In a five-day week, daily working hours are not to exceed nine hours and in a six-day week, daily working time is limited to eight hours. A meal interval of 60 minutes applies after five hours of work. A lunch break of a minimum of half an hour applies if so agreed in the contract. These conditions apply irrespective of the industry. It is worth knowing that higher management positions are not bound to these work hours. Working on public holidays is permitted if there is an agreement between employer and employee and must be remunerated at double the employee's ordinary daily rate.

Annual Leave

Employees have a right to a minimum of 21 days of uninterrupted annual leave, including weekends and public holidays. Commonly 15 actual work days of annual leave are granted after one year of employment, but this depends on the position and the employer.

Remuneration

According to the HSBC expat survey, the disposable income for expatriates living in South Africa is higher than in all European countries, except Belgium. However, monthly earnings do depend on location. Posts in Gauteng are commonly paid more than equivalent posts in other provinces. Earnings for local employment are generally considerably lower than for expatriate assignments for the same jobs, as expats often receive additional allowances for housing, schooling, healthcare, pension funds and travel expenses from their overseas companies. Average salary comparisons can be found online at www.payscale.com.

Social Insurance

South Africa's social insurance provisions are basic and cover only unemployment insurance and workmen's compensation. Unemployment insurance (UIF) is carried by the employer and employee in equal parts with contributions of 1% of the monthly income each. Workmen's Compensation is carried solely by the employer for employees whose annual income is below the specified amount. Contributions to health insurance by the employer are not required by law and thus dependent on the employment contract and company policy.

TAXATION

South Africa uses a progressive tax system that adheres to international taxation standards. The tax system is residence based, which means South African residents have to pay taxes on their worldwide income irrespective of where the income has been earned. Non-residents in South Africa are subject to taxation for their income earned in the country but not for income earned abroad. Foreign taxes will be credited against any South African tax liability payable on foreign income. The South African Revenue Services (SARS) considers foreigners who live in the country for more than 91 days in a tax year to be residents for tax purposes and therefore liable for taxation in South Africa.

There are double taxation agreements with countries such as the UK, USA and most member countries of the European Union. You

Tax Structures

PAYE

With the 'pay-as-you-earn' tax method, tax is automatically deducted on a monthly basis from the salary and transferred to SARS by the employer.

Provisional TAX

Provisional tax applies to any person who receives income (or to whom income accrues) other than a salary in which case the tax is paid manually in two instalments based on estimates.

will find a listing on the SARS website, but be advised to contact an accountant or lawyer who specialises in international tax laws. SARS's special expatriate unit will advise foreigners working and earning an income in South Africa.

Income tax is paid in two forms in South Africa. Employees' tax or pay-as-you-earn (commonly referred to as PAYE) refers to the tax that is legally required to be deducted by an employer from an employee's remuneration as it is earned.

For non-salaried employees, provisional tax is a method of paying tax that ensures that the taxpayer does not pay large amounts on assessment, and the tax load is spread over the relevant year of assessment. It requires the taxpayers to pay at least two provisional amounts in advance during the year of assessment. These amounts are based on estimated taxable income. Final liability, however, is worked out upon assessment and the payments will be off-set against the liability for normal tax for the applicable year of assessment. A third payment is optional after the end of the tax year but before the issuing of the assessment.

Tax relief is available for certain expenses and benefits, such as contributions to a retirement fund, medical expenses or travel allowances. Tax exemption and various rebates may be applicable if you earn income under certain thresholds. Find out about the specific regulations in the Tax Guide published by the National Treasury, but it is highly recommended that you get professional advice from a registered tax consultant.

Tax Returns

Income tax is assessed once a year. The tax year for individuals runs from 1 March until the end of February. If you have an annual income amounting to more than R120 000 from one source of employment per tax year, it is mandatory that you file a tax return. Tax returns can be filed either manually by mail, at the revenue services' offices or electronically online via e-filing. Joint filing for spouses or life partners is not available. Tax payers are not required to submit supporting documents with their returns unless they have been especially requested to do so by SARS. Only copies of the original documents should then be sent in for assessment, and you should keep the originals for at least five years. Income tax rates are adjusted annually. Transparency in tax documentation is rated highly in South Africa. The country's budget documents are among the most transparent and detailed in the world. The Open Budget Index Survey ranks South Africa in 2012 the second best, after New Zealand, out of 100 countries.

RETIREMENT

In South Africa there is no official retirement age. Employees can retire at any age agreed on in a work contract or, if no age is specified, the time for retirement is decided between the employer and employee. Usually, the age for retirement ranges between 60 and 65 years. If you decide to retire and invest in South Africa, a retired person's permits must be applied for before your planned move to South Africa. Proof of financial security in the form of a lifelong pension or capital income of not less than R20 000 per month is required. Retired person's permits are usually granted for up to four years, but they may be renewed. It is also possible to apply for permanent residency.

Be warned that some countries will freeze a pension scheme if the expat or pensioner does not have ordinary residence in the home country. Other countries will let people draw money from their pension fund regardless of where the retired person lives. Make sure you follow your country's regulations regarding payment into and out of pension funds, and contact an expert regarding the implications for your retirement and pension funds before moving.

As many employers no longer offer any form of company pension scheme, expats often have to make provision for their own retirement income. It is very important therefore to have retirement plans in place. As there are many legalities and tax issues to consider, it is highly advisable that you consult an expert in solutions for financial retirement and tax planning.

According to the *Global Post Index 2010,* South Africa is one of the ten most popular low-cost places for retirees. The rolling hills of the KwaZulu-Natal Midlands are a popular choice for retirement with numerous housing options in estates and retirement villages in scenic settings.

In all the major cities you will find nanny and au pair recruitment agencies. Through networking at local schools and church communities you can find reliable babysitters.

HELP AT HOME

There are many jobseekers available to ease your workload at home. Domestic workers, also called chars, can help with many household jobs. It is recommended that you only hire someone who comes with references. Jobseekers also offer help with gardening, cleaning, childminding and many other tasks. Recognised refugees and asylum seekers are permitted to seek employment in terms of section 27(f) of the Refugee Act and are often hired as gardeners, domestic helpers, cooks or childminders. Always investigate references from former employers and negotiate a contract. Contracts should state daily, weekly or monthly payments, working hours, annual leave, allowances and termination regulations. Unemployment insurance of 2% of the wage (1% by employer and 1% by employee) has to be paid if your helper is working more than 24 hours a month for you. Employers usually supply work clothes, meals and equipment as well as transport costs. Medical insurance and payments to pension plans are usually not paid but can be deducted on agreement from the employee.

Minimum wages apply to domestic helpers. The minimum monthly wage in 2013 for domestic workers working more than 27 hours and less than 45 hours per week ranged between R1056.35 – R1746.00 depending on the area. Please bear in mind that this is considered the bare minimum to survive and it is hardly possible for a domestic worker to sustain a family on this amount. In general, R150–200 per day is considered average reimbursement for general household help, working eight hours a day including a break of 30 minutes.

Childminders and au pairs are widely available in South Africa, and posts are often taken on by freshly graduated school leavers as part of a gap year or work experience. They usually study at distance learning facilities or enjoy their free time in the mornings while the kids are at school or kindergarten and then share the childcare with you in the afternoons. It is an advantage that the au pairs are usually from the area, are well versed in the expectations of the schools and are able to provide useful help with local languages and common customs. They also have a wide network of support from their family and friends should some unexpected situation arise while they are caring for your children when you are not around. Strict work regulations and laws, as described above, apply to foreign au pairs.

Payment for au pair services varies according to times and workload. Average hourly rates range between R40 and R60. Fulltime au pairs (40 hours a week) with their own transport get paid between R6 000 and R8 000 per month. If you provide a car, the salary usually ranges between R4 500 and R6 000 per month. Costs for babysitting services depend on the sitter's experience and the age of the children. Average hourly rates range between R30 and R50.

RESOURCES

General Information

Dept of Home Affairs: www.dha.gov.za
Department of Labour: www.labour.gov.za
Official B-BBEE portal: bee.thedti.gov.za
Statistics SA: www.statssa.gov.za
SEDA: www.seda.org.za
Industrial Development: www.idc.co.za
UIF: www.ufiling.co.za
SAQA: www.saqa.org.za
www.southafricanbusiness.co.za
www.www.siyayaskills.co.za

Taxation

Revenue Services: www.sars.gov.za
Tax Guide: www.treasury.gov.za
Tax Calculator: www.pastelpayroll.co.za
Labour Guide: www.labourguide.co.za
Chartered Accountants: www.saica.co.za

Doing Business

Business Registration: www.cipc.co.za
Business Survey: www.doingbusiness.org
Franchises: www.fasa.co.za
Labourwise: www.labourwise.co.za
Retirement: www.saarp.net

Accounting and Auditing

www.alexanderforbes.co.za
www.deloitte.com
www.ey.com
www.gt.co.za
www.kpmg.co.za
www.mazars.co.za
www.pwc.co.za

Volunteering

www.charitysa.co.za
www.gooverseas.com
www.magister.co.za

Job Search

www.jobs.co.za
www.careejet.co.za
www.careerjunction.co.za
www.brick7.co.za
www.bizcommunity.com
www.jobmail.co.za
www.ioljobs.co.za
www.bestemployers.co.za
www.top300.co.za
www.bestjobs.co.za

Childcare Agencies and Information

www.aupairsa.co.za
www.aupairlink.co.za
www.saapra.org.za
www.supernannies.co.za
www.careway.co.za
www.helpersathome.co.za

Retirement

Retired Persons (SAARP): www.saarp.co.za
Retirement Funds: www.irf.org.za

Recommended Reading

Global Africa Network (2012) *South African Business*. GAN. Also available online

Jull, Ian (2006) *The Small Business Survival Handbook*. David Philip Publishers

McLeod, Guy et al. (2011) *Starting Your Own Business in South Africa*. Oxford University Press

Mokura, Moki (2010) *South Africa's Greatest Entrepreneurs*. PSD Promotions

Zulu, Thambani (2010) *Risk and Reward*. Tafelberg Publishers

'You have to have goals; you have to have dreams. You have to work at what you believe in and you have to believe in yourself.'

~ Natalie du Toit, swimming gold medalist

EDUCATION

The South African constitution states that everybody has the right to basic and further education. The government is obliged to take reasonable measures to make education available and accessible to all, including adult basic education.

Basic education, or General Education and Training (GET) is education from grades 0 to 12. This basic education is provided by pre-primary, junior primary, senior primary and secondary schools in both state and private sectors. Primary schools run from grades 0 to 7 while secondary schools or high schools offer education generally from Grade 8 upwards. The Grade 0 year is a reception year and sometimes referred to as Grade R.

From Grade 10, learners can either continue to Grade 12 (popularly known as 'matric') or continue their vocational education through Further Education and Training (FET) colleges. Some schools offer a post-matric year to help bridge the gap between school and university. Higher education is available to students who satisfy the entrance requirements of academic universities, colleges and 'universities of technology'.

The language of instruction at the majority of schools is either English or Afrikaans. Most primary schools in South Africa are co-educational, while many high schools, especially private schools, offer single sex education. Boarding facilities are provided by some schools, particularly high schools.

The quality of schooling varies considerably. Public schools (referred to as state schools), private schools (referred to as independent schools) offer education of varying standards. Almost 95% of South African children attend state schools, some of which are excellent, but many foreigners in the country opt to send their children to independent schools, which include international schools.

The public education sector is said to be under-funded, with under-qualified teachers resulting in poor teaching and low pass rates. Education levels have, however, increased

Improvement
in Education
Population 20 years & older

	2011	No schooling	Matric Pass	Tertiary Education
	2011	8.6%	28.9%	11.8%
	1996	19.1%	16.3%	7.1%

(Source: Statistics SA, 2011)

Michaelhouse School, KwaZulu-Natal Midlands

significantly over the last decade. South Africa spends about 6% of its GDP on education, which is on a par with funding in most European states, the USA, the UK and Singapore.

Government funding is available to all state schools. Sixty per cent of all learners attend the so-called 'no-fees schools' found in disadvantaged communities.

In the remaining 40% of schools, the learners pay school fees, which complement the running costs of the school. As a result, state schools in the more affluent areas are in a position to offer superior facilities, many of which are on a par with private schools at a fraction of the cost to parents.

The standard of education in private schools is often regarded as higher than in state schools. There are, however, state schools that are renowned for excellent facilities, quality education and high exam pass rates.

Most expatriates opt to send their children to independent schools. Usually the private educational institutions that offer English-medium tuition are preferred by foreigners, as are those that offer continuity in their child's education or incorporate an international education curriculum such as the International Baccalaureate or Cambridge curriculum.

Selecting a School

1. Arrange to visit the various schools in your preferred area.

2. Attend the open days at various schools to get a feel for the school's offerings and ethos.

3. Once you decide on a particular school, apply to the school for a place.

4. Pay a registration fee and/or deposit to reserve your child's place.

5. Apply to Home Affairs for a study permit with the school's written confirmation of acceptance.

6. For final registration at the school, you are required to produce the child's passport with a valid study permit. Regulations are inflexible and strictly enforced.

7. Give the school a copy of the child's passport and study permit.

When planning your child's schooling options you should consider your next possible posting. It might be wise to enquire about boarding schools either in South Africa or your preferred country for both stability and consistency in the teaching approach and environment. To avoid disappointment, you should apply for places at your preferred schools as early as possible. It is also recommended that you apply for a study permit prior to moving to South Africa.

SCHOOL SYSTEM

Pre-school Education

The term 'pre-school' refers to both the compulsory reception year, or Grade 0, as well as other early schooling years, as many parents choose to send their children to 'school' from the age of two or three. Prior to this, children are sent to playgroups and day-care facilities if the parents work. Privately owned or community supported nursery schools, kindergartens and pre-schools are widely available. You can choose from a wide range of facilities with various opening times. Group sizes are usually small, with around 20 children to one teacher and one classroom helper. Many primary schools not only offer their own pre-school facilities but are also affiliated with various nursery schools in the area. It is highly advisable to apply as early as possible at a pre-school affiliated with a popular primary school if you have preferences for a state school outside your catchment area or in the private system. Should you look for early education programmes using Maria Montessori's teaching methods or Rudolf Steiner's Waldorf principle, then there are over 300 Montessori pre-schools and 17 Waldorf schools in the country.

Primary School Education

The age for entering Grade 0 is four turning five by 30 June in the year of admission. Exceptions can be admitted at an older age if this is justified, and many schools offer school readiness testing if later or earlier admission is desired. Primary schooling normally encompasses grades 0 to 7. Some schools offer all these grades, but in some cases there are separate schools for the junior primary or foundation phase (grades 1 to 3) and the senior primary or intermediate phase (grades 4 to 7). The reception year (Grade 0 or R) may also be offered at a primary school or in a separate pre-primary school. School policies in the private sector will differ in their admission requirements. Enquire specifically about entrance criteria at the schools you are interested in.

High School Education

Secondary or high school education starts with Grade 8 and usually continues to Grade 12. Grades 8 and 9 are often termed the junior high or junior secondary years. A few private schools start high school with Grade 7. The compulsory basic education phase ends at Grade 9. Learners who exit the school system at this stage may qualify to continue at a Further Education and Training (FET) college. Grades 10 to 12 fall into the optional Further Education and Training (FET) phase and are termed the senior secondary or senior high school years. At the end of Grade 12, which is the final year of schooling, learners in the state system take the National Senior Certificate (or 'matric') examination.

Matric School Subjects

Compulsory

Home Language
First Additional Language
Mathematics or Mathematical Literacy
Life Orientation

Additional

At least three subjects out of a wide variety including social or natural studies, technology and arts.

Matriculation

The National Senior Certificate (NSC) is commonly referred to as a 'matric'. A Matriculation Endorsement is received when the required standard is achieved and is an entrance requirement for South African universities and colleges and some universities overseas. These exams are accepted mainly in countries where the high school ends after 12 years of education. Further study options depend on the subject choice for the senior certificate and the pass mark.

Curriculum

All schools follow the South African National Curriculum. Some state and most private and international schools add additional elements to the South African curriculum or teach according to a foreign or international curriculum with additional elements from the South African curriculum to meet the foreign international curriculum.

There are two main examining bodies for the National Senior Certificate (NSC): the state examination set by the Department of Basic Education and an independent examination set by the Independent Examination Board (IEB). All schools, including independent schools, must adhere to the assessment standards set by Umalusi, the South African Council for Quality Assurance in Education. Umalusi is also responsible for the accreditation of both institutions and programmes in South Africa. At state schools and several private schools, annual national assessment tests and national benchmark tests are taken in grades 1 to 6 and grade 9 to assess performance in specific grades and subjects.

Many private schools opt for the Independent Examination Board (IEB) rather than the state National Senior Certificate. The resulting qualifications are equivalent, although the independent examinations are considered by some to be of a more rigorous standard than the state examinations. The National Senior Certificate (NSC) examination in Grade 12 is a prerequisite for employment in certain occupations in South Africa. To gain entrance into degree courses at university in the country, the basic pass for the matriculation endorsement is an aggregate mark of 50% in four subjects, which must include the home language. There are various grades of pass that entitle the candidate leaving school either to seek employment or to study further at a college or university.

Should your child wish to take up further studies after finishing high school in South Africa, it is important to find out the entry requirements of your preferred institutions for tertiary education. Thus, it is highly recommended that you enquire about the different approaches to education, the content of the curriculum and the school's choice of final examination when deciding on which school you choose for your child. An international exam, such as the A-levels of the Cambridge International Examination can be achieved at various independent schools that adhere to the Cambridge Education System. Some international schools, such as the German or French schools, offer courses for foreign certificates, such as the *Abitur* or the *Baccalaureate*. People who pass these exams are usually granted matric exemption from HESA (Higher Education of South Africa) so these final exams are accepted as qualifications to study at local universities as well.

Subjects

Basic knowledge is taught in the traditional school subjects. From the Grade 10 year, the learner is required to choose at least seven subjects, which are then carried through to the National Senior Certificate examinations. The first language of instruction (usually English, Afrikaans or an African language) and a compulsory first additional language (usually English, Afrikaans or an African language) are taught from primary school. A third language can sometimes be chosen as a subject at high school level. Life Orientation is a compulsory subject for all school years. Life Orientation is an inter-disciplinary subject for wholesome education and includes physical education, career perspectives, wellbeing and citizenship education as well as community service. From Grade 10 learners must also choose between pure Mathematics or Mathematical Literacy, a subject that teaches basic mathematical concepts referring to everyday situations. The additional three subjects can then be selected from a variety of areas including Technology, Art, EMS (Economic Management Sciences), HSS (Social Studies) and the sciences. The selection of subjects available is dependent on what the school offers. Many private and state high schools and colleges offer short courses and programmes for independent diplomas and certificates, some of which are internationally recognised.

SCHOOLING

School Year

The South African school year starts mid-January and ends at the beginning of December. The school year is divided into four school terms, with an autumn break in April, a longer break in winter at the end of June/July, a spring break at the end of September and a long summer break of around five to six weeks in December/January. The state schools adhere to a prescribed school calendar. Take note that the school terms and holidays for the coastal provinces and the inland provinces differ. Each independent school sets its own school calendar and the term dates will vary from school to school. International schools, in particular American schools, may have dates correlating with the home country's school calendar instead of the South African school term dates.

School Hours

School generally starts early in South Africa, mostly between 7h00 and 8h00. School ends usually between 12h00 and 13h00 for Grade 0 to 2 pupils and between 14h00 and 15h00 from Grade 3 upwards. Many schools expect the children to take part in at least one extra-mural activity per week, which is over and above the set school hours. After-hours care facilities and homework support are offered for a fee at many schools.

Discipline

The discipline policy and ethos vary from school to school and are regulated by the school's own code of conduct, which is signed by the learner, parents and the school on admission. South African schools tend to be strong on discipline. Many schools have strict rules and guidelines for dealing with bullying in their schools. In terms of the Schools Act, corporal punishment is illegal.

In Science classes, learners often do practical tasks, which include dissections and chemical or physical reaction experiments with a variety of equipment and apparatus. Private schools, especially, offer excellent facilities such as science or language laboratories and computer rooms. Some schools even house a fully equipped theatre.

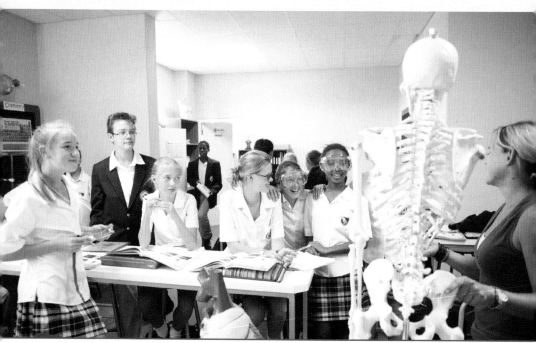

School Registration

In South Africa, you are free to register your child in the school of your choice. For acceptance in a state school, the children generally have to live in the catchment area of that school. When applying at either a popular state school or a private school there are often long waiting lists.

Fees

State-aided schools with smaller classes of about 25–35 learners cost between R6 000 and R30 000 per year, while fees for private schools can be as high as R70 000 per year. Both state and private schools use the revenue from fees in various ways. Some will employ additional teachers, while others use the fee income to provide better facilities, additional extramural activities or perhaps after-care. Fees for boarding facilities are over and above the tuition fees. Many private schools also require you to pay a deposit in the form of a non-refundable development levy.

Parental Involvement

Parents can play an integral part in schooling. This manifests in how the school is run and how it can offer the best education in the interests of the children of the community. In state schools, the school governing body (SGB), which comprises the school management team and elected parent representatives, governs the management of the school. This includes, amongst other responsibilities, the school finances and school policies. Schools also have a parent teacher association (PTA), which is a committee that includes teaching staff and parents. The responsibilities of the PTA include addressing communication issues, raising funds for the school and designated school charities and facilitating community-building events.

Uniforms

Uniforms are mandatory in state schools and in most private schools. The style is dependent on the school, and uniforms can be bought in the school's own uniform shop or at specified outlets.

School Registration Documentation

☐ An unabridged birth certificate in one of the official languages or with a certified translation

☐ A transfer card from your last school. This applies only if you transfer inside South Africa

☐ The most recent report from the previous school

☐ A study permit if you have a temporary residence permit

☐ An up-to-date immunisation record

Transport

Transport to and from schools is usually organised by the parents themselves. Lift clubs are often in place for parents sharing the transport of their children during the daily school run. Only a few schools offer transport by school bus or shuttle. Enquire at your school if there is an existing lift club programme in which you can participate. Many people use unaffiliated school shuttle services.

School Meals

For day learners, most state schools in the more affluent areas have some kind of cafeteria (or tuck shop) where children can buy drinks, snacks and basic lunch options. Only a few schools, mostly private ones, have a canteen that offers cooked meals.

Student Card

Pupils and full-time students above the age of 12 years can apply online for an international student card. This card, issued for a minimal annual fee, is recognised in South Africa and offers student discounts when visiting attractions or travelling in the country. (See www.isic.co.za for details.)

EDUCATION FOR EXPAT CHILDREN

Non-South African learners need a valid study permit to take up schooling or studies in South Africa. Study permits have to be applied for at the Department of Home Affairs either in the country or at the foreign mission before immigration.

The process of getting a study permit can be quite long and applications can take three months or longer to be approved. A study permit must be applied for well in advance, as schools are required by law to check the immigration status of their learners. It is illegal to have a child attend school without a valid study permit. Principals will not hesitate to send a child home if he or she does not have a valid permit or has only a pending permit. For help with obtaining a permit, assistance can be obtained from one of the recommended immigration practitioners.

There are several schools in South Africa that follow an international or foreign curriculum that specifically supports the special needs of expatriate children. Having classmates from their own home country and speaking their home language enable children to adjust faster and socialise more easily.

Some international schools and various independent schools in South Africa offer the Cambridge International Examinations (CIE). These schools work according to a British curriculum set by the CIE, which is part of the University of Cambridge. At these schools children can get an International General Certificate of Secondary Education (IGSCE), which is written at the end of Grade 10 or beginning of Grade 11, the AS-level exam in Grade 12 and the A-level, which is offered after an additional year of instruction. The A-level is a pre-requisite for study at most universities in the UK and is an entrance requirement for most universities overseas.

The International Baccalaureate (IB) is an international final exam that is offered at IB World Schools and is accepted at most institutions of higher education around the world. The Australian General Achievement Test (GAT) and an equivalent VCAA exam set by Victoria, Australia is written by learners at some international or independent schools, such as the Crawford Schools. American international schools teach according to the American curriculum and offer the standard Scholastic Aptitude Tests (SAT). While French schools in the major cities offer the French Baccalaureate and German schools the German Abitur, both include bilingual education and, in addition to their national curriculum, also teach according to the South African national curriculum.

Study Permit Documentation

- [ ] Valid passport
- [ ] Unabridged birth certificate, with translation if not in English
- [ ] Official letter of acceptance from the educational institution
- [ ] Written permission from the parents or the sole custody parent if the learner is a minor.
- [ ] Medical certificate
- [ ] Chest x-ray for learners over the age of 12
- [ ] Proof of medical cover recognised in South Africa
- [ ] Proof of sufficient funds to cover tuition fees, subsistence and incidental expenses
- [ ] Valid return ticket or repatriation guarantee

DEALING WITH DIFFERENCE

Children who are raised in a different culture to that of their peers will encounter various challenges as opposed to the children who grow up in their home country. Families from overseas often do not have easy access to a flexible and stable support network, particularly in the early years of the relocation. International school communities are very experienced in supporting families with an international background. They provide an extensive internationally orientated education and often make special provisions for specific language requirements.

Language Needs

At most schools, pupils will need to be able to understand and communicate in English or Afrikaans as these are the main mediums of instruction. Either English or Afrikaans is taught at first or home language level, while the other is considered a first additional language (a second language at a lower language skills level). If your child needs a private tutor to improve English language skills in order to follow the classes, your school or the British Council will be able to advise. If a learner has lived in South Africa for less than five years before writing the matric exam, he or she will be exempted from the requirement to take any of the eleven official South African languages as the 'first additional language' and can choose an alternative language or subject instead. Be advised to check with the Department of Education and your school to be sure about the current regulations.

Only select schools offer specific foreign language instruction such as French, Spanish or German. However, certain schools offer special extramural foreign language instruction or special language support for international learners. Foreign language tuition is primarily provided by independent tutors or by instructors who work in affiliation with foreign cultural institutes such as the *Alliance Française*, the *Società Dante Alighieri* or the Goethe Institute.

Special Needs

Primary education for mentally and physically challenged children is usually provided in special schools. Mainstreaming special needs children is done in some schools, but not all are prepared to offer inclusive education with facilities for kids with special needs. There are only a handful of special schools for children with severe disabilities or special needs. Most schools catering for pupils with a wide range of special needs, such as children with autism, ADHD, ADD or cerebral palsy, are located in the major cities. Bear in mind that places are scarce in many of the special needs schools and it is advisable to reserve your child's place early.

Special schools or enrichment courses for the specific needs of gifted children are very rare. Only Radford House primary school in Johannesburg currently caters especially for the needs of gifted children. Enquire with Mensa SA about special events for gifted kids and parents.

TERTIARY EDUCATION

There are 23 public universities in South Africa and numerous private colleges, which offer a wide variety of courses from certificate and diploma courses to doctoral degrees. Higher education institutions also offer many educational programmes and extra-curricular activities, clubs, societies and events. South Africa is one of the most popular destinations for international students. About 7% of the students in the country are foreign students, and a quarter of these are in the country to pursue postgraduate studies

Universities offer bachelor's, honours and master's degrees and doctorates. A bachelor's degree takes three years to complete but more specific career-oriented bachelor programs take four years or longer. Honours degrees are earned after another year or two of study, and master's degrees and doctorates follow.

English for Universities

1. International English Language Testing System (IELTS): A score of 6.0 for undergraduate students and 7.0 for graduate students

2. Test of English as a Foreign Language (TOEFL): A score of a minimum of 550 points

3. Cambridge Certificate with a pass in English at AS level

4. International Baccalaureate with pass in English

5. Any examination that is on par with the South African National Senior Certificate exam: A pass in English

Courses at local universities are taught in English and some in Afrikaans. Thus, foreign students from non-English speaking countries must provide proof of proficiency in English.

The fees for higher education vary depending on the institution, its location and reputation as well as the chosen program. The fees for foreign students are not subsidised and hence course fees are significantly higher for students with a temporary permit than for permanent residents or South African citizens.

A matriculation endorsement is required for admission to a university. Further entrance requirements depend on the specific study programme. Entry requirements for degrees are based on a points system, which correlates with the South African school subjects. Every institution has its own entry standards and admission policies. For more information about diplomas and degrees and how they correspond to international standards check with the South African Qualifications Authority (SAQA). This statutory body ensures that South African qualifications are of excellent quality, and are internationally comparable.

It is advisable to write the NBT or National Benchmarking Tests, which are set by the universities and tested at various times in various venues throughout South Africa during the year.

Student support offices at the universities and colleges will be able to provide advice on their education programmes and requirements.

Universities usually have student residences for accommodation, but places are limited and may be subject to specific entry requirements and/or a waiting list. Private colleges rarely have student accommodation.

Private university colleges, such as Varsity College, offer tuition support and a campus environment for students studying towards a degree or diploma. This option is possibly a viable alternative for international students who do not qualify for entrance to a state university.

UNISA, one of the largest open distance learning universities in the world, was the first of its kind in the world.

The University of Cape Town's Graduate School of Business (GSB) is ranked the top business school in the world regarding value for money for its full-time MBA program. It also ranks 54 in the top 100 business schools in the world. *(Global MBA Rankings, 2012)*

International students cannot register at their chosen university if they do not have a valid study permit. Remember that study permits are only valid for one specific educational institution and a change of institution requires a new application.

Foreign students are allowed to work part-time up to 20 hours per week during term time as part of practical training. A special endorsement of study permit is needed.

Management Schools
The quality of management schools in South Africa is commended in various surveys and South Africa ranks 13th out of 142 countries for these schools. *(Global Competitiveness Report 2011/2012)*.

MBA Programmes
South Africa's top business schools offer prestigious MBA programmes that are highly regarded worldwide. The top university business schools in South Africa are Pretoria's Gordon Institute of Business Science, Wits Business School, University of Cape Town Graduate School of Business and University of Stellenbosch Business School, but there are various other excellent private universities that are solid performers in many programmes.

Adult Education
Further Education and Training (FET) is also available for adult learners. Private institutions, technical colleges and community colleges also offer diplomas and certificates and provide evening classes, part-time courses and full-time studies for the adult population. Subjects range from local African languages or qualifications useful in the tourism sector to graphic design and computer courses.

Outside School

Homework Help

After-care facilities and supervised homework centres are available at most schools for a monthly fee, especially in the junior primary years. Private homework support centres are rare and mainly located in the more affluent suburbs. There are, however, tutors for private lessons as well as independent after-school programmes such as MasterMaths or the Kumon study centres. Enquire with your school for further details.

Boarding Schools

There are several excellent boarding schools in South Africa and many South African families send their children to boarding school, particularly for the high school years. Boarding schools are popular with many expatriates as they offer an opportunity to grant some stability and a safe environment for young learners. You should investigate the particular school's facilities and its environment to match the school to your and your child's needs. Boarding costs range in the region of R20 000 to R50 000 per year, and are paid over and above the school fees.

Extramural Activities

Schools usually offer a comprehensive after-school schedule of sports and cultural activities as well as various outreach and leadership opportunities for pupils. Depending on the school, the fees for these facilities may be included in the annual school fee or will be charged as additional costs. Popular school sports such as swimming, hockey, netball, soccer, cricket and rugby are often included in school fees, but tuition for activities such as golf, judo, karate, ballet or music is usually charged over and above school fees.

Summer Camps

American-style summer camps are gaining popularity with families in South Africa. Various providers such as Kings Camps, Kidz Get Wild and Sugar Bay offer camps and activities during the school holidays in the cities or at holiday venues around the country. The duration and fees for these camps vary. These camps as well as various workshops, drama classes or sport clinics offer a good opportunity for socialising between local children and other international children.

RESOURCES

General Information

Basic Education: www.education.gov.za
Higher Education: www.dhet.gov.za
Portal: www.thutong.doe.gov.za
www.equaleducation.org.za
www.studysa.co.za

School Directories

www.isasa.org
www.saschools.co.za
www.schoolguide.co.za
www.schools4sa.co.za

Independent Schools

Abbotts Colleges:
www.abbotts.co.za
Cambridge Education: www.ace-sa.co.za
Curro Schools: www.curro.co.za
Crawford: www.crawfordschools.co.za
IB World Schools: www.ibo.org
IEB Schools: www.ieb.co.za
IES Schools: www.iesedu.org
Montessori: www.samontessori.org.za
Muslim Schools: www.ams-sa.org
Reddam House: www.reddamhouse.org.za
Waldorf Schools: www.waldorf.org.za

Language Schools

Alliance Francaise: www.alliance.org.za
British Council: www.britishcouncil.org.za
EduSA: www.edusouthafrica.com
Eurolingua Institute: www.eurolingua.com
Goethe Institut: www.goethe.de
Societa Dante Aligheri: www.ladante.org

Home schooling

www.educatesa.co.za
www.south-african-homeschool-
curriculum.com
www.tuisskolers.org

Learners with Special Needs

www.napsa.org.za
www.included.org.za
www.mensa.org
www.radfordhouse.co.za

Career Options and Study Facilities

www.careerplanet.co.za
www.mydreamcourse.co.za

Tertiary Education

Higher Education (HESA): www.hesa.org.za
Higher Education (IIE): www.iie.ac.za
MBA programmes: www.mba.co.za
Business Schools: www.aabschools.com
University of South Africa: www.unisa.ac.za
Varsity College: www.varsitycollege.co.za

International Study Abroad

www.studyabroad.com
www.aifsabroad.com
www.studiesabroad.com

Summer Camps

www.kgw.co.za
www.kingscamps.org
www.sugarbay.co.za

Recommended Reading

Independent Education Magazine:
www.ieducation.co.za

Child Magazine: www.childmag.co.za

Kokot, Shirley (1999) *Help our Child is
Gifted*. Radford House

Van de Ruit, John (2005) *Spud*. Penguin

'Education is the most powerful weapon
which you can use to change the world.'

~ Nelson Mandela

'Work is good, provided you do not forget to live.'
~ *African proverb*

LEISURE

FOOD

The vast array of foodstuffs available in South Africa caters for every taste and you will be spoilt for choice. Also, due to the favourable climate, a wide variety of locally grown and harvested produce is available.

Many refer to the traditional South African cuisine as 'Cape Dutch cuisine' or 'Cape Malay cuisine' but there is much more to the local cuisine than *bobotie* and *boerewors*. Traditional cuisine is also influenced by the cooking and preserving methods of the first African inhabitants and those of the early settlers, their slaves who originated mainly from Malaysia and Indonesia, and later the indentured labourers from India and China. Exotic spices, such as nutmeg, ginger, chilli, coriander (also called *dhania*) and allspice are dominant in the local cuisine.

Many meals consist of chicken, lamb, beef, pork and game, such as ostrich or kudu. South Africa's 'Karoo lamb' is renowned for being the best lamb in the world. The meat has a distinct flavour, which results from grazing on the vegetation of the Karoo region. For a long time South African food consisted of freshly hunted game of all kinds, cooked in stews, grilled on a fire or dried to preserve it. To keep fresh meat from wasting it was often salted, dried and cured or smoked, resulting in biltong or *droëwors* (dried sausages).

Nowadays, getting together for a *braai* (barbeque) is a popular pastime. In some townships the locals use the Zulu term *shisa nyama* to describe an informal barbecue on the street outside a butchery.

Vegetarians and vegans can also find many a culinary treat in the local cuisine. Typical vegetables in South African dishes include carrots, beetroot, cabbage, spinach, pumpkin, butternut squash, *brinjal* (aubergine), broccoli, green beans and tomatoes.

Delicious fruit is available in abundance, such as mangos, pawpaws, granadillas (passionfruit), pineapples, bananas, lemons, oranges, *naartjies* (tangerines), guavas, litchis and avocado pears. Many of the fruit are available as dried fruit in strips or little cubes at local markets and farm stores. Corn or maize, which the locals call *mealies* (or *mielies*), has long been the staple diet for the indigenous people. *Mealies* and beans form the basis of many meals.

....

South Africa has the longest wine route in the world stretching more than 850 km from Cape Town to Port Elizabeth.

Seafood is widely available especially at the coast. As South Africa is surrounded on three sides by oceans, there is an abundance of fresh seafood. A large variety of fish such as dorado (sea bream), hake, tuna, baracuda, prawns, calamari (squid) and the South African specialties snoek and crayfish are available. Trout is a popular fresh fish and Knysna oysters are known worldwide.

South Africa has adopted international food standards. Regulations require that ingredients, common allergens, a nutrient analysis, a batch number or code and a use-by date must be listed. Be aware that sugar products in South Africa are produced from sugar cane and not from sugar beet and that white and brown bread, flour and maizemeal are usually fortified with vitamins. Also, be aware that not all dairy products are hormone free.

Halaal and kosher food items are widely available and clearly marked in the bigger supermarkets. In addition, all McDonald's outlets and several branches of KFC, Wimpy or Nando's are certified and approved by the Muslim Judicial Council. In major cities you will also find Jewish community shops that sell kosher food.

Local is Lekker

Meats

Ostrich, Karoo Lamb, Springbok, Kudu, Biltong

Drinks

Rooibos Tea, Pinotage, Marula Liquor Don Pedro, Tizers

Fruits

Naartjies, Avocados, Pawpaws, Mangos, Pineapples

Fish

Snoek, Crayfish, Kingklip, Tuna, Rainbow Trout, Squid, Oysters

Vegetables

Gem Squash, Brinjals, Chillies, Sweet Potatoes, Butternut, Pumpkin

The water is safe to drink in most areas of South Africa. In the more remote regions it is advisable to drink bottled spring water or sparkling water, which is widely available. Alternatively, you might choose to boil and cool tap water to sterilise it or utilise water purification tablets. In such instances, keep the water in the fridge and use it within a day. Home water filtration systems are also available.

On the Braai

Braai

The South African equivalent of a barbeque is a braai, where you will usually find beef, lamb or chicken and even fish. National Braai Day is celebrated on Heritage Day, a public holiday on 24 September.

Boerewors and Pap: Farmer's sausage made with ground beef, spices and herbs served with *mieliepap* (stiff cornmeal porridge also called *putu*) is an old-time favourite

Pot bread: Also called *potbrood*, this bread is baked over a fire in a cast-iron pot often with *mielies* or beer as ingredients

Potjiekos: This traditional meat stew is cooked for several hours in a three-legged cast-iron pot, called a *potjie*, over an open fire

Sosaties: Marinated meat grilled on skewers like satays, often called kebabs. Usually made with chicken and beef

Mielie (or Mealie): The South African term for corn on the cob

Seafood

Crayfish

The West Coast rock lobster is called crayfish or *kreef* and is available between November and March along the coastline from Namibia to the Eastern Cape. Licences to catch this protected species can be purchased at local post offices

Kingklip: White regional game fish

Snoek: A regional game fish with white oily flesh and a distinctive taste, which is frequently smoked and is popular as a pâté

Tuna: This fish species is caught mainly between May and September and served seared. Tinned tuna is also popular

Smoked Trout: Locally farmed Rainbow Trout either *braaied* or as a pâté

Squid: Eaten as 'calamari steaks' or sliced into 'calamari rings'

Between Meals

Biltong

A popular snack speciality made of salted and spiced dried meat, similar to beef jerky. *Biltong* can be bought in most supermarkets, at farmers' markets and special *biltong* stalls in shopping centres

Droëwors: Dried strips of thin boerewors made with beef or game meat

Samoosas: Traditional South Asian and Indian fried triangular pastry parcels stuffed with a spicy meat or veggie filling

Chips: When South Africans refer to chips they are referring to either a packet of snack crisps or hot fried potato strips, otherwise known as French fries or pommes frites

Sarmi: Local slang for a sandwich

Bredie: A soup or stew made with vegetables and meat

Venison: Venison is flavourful and very low fat game meat. South Africans refer to the meat from buck such as impala, kudu, eland, gemsbok, springbok, blesbok or from warthog as venison

Morogo: Wild spinach braised together with onions and often mixed with *mieliepap*

Ostrich: A healthy red meat, which is popular due to its low cholesterol but high protein content

Dinner Time

Bobotie

This classic Cape Malay dish is baked with ground lamb or beef, raisins, turmeric, curry powder and an egg custard topping. It is usually served with yellow rice

Local
Favourites

Bunny Chow

Taste a bunny chow when in Durban. This uniquely South African meal is served in many street outlets and consists of a hollowed-out bread loaf filled with delicious hot spicy Indian curry

Take-away Meals

Gatsby: A bread roll filled with steak or Cape Malay curry and lots of spicy sauce and soggy chips

Slap Chips: Hot but soft and sloppy potato chips, often drenched in sauce or vinegar

Breyani: This spicy dish, also called *biryani*, is made with rice, lentils and a unique spice mixture forming a base for meat, vegetables or fish

Malva Pudding: An apricot flavoured sponge pudding with sweet syrup served warm, often with custard

Rusk: A sweet or plain biscuit bread, sliced thick and baked until hard, dry and crisp, which is dunked in coffee before eating

Vetkoek: Fried dough, similar to donuts, eaten with syrup or a savoury filling

Koeksisters: This popular Afrikaner treat is made by plaiting dough strips together and soaking them in syrup

Don Pedro: An after-dinner drink of cream and vanilla icecream mixed with marula liquor or whisky

Treats

Melktert

A sweet milk tart sprinkled with cinnamon, similar to a custard tart, with a thin pastry base

A café in South Africa is usually a corner store and not a coffee shop!
The typical café sells basic provisions, such as bread, milk and convenience foods. The prices are higher than supermarket prices.

BUYING FOOD AND GROCERIES

Food shopping is usually done at various supermarket chain stores and retail outlets. The freshest food can be found at the weekly farmer's markets or directly from the farms. Farm shops, called *padstals*, are often located along country roads. Fresh locally-produced food and delicacies can also be found at slow food markets, which are held on weekends at various venues in city parks, suburban community halls or farms in outlying areas. Fresh sustainable fish can be bought at local fisheries.

Organically grown fruit, vegetables, free range meat and eggs are widely available. In major supermarkets there are also health food ranges with special wheat-free, gluten-free and dairy-free products. You will find soy, rice and goat milk products at Pick n Pay and Woolworths outlets and other speciality health food stores. A local nutritionist or dietician will advise on special products or you can find out about supplements at local health food stores. Baby food can be found at supermarkets, and organic baby food is best sourced at local health stores.

Prices for basic foodstuffs are lower in South Africa than in many countries overseas. Basic food items such as brown bread, milk and maize flour are VAT exempt and subsidised by the government. Many food items that expats consider essential for their diet are, however, more expensive. Imported food like coffee, biscuits and cheeses are available at elevated prices. If you are looking for foreign delicatessen food and cannot find it in the local shops, enquire in your community about foreign food importers and delis.

Takeaways

Fast food outlets and convenience stores at petrol stations sell takeaway food. Pizzas, burgers, fried or grilled chicken and Chinese dishes are particularly popular. Many restaurants, particularly the Italian and Chinese restaurants, offer takeaway food, but it is advisable to order well in advance. Many supermarkets have ready-made cooked meals and salads, which are as good as wholesome home cooking.

Professional delivery companies servicing several restaurants in an area provide door-to-door deliveries. You will usually have a wide range of options for takeaway meals. You can place the order via phone and request the delivery at an arranged time.

MEALS AND DRINKS

South African cuisine offers a wide variety of food options during meals. Locals often breakfast on porridge made from oats or mielie meal or toast with butter and marmalade or jam, others enjoy yoghurt and cereal or the more savoury bacon and eggs. Coffee, tea or fresh juices are usually consumed. Toasted sliced bread is a standard staple and French baguettes, croissants, muffins and wholemeal or dark rye breads are widely available, although in rural areas you will mainly find sliced white or wholemeal bread and white bread rolls. Rusks are popular, and can be eaten by dunking them in your cup of tea or coffee.

For lunch, sandwiches or wraps and salads are popular. Soft drinks and squash as well as coffee or tea are often consumed while fruit juices are not as common even though a wide range of delicious local juices are available in shops. Dinner options vary widely from hot dishes to cold platters and salads.

Meal Times

Breakfast
Breakfast is usally eaten between 7h00 and 9h00.

Mid-morning Break
A short coffee or tea break is often taken around 10h00.

Lunch
Lunchtime is usally eaten between 12h00 and 14h00.

Dinner
The evening meal is eaten fairly early, usually between 18h00 and 20h00.

Non-alcoholic Drinks

Bottled water, either still or sparkling, is often flavoured and widely available. Tap water is usually drinkable and supplied free in restaurants. Soft drinks or sodas, which are also called 'cool drinks', include fizzy carbonated sweetened drinks such as Coca Cola, Fanta, Sprite, Seven Up, TAB or various fizzy apple or grape juices such as locally produced Appletizer, Peartizer and Grapetizer. Smoothies and milkshakes are made with either fruit or fruit flavours.

Although locals often drink instant or filter coffee, specialty coffees such as cappuccino, coffee latte or espresso are widely available. Popular teas available include English breakfast tea, also referred to as black tea, Ceylon tea, *rooibos* tea and a variety of herbal infusions. Trendy sidewalk cafés where coffee is made by trained baristas are more and more common in the business districts and tourist centres. Hot chocolate or Horlicks and Milo, both of which are made from malt and added to milk, are popular, especially with children.

Rooibos tea is recognised for its antioxidant property and health benefits. It is caffeine free and low in tannin content. The *rooibos,* or redbush, plant, *Aspalanthus linearis*, is indigenous only to South Africa's Cederberg mountain region roughly 250 km north of Cape Town. The dried needle-like leaves of the hardy bushes have a distinctive sweet aroma and flavour.

Melting Pot

South African cuisine is a true melting pot of different cooking styles influenced by the many cultures living in the country. Influences are diverse and range from the initial indigenous cultures through those introduced by the early settlers to the more recent influences of Europe's fine dining and coffee culture, the American trend in fast food and the Asian liking for raw fish and sushi bars.

Africa

The original inhabitants of the region were the *strandlopers* along the Cape coast and the San in the interior. These people were hunter gatherers who passed on their tradition of preserving fresh foods in salt and cooking over open fires, as well as the use of the *rooibos* plant and other medicinal herbs in food. Influences from the northern African countries can be found in the use of flat breads and *pap* (maize porridge).

France

The French brought with them their love for fine pastries and good wines. French bakery items, such as the baguette, called simply French loaf, croissants, macaroons and *pain au chocolat* (chocolate pastries), are widely available.

Malaysia

The Cape Malay cuisine has its roots in the cooking styles of the Malayan slaves who adapted their dishes to the palates of the early settlers. The resulting South African versions of their spicy dishes are milder and sweeter than the original Asian dishes. Foods introduced include the Indonesian satay sticks, also called *sosaties*, and *samoosas*. Malay dishes never use pork or alcohol, as they usually obey the Muslim religious rules.

England

The British settlers brought with them their love for roasts, potatoes and puddings. Puddings are traditionally based on British cake recipes of sweet and syrupy baked puddings, such as brandy pudding or malva pudding. Carveries, which are a selection of roast meats with roast potatoes and gravy, are the centre of most buffet spreads. Fried fish and chips are found on many menus.

Portugal

The Portuguese introduced the spicy taste and flavour of *peri peri*, or piri piri (African bird's eye chillis) and chilli. *Peri peri* chicken 'flatties' or prawns are signature dishes at many restaurants.

Netherlands

When the Dutch first arrived, they brought with them skilled horticulturists and farmers who planted the first gardens and vineyards in and around Cape Town. Their influence is recognisable in many traditional Afrikaans dishes, called *boerekos* (farmer food), in particular *potjiekos* and *braais*. Sweet breads and jams often complement grilled meats or fish, and root vegetables are used widely. Signature sweet recipes include *koeksisters*, *melktert* (milk tart) and *vetkoek* (fried dough).

Greece

Greek pita and feta cheese are available, and feta is a standard ingredient in most green salads. A variety of coffee shops are owned by Greeks, serving traditional *baklava* or other Greek pastries.

Italy

Italian pizzas and pasta are particularly popular. The South African variation of the original pizza often has a thicker, softer crust with numerous toppings. Pasta (noodles) is rarely homemade and usually served with a lot of sauce. Spaghetti bolognaise or lasagne can be found on most menus.

Germany

The German settlers, with their love for sausages and meat products, prompted the creation of the *boerewors* (farmer's sausage) and many traditional German sausage, using pork and veal, can be found in the country. Dark breads, made by skilled master bakers, and even *Brezeln* (pretzels) are widely available.

India

The indentured Indian labourers, settling along the eastern coast, maintained their spicier dishes and did not compromise their hot curries the way the Cape Malay people did. Indian dishes are often made with chicken, lamb, vegetables or beans and are very popular, especially in the KwaZulu-Natal region. Various condiments and sauces such as *dhal,* fruit-based chutneys and *sambals* accompany the curry dishes to complement the tastes and tame the hot spices. *Breyani* is another typical Indian dish of baked rice made with meat or vegetables, lentils and a unique mix of spices.

Asia

Typical Chinese dishes are available at Chinese restaurants. Chinese food produce can be sourced at Chinese supermarkets or local Chinese shops. Sushi is growing in popularity and is available in restaurants, at fresh food counters in local supermarkets and as takeaways. Thai food is available in both Thai restaurants and more recently in fusion-style cuisine. Stir fry with rice or noodles is a popular menu item.

Haute Cabrière Cellar Restaurant, Franschhoek Valley

Wine

South Africa not only produces delicious food but also first-class wines. South Africa's winemaking tradition is over 350 years old. The first grapes were harvested in South Africa in 1659, long before wine was cultivated in the Americas, Australia or New Zealand.

Wine is cultivated by more than 500 cellars in various regions around the country. The foremost wine regions are considered to be the Cape Winelands, which includes the Stellenbosch, Franschhoek and Paarl regions, the Robertson and Worcester wine region and the Breede River Valley. The Breedekloof area and the Olifants River Valley are currently the regions producing the most wine. The Northern Cape's Orange River Valley is also known for excellent wines. Today, South Africa is recognised as the leader in sustainable and ethical wine production in the world and won the prestigious Fairtrade Award in 2011.

Most of the wine varieties cultivated in South Africa today were originally imported. Noble varieties such as, Sauvignon Blanc and Chardonnay grapes, produce excellent white wines in the local climate, and Shiraz and Pinot Noir are the dominant red varieties. Six crossings are unique to the country; the most renowned of these is Pinotage.

Fortified wines include port and sherry. Sedgwick's Old Brown Sherry has a sweet taste and nutty brown colour and has gained cult status among many South Africans across race, age and income.

Award-winning sparkling wines are also produced in the Cape Winelands. Among the most popular 'bubblies' are the ones produced by Pongracz, Boschendal and J.C. Le Roux. Graham Beck sparkling wine was enjoyed by both former South African president Nelson Mandela and American president Barack Obama when they celebrated winning their respective elections.

> Pinotage is a unique blend between the red Pinot Noir grape and a red Cinsaut or Hermitage grape and was first harvested in South Africa in 1925. Today Pinotage wines are also cultivated in other countries, such as New Zealand and California. This deep red wine has a smoky and earthy flavour, which is especially suited to venison and the South African *braai*.

Beer

Beer has a long tradition in South Africa and was enjoyed by the locals long before the white settlers arrived in the 17th century. Originally it was brewed from grain, corn and fruits. *Umqombothi* is a traditional beer made from maize, sorghum and yeast and is still self-brewed and enjoyed in the townships. Commercially brewed beer is widely available in pubs, restaurants and bottlestores throughout the country. The alcohol content of South African beer, at around 4 to 5%, is higher than in the USA and the UK. Local brands include Castle and Carling Black Label. Local apple ciders and ales are popular. Today, lager beer is more widely available than draught and many foreign brands are available in South Africa. Namibian beers such as Amstel, Hansa and Windhoek, which are brewed according to Dutch and German standards are very popular. South African Breweries (SAB) is the world's second largest brewery.

Spirits and Liqueurs

Brandy is a South African favourite, with brands ranging from the award-winning KWV brandy, which was judged Best Brandy in the World at the International Spirits Challenge (ISC) awards, to the infamous everyday Klipdrift. In addition to locally made whisky and rum, South Africans spirits include Mainstay, a spirit made from sugar cane.

Various cream liqueurs are made locally. Amarula, which is exported worldwide, is made from marula fruits found in the Limpopo Province. It was awarded the prestigious trophy for the Best Liqueur in the World at the International Wine and Spirit Awards.

You may also come across the strong home-made moonshine liquors. *Mampoer* is made from fruit such as peaches and marula and *witblits* is made from grains. These liquors may have lower alcohol content than similar moonshine spirits produced overseas, but the percentages of alcohol range from 50% to as high as 80%. Historically, both spirits were made by farmers with left-over produce, but they are growing in popularity due to their distinctive taste. These drinks are not for the faint hearted and you should only taste homemade brews if you know where and how they were distilled.

Visit a Microbrewery in the KZN Midlands

Taste Liqueur from the Marula Tree

Enjoy Local Hospitality

EATING OUT

South Africa has many chefs hailing from some of the world's top restaurants, so eating out can be a very special treat. You can expect cooking styles to range from traditional fare to Asian-inspired spicy dishes and international fusion-style cuisine. Whether you decide to go out for a quick snack or want to have a sumptuous meal at one of the many fine dining restaurants, you will be amazed by the variety of delectable food on offer. To dine at some of the more popular restaurants, it is advisable to book a table in advance, especially if you are a bigger group or plan to dine out on weekends and during peak holiday periods.

Most restaurants are child friendly. Many places offer children paper and pens or toys to keep them busy and many family-orientated restaurants have a secure children's play area with sandpit or jungle gym.

Most restaurants offer a wide variety of dishes for every taste, and seafood restaurants are popular. Fish platters can be ordered in many places and fish, chicken or steak combos are popular menu items. The more adventurous eaters will find typical African food where it is possible to taste game, such as crocodile, springbok or kudu meat, as well as typical dishes from the rest of the African continent. For the eater who wants to stay within his/her comfort zone, there are numerous foreign specialty restaurants and international chains of fast food outlets, bars and coffee shops. But make sure you get to try some typical South African specialties too.

There are various restaurants offering African traditional dishes, such as Moyo, which has branches countrywide, Mama Africa or GOLD in Cape Town CBD and Legotla in Sandton, Johannesburg. Here you will be served typical local dishes, often with delicacies representing the whole African continent. Traditional music with drums or marimbas often accompanies the dining experience.

When going on a safari, you will have the opportunity to experience a typical *boma* dinner in the bush. There you will be served South African food under the stars and dinner will often be accompanied by entertainment from local dancers or musicians. A *boma* dinner at one of the many game reserves is a memorable bush experience.

Five out of the top ten South African restaurants are located in the Cape Winelands and three of them are in South Africa's unofficial foodie capital, Cape Town. *(Eat Out, 2012)*

Opening Times

Opening times vary greatly between establishments. Many restaurants open only for lunch and dinner and the kitchen closes between meals. Often there is a day of rest, usually on a Monday. In hotels there is usually a bistro or coffee shop open all day. Coffee bars and restaurants in shopping centres are usually open seven days a week from 9h00 until around 21h00.

Payment

Most restaurants accept credit and debit cards issued by both domestic and foreign banks. Handheld terminals are used for the card payment. If terminals are not brought to the table, accompany the waiter to the payment point to avoid potential fraudulent transactions. Although uncommon, card-cloning syndicates have been known to operate via waiters in restaurants.

Tips

Although tipping is voluntary, waiting staff earn only a minimum wage and are reliant on your tips. Tipping is commonly calculated as 10-15% of the bill. Note, however, that for tables of eight or more diners the establishment may automatically add the tip to the bill and it is advisable to check before making payment.

Dress Code

This is dependent on the restaurant. Most restaurants do not have a dress code and casual attire is accepted. However, the more formal establishments, clubs and fine dining restaurants require a collared shirt, long trousers and closed shoes for men.

Bring-your-own/Corkage Fees

You can take your own wine to many restaurants. The corkage fee is usually around R30 per bottle. Wine estates usually do not allow foreign wine to be brought onto their premises.

Smoking

Smoking in public spaces is illegal and only allowed in specially designated areas. Most restaurants are completely smoke free or they have a designated smoker's section.

Leftovers

It is common to request your leftovers be wrapped to take home and most restaurants will gladly pack your uneaten food into packaging commonly referred to as a 'doggie bag'.

Pets

Restaurants do not allow dogs and other pets into their premises as this is against health regulations. You might, however, find that many coffee shops or bistros with outdoor dining areas will offer water bowls for your pooches.

Water

Bottles of still or sparkling water are frequently supplied on the table when you arrive at the restaurant. These are usually not complimentary and will be charged for if opened. It is, however, safe and acceptable to order a glass of normal tap water, with or without ice and a slice of lemon.

Sustainable
Seafood Guide

Most Sustainable

Best Choice
Angelfish, Snoek, Squid, Yellowtail

Reason for Concern

Think Twice
Abalone, Sole, Swordfish, Dory

Unsustainable or Illegal

Don't Buy
Galjoen, Musselcracker, Steenbras, Stumpnose

(Source: SASSI, Consumer Seafood Pocket Guide, 2012)

TOURS AND FESTIVALS

South Africans enjoy celebrating the fresh harvest of their local crops. Many food festivals are held annually. These include the oldest food festival, the Cherry Festival in Ficksburg, which began in 1967, and others such as the Oyster Festival in Knysna in July or the Olive Festival in the Riebeek Valley in May. Beer and whisky festivals are celebrated at various locations during the year, and, during the wine harvest months of February and March, there are wine festivals in many wine-producing towns.

If you want to gain more insight into South African home cooking, book a cooking class with one of the many fantastic South African chefs, such as Cass Abrahams, Justin Bonello, Reuben Riffel or Jenny Morris, who offer their tips and share their expertise in local cuisine. You can also learn how to cook typical Cape Malay meals in Cape Town's Bo-Kaap or how to cook a traditional breyani in Durban. Guided gourmet food and wine tours in the Cape Winelands can be booked through various service providers.

The Beer Route in KwaZulu-Natal is known for its many microbreweries where you can experience the art of beer brewing and taste the artisan beer. The South African Breweries World of Beer Tour in Johannesburg is well worth a visit.

Township tours give you some insight into the daily meal options of the local South Africans. Countrywide, tour operators offer township tours that include a visit to a shebeen. A shebeen is a place where people from the township meet for drinks. At Mzoli's in Guglethu near Cape Town, Wandies Place in Soweto near Johannesburg and Maxis in Umlazi near Durban you can experience township food in safe surroundings with a vibrant atmosphere. Sometimes you can even book to learn how to cook typical South African meals during a township tour. It is advised that you only visit or stay in townships with a reliable guide. Shebeen visits should be booked through an official South African tourism agent.

Visit an Indian Food Market

Join a Cooking Class

Dine With the Locals

RESOURCES

Food Facts and Recipes

Food24: www.food24.com
Africhef: www.africhef.com
Yuppiechef: www.yuppiechef.com
Association for Dietetics: www.adsa.org.za
Food Advisory: www.foodfacts.org.za
Cheese Guide: www.cheesesa.co.za
Seafood Guide: www.wwfsassi.co.za

Restaurant and Wine Guides

www.eatout.co.za
www.dining-out.co.za
www. rossouwsrestaurants.com
www.restaurants.co.za
www.wininganddining.co.za
www.safoodandwineblogs.com
www.wine.co.za
www.wosa.co.za

Special Diets

Gluten Free: www.glutenfreesa.co.za
Halaal Food: www.zabihah.com
Kosher Food: www.yeahthatskosher.com
Vegan Food: www.vegansa.com
Cheese Guide: www.cheesesa.co.za

Grocery Shopping for Expats

www.germangoods.co.za
www.azenfoods.co.za
www.carluccisdeli.com
www.frandaleimports.co.za
www.treasures4u.co.za
www.uke.co.za

Takeaway Delivery

King Delivery: www.kingdelivery.co.za
Mr Delivery: www.mrd.com

Cooking Classes and Gourmet Tours:

www.africanrelish.com
www.andulela.com
www.capefusiontours.com
www.luhambotours.com
www.southafricanfoodies.co.za
www.tlpchef.co.za

Recommended Reading

Jan Braai, (2013) *Fireworks*. Bookstorm

Cheifitz, Philippa (2009) *South Africa Eats*. Quivertree Publications

Pieterse, Marita (2006) *Four Seasons: Cooking Throughout the Year in South Africa*. Struik

Platter, John (2012) *Platter's South African Wines*. John Platter

Smit, Sannie & Fulton, Margaret (2010) *The A-Z of Food and Cookery in South Africa*. Random Struik

Abrahams, Cass (2008) *Cass Abrahams Cooks Cape Malay*. Metz Press

Brookdale Health Hydro (2012) *Heavenly & Healthy Foods*. Brookdale

Van Wyk, Magdaleen (2007) *Complete South African Cookbook*. Struik

Van Zyl, Dine (2012) *The Great Boerekos Book*. Dine van Zyl Publications

Food and Lifestyle Magazines:
Food & Home, Food & Wine, Fresh Living, Taste, Top Billing and other food and lifestyle magazines are available at shops and online from
www.amazon.com / www.kalahari.com

'A good braai explains the great mystery of why man found fire.'

~ James Clarke, journalist

SHOPPING

South Africa is a shopper's paradise. The relatively favourable exchange rate makes shopping in South Africa fun and affordable for most expatriates. From rural farm stalls and convenience stores to gigantic hypermarkets and upmarket shopping malls, you will find shops for every need and budget.

In recent years many shops have moved out of the city centres, and now huge shopping precincts are found in many suburbs. Smaller towns and rural areas usually have a grocery store and sometimes a bakery and butchery, but for more comprehensive shopping facilities, you would have to travel to the bigger cities.

Canal Walk Shopping Mall in Cape Town and The Gateway Theatre of Shopping in Umhlanga, KwaZulu-Natal are, with more than 380 shops, the largest shopping centres in Africa. Spacious shopping malls house fashion boutiques, chain stores and supermarkets as well as banks, foreign exchange bureaus, book and music stores and a post office all under one roof. In these centres you will also find restaurants, coffee shops and food courts. Many malls even have cinemas, a theatre and exhibitions. There are often medical centres and dental practices in or adjoining the malls. In many villages, towns and in some cities you will find weekend markets selling arts and crafts, antiques or bric-a-brac. Slow food markets and farmers markets offer organic locally produced foods. Second-hand markets are becoming more and more popular.

Factory shopping is also a popular pastime for many South Africans. In many cities, you will find factory outlets in which you will find factory seconds or surplus ware of high quality at a fraction of the price you would normally pay in the shops or department stores.

Round-the-clock shopping for basic provisions can be done at petrol stations with forecourt shopping facilities. Service stations with convenience stores are mainly located along the main arteries in bigger towns or along the major highways. For 24-hour pharmacies, contact a hospital in your area.

In general, shops accept cash or debit/cash cards and major credit cards for payment. South African currency cheques and foreign currency cheques, such as traveller's cheques are rarely accepted in shops. Traveller's cheques should be cashed at foreign exchange bureaus before shopping. Automatic teller machines (ATMs) are found in all major shopping centres.

....

Cape Town is rated one of the 30 Best Shopping Destinations in the World.
Tripadvisor, 2012

Canal Walk Shopping Centre

In South Africa, 14% VAT is added to all goods and services, with the exception of certain basic grocery items, such as bread, milk, fresh fruit and vegetables. VAT is a sales tax that is placed on the sale of goods and services. The displayed price is almost always inclusive of VAT, and all invoices and till receipts will reflect the total VAT payable on the transaction. Visitors and temporary residents older than seven years of age can claim a VAT refund for items purchased in South Africa. Many reputable shops, and most jewellers, antiques shops and galleries will be able to assist with VAT refund claims and the required documentation. The price of the product must exceed R250 and you will need the original tax invoice for the items. Credit card slips usually suffice. A commission applies. The items must then be exported within 90 days. When leaving South Africa, you need to show your purchases to the officers at your point of departure before checking in your luggage.

The Consumer Protection Act implemented in 2010 regulates and protects the customer and the customer's rights. With this new act, South Africans have become amongst the most protected consumers worldwide. Should you have a complaint, contact the Consumer Centre at the Department of Trade and Industry (DTI) or the National Consumer Tribunal for advice. There is also a valuable consumer information website called 'Hello Peter' that provides a wide range of insight regarding consumer complaints and compliments.

The Proudly South African 'buy local' campaign is an initiative to stimulate the national economy. It encourages consumers to shop for locally made products and services.

Average Prices

R20
2 litre Milk

R9
330 ml Local Beer

R90
Plain T-shirt

R13
75 ml Toothpaste

A–Z OF SHOPPING

Alcohol

Alcohol is sold at bottle or liquor stores. Supermarkets often stock wine and champagne, but never beer or liquors. You cannot buy alcohol on Sundays or public holidays in certain provinces and stores often do not sell any alcohol after hours.

Antiques

Due to South Africa's colonial history, there are beautiful genuine antique articles to be found in little antique shops all over the country. Most antique dealers will have an assortment of English, French and Dutch furniture, stoneware, jewellery and collectables. You might even be lucky enough to find some antique Cape silverware, teak and brass cutlery or ebony and satinwood furniture.

Appliances

Modern kitchen appliances from popular international brands are available. However, it is often difficult to find a service company that can repair newer models of appliances that may not yet be available in South Africa. Shops offering a wide range of household appliances include Checkers House and Home, Game, Makro, Hirsch and Dion Wired.

Arts and Crafts

You can find a wide range of collectables, ornaments, sculptures and local artefacts made of wood, stone, leather, beads and semi-precious stones. These are sold at curio and souvenir shops in the cities or near attractions but they are also available from street vendors, crafts and flea markets, where you will find many bargains.

Baby Needs

Baby clothing is available in department stores and boutiques. There are unique local children's clothing designers, such as Keedo, Balu, Bug Zoo, Naartjie or MooMoo Kids. Organic cotton clothing is available as well. Furniture for babies and children can be sourced at furniture stores or made to order. Plastic toys, bottles and baby accessories can be found at special megastores Babies R Us and Babycity. Educational toys made of wood are becoming more popular and are now available at selected stores.

Bookshops

The selection of books in languages other than English or Afrikaans is quite limited. Foreign books are best ordered online. Some of the major bookstores, such as Van Schaik, Exclusive Books or Adams, have a small section of foreign newspapers and magazines. You can order most books online, often at discounted prices and sometimes even with free delivery.

Cellphones

Cellphones and simcards or microcards are available directly from the cellphone providers as well as at various department stores. Pre-paid options and various fixed-term contracts are available. You have to register your simcard according to RICA regulations. Proof of South African residential address and passport are required for registration. Airtime can be purchased either online directly via the banking websites or at most convenience stores and supermarkets.

Chemists and Pharmacies

Most medicines are available in South Africa, but it is advisable to bring unusual prescription medicines with you. Independent chemists and the chemist chain stores of Clicks, Durbell and Dis-Chem sell a wide range of toiletries, over-the-counter medicines and cosmetics. Pharmacies (*apteek* in Afrikaans) are often located in shopping centres in suburban areas and in hospitals and medical centres. They usually stock international brands of medicines, generics, specialised skincare products and cosmetics and toiletries.

Christmas Decorations

Christmas decorations are sold from as early as October in supermarkets and chain stores. Many people resort to buying artificial Christmas trees, which are also available from the hypermarkets or stores during the pre-Christmas season. Fresh trees, sold by street vendors along main roads in the cities, do not last very long as the festive season falls in the summer months. The tree species sold in South Africa have very long needles and are not as easy to decorate.

Cosmetics

Cosmetics, including make-up, skin- and bodycare products of major international brands, can be bought locally in major chain stores and smaller health and beauty shops. Chemists and chain stores, such as Edgars, Stuttafords, Truworths, Foschini and Woolworths usually offer a wide variety of beauty products in their cosmetic and fragrance departments.

Clothing

Most of the international clothing brand stores are located in the big shopping centres. The most exclusive designer fashion shops are located in the V&A Waterfront Shopping Centre in Cape Town, Sandton City in Johannesburg and Gateway Shopping Centre in Durban. Local and international designer brands can be found in these shopping centres. Fashionable designer clothes are comparably cheap and can be bought for sometimes up to 50% less than overseas prices. Clothes for bigger sizes can be found at Donna Claire women fashion stores and at Woolworths, Milady's and Stuttafords. School clothes are usually purchased or ordered from the school's designated suppliers.

Curtains and Blinds

Local home decor stores will measure for and make fabric curtains and roman blinds. It is advisable to oversee the installation. Wooden blinds and American shutters are available. DIY and home stores stock a small range of ready-made bamboo blinds or aluminium slatted blinds, mainly in basic colours. Stores, such as Mr Price Home, @home, Game and Woolworths, sell ready-made curtains in limited styles.

Cycling

Bicycles and cycling accessories and repairs are offered at major sports equipment stores and smaller specialist stores.

Sandton Craft Market

Department Stores

Edgars, Stuttafords, Foschini, Truworths and Woolworths are the major department stores and have chains countrywide. They are located mainly in major shopping centres.

DIY and Hardware Stores

For your DIY shopping, you might want to try Brights, Cash Build, Builder's Warehouse, Builder's Express, Mica and Pennypinchers, which all have stores across the county. They often help to locate and recommend reliable builders in your area.

Dry Cleaners

You will find dry cleaners in the suburbs and most of the malls. Some dry cleaners will pick up and deliver. Hotels and temporary accommodations also usually offer a laundry service and dry-cleaning facilities. Charges vary widely.

Electronic Equipment

Quality electronic equipment is available, but the prices are comparable to or even higher than prices internationally. Various computer stores offer a wide range of computer hard- and software. A basic selection of computer accessories and games can be also be found at Game, Incredible Connection, Dion Wired, Makro, Trade Centre and music stores.

Fabric Stores

There are various shops selling fabrics for curtains and blinds. However, there are few stores that specialise in selling fabric for dress-making. Tailors can advise on and order suitable fabric and make clothing such as shirts or suits to measure.

Flowers

You can buy fresh flowers at markets, florists, supermarkets end even convenience stores at petrol stations. At florists you can either get fresh arrangements or order bouquets and special arrangements in advance. Prices and delivery options vary widely. Tulips and orchids are very expensive, while local flowers are available at bargain prices in season. Some florists offer special deliveries.

Framing

Local DIY stores offer small ranges of frames. Finding ready-made picture frames is difficult. Framing is expensive in South Africa, and you should enquire about expertise in framing precious paintings or repairing expensive frames in your area.

Furniture

There are many furniture shops and outlets as well as several DIY or furniture warehouses like Home & Garden, Wetherlys, Furniture City, Hirsch's and Patio Warehouse. Interior aficionados will find outlets mainly in the light industrial areas. Solid pine furniture is easily available but, if you want furniture in other types of wood, you may have to have it custom made or have it imported. Bedroom and kitchen cupboards are almost always built in.

Golfing Equipment

There are specialised stores supplying golf equipment and well-priced accessories. The Pro Shop, Golfer's Club and Sportsman's Warehouse are the biggest chain stores. Golf courses and driving ranges often have golf shops as well.

Garden Centres

Nurseries and garden centres (*kwerkery* in Afrikaans) sell a wide range of indigenous and popular exotic plants. They also usually have a limited range of garden pots, tools and accessories. Often they incorporate farm stalls, coffee shops, children's play areas and sometimes even a pet zoo. South Africa's biggest garden centres are Garden Pavillion, Builder's Warehouse gardening centres, Stodels and Floradale.

Grocery Shopping

Supermarket and hypermarket chain stores such as Pick n Pay, Shoprite Checkers, Spar and Woolworths have a wide variety of goods. Woolworths is particularly popular with expatriates, as they have a high standard of fresh food and ready-made meals. Farm stalls sell fresh produce from local farmers and delicatessen foods. There are also many smaller convenience stores, like 7Eleven or Quickspar stores. Fruit & Veg City and the Food Lover's Market offer fresh local produce and a variety of local and international delicatessen foods.

Health Food

Health food stores are found in many shopping centres. They stock local and organically grown products for almost every dietary requirement. Some also carry international brands. Often they will help source and order your preferred dietary products.

Hair Care

Hair salons or barber shops are situated in almost every shopping centre. Some stylists offer a mobile service or work from home. Appointments should be booked in advance to avoid disappointment. In most salons, international brands are used for hairstyling products and the styling costs vary widely. It is custom to tip the shampoo lady. Some hair salons also offer beauty treatments, like pedicures and manicures, while you wait.

Home- and Tableware

Homeware for bedroom, bathroom and kitchen is available in home stores such as @home, Boardmans, Home ETC, Mr Price Home, Sheet Street, Home Depot, Loads of Living and House & Home.

Jewellery

Local jewellers sell stunning manufactured pieces made of precious metals and gems, especially jewellery with diamonds or precious stones such the blue African tanzanite stones. In some of the diamond stores such as Shimansky, Uwe Koetter and Jewel Africa in Cape Town or Schwartz Jewellers in Johannesburg you can take guided tours through the workshops. Browns Jewellers, Mark Solomon, Arthur Kaplan and Wolf Brothers are the biggest jewellery and watch retailers in the country. Most jewellers will design custom-made pieces.

Sandton Craft Market

Maternity Wear

Clothes for pregnant women can be found in dedicated areas in department stores such as Woolworths and Edgars or, alternatively, in speciality maternity wear retailers such as Kids Emporium or Cherry Melon. Consider ordering online or bring maternity stockings, underwear or special maternity support wear from home.

Musical Instruments

Both purchasing and renting musical instruments is relatively expensive in South Africa. Good quality second-hand instruments are available. Transporting your piano from overseas is not recommended. Instruments can also be rented on a monthly basis. Local music teachers can advise you on where to source instruments in your area.

Music and Computer Games

Musica or Look & Listen stores sell popular CDs, DVDs and electronic games as well as a small range of equipment. They are located in many shopping centres. Smaller centres often house smaller shops selling only the most popular CDs and DVDs or discount disks.

Organic Food

Fresh fruit and vegetables, which are grown organically, can be bought at supermarkets, Fruit & Veg City and the Foodlover's Market branches and weekly farmers markets. Food baskets with organically grown food can be ordered online at various suppliers.

Outdoor Clothing and Equipment

There are many stores that specialise in outdoor clothing, shoes and equipment such as Cape Union Mart, Due South, HiTec and Outdoor Warehouse. Campworld stores also sell trailers and caravans and offer on-site repairs.

Pet Supplies

You can source pet food at the local supermarkets or pet store. Pet shops also sell a wide range of food, accessories and care products for your pet. There are many veterinary practices, and most also sell pet food and products.

Photo Printing and Equipment

A good range of photographic equipment is available. Consider importing specialised equipment and accessories from home. Digital image print shops are located in most shopping centres and will also take and print passport photos.

Plastic Products

Plastic products, like storage containers and household boxes, are produced locally as well as imported from overseas. At Plastics for Africa and Plastic Warehouse you will find a huge assortment of storage items. Local chain supermarkets will also have an assortment of the most common household items.

Second-hand Goods

Appliances, furniture, books and clothing are available in various second-hand shops. However, online shopping for these goods at Gumtree or bidorbuy is very popular.

Shoes

High quality leather shoes can be sourced locally, although most designer footwear is imported and will cost more than you would pay overseas. As good quality shoes are quite expensive, many expatriates purchase shoes on their home visits. Summer footwear is widely available. It is quite difficult to find a good range of children shoes. Green Cross stores have a limited children's shoe range.

Sports Clothing and Equipment

Sporting attire and equipment is available from various stores such as Sportsman's Warehouse and Mr Price Sport. Here you will find treats that you would have to pay considerably more for overseas. Shopping for trendy and fashionable beachwear is fun to do along the popular coastal areas. It is sometimes difficult to source equipment and accessories for less popular sports, such as roller skating, volleyball, basketball or ice hockey.

Surfing Equipment

Surfing equipment and accessories are usually not found in the regular sports stores. Coastal towns have many surf shops with special equipment. Premium surfboards are manufactured in South Africa.

South Africans are encouraged to buy products that bear the 'Proudly South African' logo.

Stationery

General stationery, arts and school supplies as well as greeting cards and gift wrapping paper can be found at supermarkets, CNA or PnA or speciality stationery stores. Waltons, Macro and Trade Centre chain stores sell a range of office supplies. Be aware that exercise books and files come punched with two holes. If you have American paper sizes and need paper with three holes, it will be useful to bring your own punch.

Toys

Popular overseas brands of toys are available. Toys R Us and Game have bigger ranges, and various toy factory stores import toys and games at discounted prices. Wooden or educational toys are available at various retailers.

Videos

Video stores usually operate on a membership basis and are found in suburban shopping centres. Borrowing a game or movie DVD is inexpensive in these stores. Bookshops and supermarkets often sell DVDs as well.

Sandton Craft Market

Arts and Crafts

Beadwork

The Ndebele, Zulu and Xhosa are renowned for making lovely beaded jewellery. Zulu bracelets and 'loveletters' are very popular. Some manufacturers such as Streetwires or Monkeybiz in Cape Town export their artworks internationally, and conduct tours around their workshop.

Tableware

Various local designers, such as Carol Nevin, Carmel, Meekel, Sol Art Pewter or Carrol Boyes, produce artfully crafted cutlery, table and homeware, which can be sourced in major shopping centers, galleries and some curio shops.

Shweshwe Fabrics

The originally indigo coloured fabric, which has been produced in South Africa since the 19th century, can be sourced in fabric shops and some curio shops in a range of colours and patterns.

Baskets

The Zulu are known for making stunning baskets in many styles and designs. The modern versions are made with colourful telephone wire.

Painting

Local township art is renowned for its bright and colourful paintings. You can buy these paintings in galleries or at one of the many craft markets.

Mohair

South Africa is the world's biggest producer of mohair wool from Angora goats, and lovely wool products are available for sale at various outlets.

Pottery

In South Africa, you will find stunning brightly decorated pots made from mud and clay, such as the traditional pots of the Venda people, which are painted with colourful geometric patterns. There is also pottery in many different designs, such as the ceramic Dlamini figurines made in KwaZulu-Natal.

Carvings

Local wood is used by the Venda people to make beautiful spoons, bowls, trays or walking sticks. However, most of the carvings sold in South Africa are made by craftspeople from Botswana, Mozambique or Zimbabwe.

Candles

Swazi candles are renowned for their craftsmanship. Candles in many colourful designs and special shapes can be found also at Kapula Candles in the Cape Overberg.

Colourful Rugs and Carpets

These are handmade in many designs by talented weavers. Several companies like KwaZulu Weavers, Ilala Weavers, Hilmond Weavers and The Kraal Gallery specialise in hand-woven rugs.

| Shopping Hours | The bigger shopping centres are usually open seven days a week from around 9h00 until as late as 20h00. In rural areas or in the city centres, shops are usually open from 8h30 until 17h00 on weekdays, and are closed on Sundays. Most shopping centres open on public holidays, with the exception of Christmas Day and, possibly, Good Friday. |

Shopping
Tips

| Haggling | Haggling (or bargaining) in chain stores is not an accepted practice. At markets and informal trading areas the vendors are known to inflate the prices in anticipation of the haggling process. Bear in mind that many crafts people are reliant on their sales to support their families, and you should be careful not to exploit them in the bargaining process. |

| Take Your Own Bag | In supermarkets, and certain other stores you will need to pay for plastic bags if you do not have your own bags or basket when you do your grocery shopping. You will be charged for the number of plastic bags the packer uses for your purchases. Plastic bags cost between 30c and 50c depending on store. |

Return Policy

Make sure you know the return policy before you purchase goods, as the return policy will differ between stores. Returns are usually granted, provided the goods are in their original packaging and you present the sales slip. Refunds are not always offered; instead many shops exchange the purchase for alterative merchandise or offer a credit or vouchers for use towards future purchases.

Parking

Off-street or parking in malls is usually charged at an hourly rate. Some shopping centres offer an initial period of free parking. In many parking areas you may also find 'car guards' who will be grateful for a small tip (R2–R5) when you return.

Store Cards

Major stores offer their own credit cards, which are associated with special store deals and payment terms. With some store cards you can accumulate loyalty points, which can be exchanged for discounts, rewards or vouchers or even donated to a charity or school (such as the MySchoolCard). Some bulk retail stores such as Makro require you to register for a special access card.

Special Offers

To see the current special deals refer to the weekly community newspapers and the advertisement sections or inserts that are usually delivered to your door free of charge. Several free publications with special deals for stores in your area are delivered to your postbox.

RESOURCES

Business Directories

www.yellowpages.co.za
www.hotfrog.co.za
www.mbendi.co.za
www.cylex.co.za
www.brabys.com
www.yalwa.co.za
www.rainbownation.com

Consumer Advice

www.thedti.gov.za
www.thenct.org.za
www.hellopeter.com
www.pricecheck.co.za
www.taxrefunds.co.za

Groceries Shopping

Pick n Pay: www.pnponline.co.za
Woolworths: www.woolworths.co.za
Checkers: www.checkers.co.za

Books and Music

Look & Listen: www.lookandlisten.co.za
Musica: www.musica.co.za
Kalahari: www.kalahari.com
Amazon: www.amazon.com
Exclusive Books: www.exclus1ves.co.za

Online shopping

Loot: www.loot.co.za
Want it all: www.wantitall.co.za
Take-a-lot: www.takealot.com
Groupon: www.groupon.co.za
Bid or Buy: www.bidorbuy.co.za
Netflorist: www.netflorist.co.za
Wine: www.winemag.co.za

Antiques

Antique Dealers: www.saada.co.za
Antiques Fair: www.naada.co.za

Classifieds

Junkmail: www.junkmail.co.za
Gumtree: www.gumtree.co.za
OLX: www.olx.co.za

Factory Shopping

www.factoryshops.co.za
www.factoryshopping.blogspot.com

Markets

Market guide: www.thislittlepiggy.co.za
www.neighbourgoodsmarket.co.za

Organic Produce

www.shoporganic.co.za
www.go-organic.co.za
www.faithful-to-nature.co.za

Expat Shopping

www.southafricanshop.net
www.expatshoppingguide.com
www.expatshop.co.za
www.hollandseproducten.co.za
www.adriatic.co.za
www.azteca.co.za
www.treasures4u.co.za

Recommended Reading

Black, Pam (2012) *The A-Z of Factory Shops in the Western Cape*. Pam Black Publications

Due South (2006) *South African Craft Sites*. Eskom-Due South

Sellschop, Susan (2002) *Craft South Africa*. Pan McMillan

Temkin, Nikki (2011) *Chic Jozi*. Penguin

'I was shocked to see tall buildings and BMWs
and to hear rap music. It's really beautiful.
It feels like God visits everywhere else but lives in Africa.'

~ Will Smith, American actor

OUT AND ABOUT

Living life to the full in beautiful South Africa is easy to do! There are many ways to enjoy living in the country, whatever your personal preferences are. The comfortable climate and abundant sunshine encourage an outdoor lifestyle and the magnificent landscape and natural beauty entice you to explore the country. You will find golf, running, cycling, watersports, camping, hiking and the social *braai* are some of the many activities that people enjoy doing in their free time.

South Africans generally love a good party and enjoy going out for drinks. It is quite common for people to socialise with colleagues after work, with or without spouses. On weekends many people get together for a *braai* and watch sport events with family and friends. Being fit and active is popular in South Africa and weekends are often spent joining activities and events that range from locally organised charity runs to some of the big international sports events. Options to participate actively are manifold. You can choose anything from leisurely walks on a beach or in a park, to team sports such as soccer or cricket. Annual running and cycling events draw huge numbers of participants of all ages and skill levels.

The nightlife in South Africa's major cities is vibrant with a lot of events taking place all year round. Options for evening entertainment range from sipping sundowners and admiring the local scenery to visiting shows or concerts. Johannesburg is often referred to as being a 'city that never sleeps', and has many exciting venues offering a variety of events. Outside of the major towns and tourist centres, however, nightlife is limited and cultural entertainment is restricted to a visit to the movie theatre, an occasional festival, dining out at a local restaurant or when in the wild, enjoying an outdoor *boma* dinner under the stars.

South Africa also has a tremendous number of unique cultural attractions and these will enlighten you about the country and its people. South Africans love to celebrate their multi-cultural heritage, so you will encounter a vast variety of cultural activities to enjoy in your leisure time. Playhouses, theatres and opera houses offer many different kinds of shows and performances ranging from classical ballet to contemporary music performances and from traditional Shakespeare tragedies to locally produced stand-up comedy such as the hilarious 'Evita se Perron' in Darling.

From cultural highlights to prehistoric rock art and modern design installations, there are numerous cultural experiences to choose from throughout the year for every age, budget and taste.

....

South African Athol Fugard is the most performed playwright after Shakespeare.

The Amphitheatre, KwaZulu-Natal

ARTS AND CULTURE

There are many interesting museums to visit all over the country, from small monuments to huge exhibition centres. Excellent collections relate to South Africa's history, natural history, arts and popular culture. Entrance to national museums is free of charge on public holidays, and many museums are closed on Mondays.

Whether you want to watch first class international dance companies, small local comedy acts or lay theatre performances, theatres offer great performances and high quality shows. Nearly all major events and shows are located in venues in and around the main business centres, but there are some smaller theatres to be found in remote towns. Many places that host cultural events offer memberships for supporters of the arts and have regular events for their members.

If you join a membership programme for a theatre, museum or society, such as 'Friends of the Opera', you usually qualify for discounts, get regular updates about new events or exhibitions and get invited to members-only previews, *vernissages* and talks, which are also good places to meet interesting people. Make sure that you visit one of the many open-air theatres or open-air movie theatres for an evening out with stunning scenery.

International performing artists and music companies regularly stage events in the major cities and a wide range of festivals take place every year catering to all tastes.

Museums to Visit

Apartheid Museum

This museum near Soweto depicts the history of apartheid in the 20th century.

Kimberley Mine Museum

This open-air museum has underground tours about the discovery of diamonds.

Maropeng Visitor Centre

Near Johannesburg and Pretoria, the centre has interactive displays on the development of humans and fossil finds.

National Museum

The museum in Bloemfontein houses the country's largest exhibitions of natural and cultural history and art.

National Gallery

Based in Cape Town, the gallery has collections of African as well as British, French, Dutch and Flemish art, complemented wtih visiting exhibitions.

Music

Singing and dancing are a big part of the traditional cultural heritage of the South African people. Out of these roots has evolved some unique South African music, such as *kwaito*, a South African version of house music mixed with gangster rap elements, *ghoema*, a Cape Malay music style with roots in traditional slave music, *kwela*, which incorporates the pennywhistle and *mbaqanga*, a mode of African-inflected jazz.

Music played an integral part in the freedom struggle. For example, partnerships between white and black musicians, such as in Mango Groove and Jaluka, challenged the apartheid regime.

South Africa also has internationally celebrated local choirs, such as the Soweto Gospel Choir and the Drakensberg Boys' Choir, and highly respected tenors and opera productions.

Live concerts and music festivals, such as the annual International Jazz Festival in Cape Town, 'Splashy Fen' in the Drakensberg or 'Rocking the Daisies' on the West Coast, draw thousands of music lovers to their remote venues. Open-air concerts are also offered at various wine estates and other venues among them Kirstenbosch Botanical Gardens in Cape Town, Zoo Lake in Johannesburg and the Botanic Gardens in Durban.

Concerts for international touring artists are generally limited to venues in Johannesburg and Cape Town, however some celebrity DJs are known to have stints regularly in some of the most prominent clubs throughout the country. Explore print or online publications such as WhatsOn, Computicket and Webtickets for information on current events.

The dynamic South African opera company, Opera Africa, has earned international acclaim, winning several international awards. Local singers, musicians and composers combine the best of classical opera with rich African sounds.

Movies

Going to the movies is a favourite pastime of many South Africans. The films are screened in cinema complexes in major shopping centres. These include Ster-Kinekor, Nu Metro and Cinema Nouveau. Tickets are reasonably priced and can be booked online or by telephone or bought at the cinema. International films, which are screened in the original language, are shown at various film festivals throughout the year. The cultural institutions also offer foreign film screenings at their venues. Special receptions are available to members of 'movie club'- programmes or at the cultural institutions. These are usually great places to mingle and make new friends.

The Soweto Gospel Choir received the prestigious Grammy Award in the category 'Best Traditional World Music' in 2004, 2007 and 2010.

Nightlife

Sipping on cocktails, people watching from a popular street-side bar or dining on delicious local and foreign specialities are great attractions once the sun is down. Venues are too many to mention and range from the popular tourist spots such as Nelson Mandela Square in Sandton and the V&A Waterfront in Cape Town to areas such as the Melville and Rosebank area in Johannesburg, vibrant Long Street in Cape Town's CBD, Camps Bay in Cape Town, Florida Road in Durban and the Port Elizabeth Pier.

For the more active night owls, a wide range of sophisticated entertainment options offer exciting nightlife experiences in the major cities. International acts and DJs make going out as fun and attractive as anywhere else in the world. Johannesburg's thumping entertainment and nightlife options as well Cape Town's stylish bar and clubbing scene offer great late night vibes. Cape Town is well known for its numerous popular upmarket bars, pubs and discotheques and the Johannesburg's scene is vibrant throughout the night. Durban and Port Elizabeth, also have more relaxed but well-established party scenes.

Age restrictions apply at most nightlife venues. The minimum age for people allowed into bars ranges between 18 and 21 years. Be cautious and watch your drinks, and when going out, you should only use a reliable transport company to take you to an event.

Gay bars and nightclubs exist in the major cities. In particular, Cape Town's De Waterkant is known for its vibrant gay scene. There are various events, such as the annual Pink Mardi Gras Festival and the Mother City Queer Project, which takes place every December in Cape Town, and the Knysna Pink Loerie Festival in April. As a result of the extravagant decorations, flamboyant costumes and fun party atmosphere, these events attract not only the gay community but visitors from all over the world. More information can be found on the *Gay Pages* or the *Pink SA Guide*.
(*www.exit.co.za, www.mask.org.za* or *www.pinksa.co.za*)

Gambling

Sophisticated and impressive casinos exist in all cities and most major towns. They offer not only gambling facilities but are also prominent venues for international touring artists performing in the country. Sun City, near Rustenburg, is the most renowned in the country and is well worth a visit.

Horse racing events take place throughout the year on weekdays and Saturdays at courses around the country. The most prestigious races are The Vodacom Durban July and the J&B Met in Cape Town. These are flamboyant affairs, where the glamorous fashions attract as much attention as the horses. Race cards are available at local convenience stores for the weekly horse racing meetings and the results are published in the daily newspapers.

The gambling industry is well regulated. Sports betting is as popular as betting on horse racing and betting outlets are found in most towns. The national rugby, soccer, cricket and golf teams attract the most interest.

SPORT

South Africans love their sport and the locals are both armchair champions and active participants. Sport is big news in the media and many conversations lead to discussion of the latest sporting developments. Popular spectator sports are rugby, soccer and cricket, and matches provide a welcome excuse for a social get-together. The opportunity to watch a game live should not be missed and will leave you in awe of a South African's patriotism, zest for life and team dedication.

Football, or soccer as it is known in South Africa, is the most popular local sport. Soccer united the nation and showcased the country to the rest of the world during the 2010 FIFA World Cup. South Africa's national squad is named *Bafana Bafana* ('The Boys'). In the local football league, known as the Premier Soccer League (PSL), the two biggest rival teams hail from Soweto. These are Kaizer Chiefs and Orlando Pirates. Soccer games have a festival atmosphere with supporters blowing their *vuvuzelas* whilst sporting colourful *makarabas* on their heads.

For many South Africans, Saturday afternoons are synonymous with a *braai* and watching rugby with friends. There is immense pride in the fact that the Springboks are previous holders of the Rugby World Cup. In addition to regular test series around the world, the annual tri-nations international competition re-ignites the ongoing rivalry between Australia, New Zealand and South Africa. There is also just as much competition and excitement around the local rugby league, the Currie Cup, where South Africans support their local provincial team.

The national cricket team, the Proteas, became the first side in the world to be simultaneously ranked number one in the International Test Series, the One Day Internationals and the Twenty20 league. National competitions are the four-day Supersport Series and the one-day matches of the Standard Bank Cup.

The 2010 Soccer World Cup is the most successful sports event on the continent to this date and attracted more than 300 000 tourists during the tournament.

Club sports are widely practised and many clubs organise regular events or competitions. Sportsclub facilities for children are not as varied as in many overseas countries, as the school sport programmes are so comprehensive and well supported. Memberships to sportsclubs are open to all and some clubs also accept occasional visitors. Although sports such as baseball, basketball, judo or fencing are not as widely practised, there are numerous clubs around the country offering facilities for their followers. The various sports associations will be able to advise on nearby clubs and coaches for the many sports activities. You will find a listing of the sports associations of the most common sports in the annexure.

In South Africa, you will often encounter people running or cycling around the suburbs or along dedicated cycle lanes, especially during the early morning or after work hours. Along the beaches, popular pastimes involve keeping fit with swimming, canoeing or surfing. Fun as well as competitive sporting events are staged every year for various fitness levels. Besides the major cycle races or marathons, you will find a host of sports, everyday activities and challenges to participate in.

Fitness centres and gyms are located in many suburbs, and joining a club is a good way to keep fit and get connected with like-minded people. Virgin Active, Planet Fitness and Curves for Women are among the biggest chains offering fitness classes and they also often have sauna and steam room facilities and an indoor swimming pool.

Many sports centres also offer squash or tennis courts for use by members. Joining dancing classes, meeting friends for a game of bowls (or *rolbal* in Afrikaans) as well as taking part in yoga or pilates groups are popular ways to relax and a fun way to meet new friends.

Watersports

South Africans love their watersports. Conditions are among the best in the world, attracting visitors from around the globe to the stunning beaches, rivers and dams. The favourable winds, especially when the strong South Easter blows in Cape Town, guarantee some of the best waves for all kinds of surfing. Sailing, waterskiing, kayaking and canoeing are popular among water enthusiasts and are practised on the many huge dams or rivers around the country. White river rafting or kloofing is done in the many wild waters such as the Orange or the Vaal rivers. Public swimming pools and waterparks are rare but usually these are well-maintained.

Top Annual Sports Events

The Dusi Canoe Marathon

The world's largest canoe marathon challenges participants to a 125 km race through the Valley of a Thousand Hills in KwaZulu-Natal.

The Cape Argus Cycle Race

This is the world's largest individually timed cycle race, and attracts cyclists to join the fun atmosphere as they ride the scenic 109 km around the Cape Peninsula.

The Two Oceans Marathon

This 56 km ultra-marathon along Cape Town's spectacular Atlantic coastline via Chapman's Peak is dubbed the world's most beautiful marathon.

The Comrades Marathon

The world's largest ultra-marathon on the road between Durban and Pietermaritzburg (92 km) entices runners to share camaraderie with people from around the globe.

The Midmar Mile

The world's largest open water swim held at the Midmar Dam near Pietermaritzburg in KwaZulu-Natal was officially recognised in the *Guinness Book of World Records*.

Golf

Golf is popular due to its relatively minimal costs compared to overseas fees. Golf courses, through their offerings of golf, fundraising and social events, are great places to meet people from all over the world and make contacts with the locals. Green fees at the golf courses vary but are considered to be reasonable. Some of the greens offer the most amazing views in the country. In South Africa, you can play at prestigious golf courses even if you are not a club member, and fees on courses vary widely, starting from as low as R300 to over R1 500. Leopard Creek Golf Course bordering Crocodile River and Kruger National Park in Mpumalanga is ranked among the top 100 golf courses in the world.

Golf at Pinacle Point

Adrenalin Junkies

There are plenty of activities for all of those who enjoy sports that make the heart beat even faster. The exhilarating experiences on offer include canopy tours in the forests, swinging down the world's highest zipline swing at Oribi Gorge, bungee jumping from Bloukrans Bridge, which boasts the world's highest bungee jump with a 216 m drop, abseiling down Table Mountain and sand boarding on beaches along the magnificent coastline. You can learn new skills or book exciting tours and daytrips with experienced guides through adventure tour operators or specialised schools.

Canopy Tours through the Forests

Relaxation and Pampering

To recharge your batteries, there are many great places to visit to revive your senses, which include beauty treatments at salons in a shopping centre in your vicinity and visits to a day spa suite. Day spas are also locally known as health hydros. The most exclusive day spas are often situated in top hotels and guesthouses such as the spa at the Oyster Box Hotel in Umhlanga, the Fairlawns Boutique Hotel Spa in Sandton or the Twelve Apostles Spa in Cape Town. There are also dedicated luxurious health resorts, that offer multi-day programmes, which include special diet and detox programmes according to the client's requirements. South Africa's health hydros, such as Brookdale Spa, are renowned for their high quality and value for money.

Relaxing Spa Treatment

EXPLORING

Going away for the weekend is a great way to explore the beauty of the country and experience the various landscapes and different cultures that make up the rainbow nation. Most areas have a wide variety of options ranging from remote camping to five-star luxury. South Africa offers superb wildlife and game reserves, magnificent mountain ranges as well as fabulous beaches and marine life. See specific suggestions for great weekend breaks in the provinces chapter.

South Africa is renowned for great game viewing. Private game reserves usually offer guided drives in specially equipped safari vehicles. South Africa's national parks also offer game drives, however game viewing is also possible on a self-drive basis and can be done from the convenience of your own car on tarred or well-maintained gravel routes. A 4x4 is usually not necessary unless you are planning off-road adventures, in which case, consider renting or investing in a suitable 4x4 vehicle. Bush walks on foot and on horseback are also offered in certain game reserves.

Safari Without a 4x4

 Addo Elephant National Park, *Eastern Cape*

 Cederberg Conservancy, *Western Cape*

 Kgalagadi Transfrontier Park, *Northern Cape*

 iSimangeliso National Park, *KwaZulu-Natal*

 Kruger National Park, *Mpumalanga*

 Hluhluwe-iMfolozi Game Reserve, *KwaZulu-Natal*

 **Nylsvlei Conservancy**, *Limpopo*

There are more than 20 national parks in South Africa besides the numerous private game reserves. The national parks are managed either by Ezemvelo in KwaZulu-Natal or by South African National Parks (SANParks) in all other provinces. Most of the parks offer reasonably priced accommodation, which usually has to be booked well in advance, especially during holiday periods. The parks also usually cater for disabled visitors. The Kruger National Park has introduced a visitor quota system in recent years to control the numbers of day visitors at the park. Make sure that you arrive early at the gates to avoid the disappointment of finding that entrance to the park is closed for the day because visitor numbers have already been reached.

If you plan to explore the country's national parks, it is recommended that you join the SanPark's Wildcard loyalty programme or Ezemvelo's Rhinoclub. The annual membership allows you unlimited access to the national parks and reserves in the country without having to pay the daily entry fees.

The Great Limpopo Transfrontier Park, which is commonly called 'The Kruger Park', is considered the world's largest conservation area and is roughly the same size as The Netherlands. The game park comprises several national parks, creating a huge 35 000 km² conservation area covering parts of South Africa, Mozambique and Zimbabwe.

Umhlanga beach, KwaZulu-Natal

BEACHES

With more than 3 000 km of coastline, there is a beach for everyone, whether you want to swim, sunbathe, surf, fish or just simply walk. The water temperature along the coastline varies widely. The Atlantic Ocean along the country's west coast does not get much warmer than 18 °C due to the Benguela current flowing up from Antarctica, while the Indian Ocean along the south and east coast can warm up to 25 °C due to the Agulhas current flowing down from the warm tropics.

There are 36 'Blue Flag' beaches and four 'Blue Flag' marinas along South Africa's coast. These award-winning beaches have a wide range of facilities and offer safe swimming in sparkling clean water. Find these beaches on www.blueflag.org.za.

Sandy beaches and numerous rock pools are an ideal opportunity for young children to explore marine life, particularly at low tide. Children should be accompanied at all times, especially as rocks can be very slippery and the barnacles and other shells can be very sharp. It is not advisable to touch any sea creatures or put your hands into rock crevices. Never swim alone and watch children closely.

Swimming in the sea is safe provided you adhere to the necessary precautions. Lifeguards are posted at the popular beaches in the vicinity of the bigger towns and holiday resorts in season, however the rest of the coastline has wild beaches with few or no amenities.

Always remember, that the sidewash, backwash and riptides can be powerful even when swimming close to the shore. Extreme caution should be taken by all, including strong swimmers, and the lifeguard instructions should be obeyed at all times.

Awesome Beaches

Western Cape

Camps Bay, *Cape Peninsula*
Boulders Beach, *Cape Peninsula*
Langebaan Lagoon, *West Coast*

Eastern Cape

Gonubie, *North Coast*
Kenton-on-Sea, *South Coast*
Humewood Beach, *Nelson Mandela Bay*

KwaZulu-Natal

Umhlanga, *North Coast*
Ramsgate, *South Coast*
Zinkwazi Beach, *North Coast*

Extreme care should be taken against both sunburn and heatstroke. Water-resistant sunblock should be used at all times and reapplied at regular intervals, even in overcast weather.

Although not dangerous, a blue bottle sting is very painful. Blue bottles resemble jellyfish and are found all along the coast. They can be identified as a small translucent blue bubble ('bottle') attached to a long thin tentacle. They appear sporadically, particularly during high tides and windy weather, and swimming should be avoided when they are present.

Contrary to common belief, shark attacks are rare events. Shark nets are erected on many beaches along the South African east coast to protect swimmers, and there have been only two serious attacks by sharks at beaches protected with shark nets in the last 30 years. Thus the number of people who drown at sea along the South African coast each year far exceeds fatal shark attacks. The KwaZulu-Natal Sharks Board in Durban holds demonstrations that provide a wealth of information on these ocean predators and you can also join their early morning boat trips to check the shark nets.

Along the Cape's False Bay, a shark spotting programme is successful in monitoring the presence of sharks on certain beaches and a system of coloured flags is used to alert bathers when a shark is seen approaching the beach. Bathers are advised to swim only at protected beaches, avoid murky water and keep out of the water at night or at twilight, when sharks are more active.

A variety of marine life can be experienced in South Africa. Southern right whales can be seen along the entire west and south coastline. Hermanus even boasts its own whale crier, who announces the arrival of the marine giants during the months of May and November. In the Western Cape you can get also close to African penguins that live in colonies at Boulders Beach near Cape Town and Betty's Bay near Kleinmond. Loggerhead and Leatherback turtles can be seen along the KwaZulu-Natal coastline between November and March, where they come to lay their eggs in the sand.

Penguins at Boulders Beach

Turtles in iSimangaliso Wetlands

Whales in Hermanus

FESTIVALS

Cultural, arts and sports festivals take place throughout the year, such as the two-day Cape Town International Jazz Festival, which attracts more than 35 000 visitors every year. For an overview of the most visited arts festivals see events pages such as www.whatson.co.za or www.sa-venues.com or subscribe to newsletters of the local theatres.

KKNK

The week-long Klein Karoo National Arts Festival in Oudtshoorn, is a celebration of the Afrikaans culture and arts. It features first-rate dance and theatrical performances as well as visual art installations every year in April. www.kknk.co.za

Arts Alive

The annual festival in Johannesburg is the major platform for young artists in South Africa and during the 'Ten Days in September' brings a wide range of theatrical, dance, poetry and music performances. www.artsalive.co.za

Jazz Festival

The Cape Town International Jazz Festival in March is a platform for some of the world's best jazz musicians and attracts more than 35 000 visitors every year. www.capetownjazzfest.com

Minstrel Carnival

The traditional street parade in Cape Town occurs in January, when locals march through the city centre dancing to *ghoema* music and displaying colourful uniforms and painted faces. www.capetown-minstrels.co.za

National Arts Festival

The world's second biggest arts and culture festival with a main and fringe programme takes place in June/July at more than 50 venues in and around Grahamstown. It is nenowned for its excellence and cutting edge productions. In 2011, more than 200 000 visitors attended the 1 200+ performances. www.nationalartsfestival.co.za

Macufe

The Mangaung African Cultural Festival in Bloemfontein is known for being the biggest and most culturally balanced showcase of African arts and culture. It is held annually in October and presents local and international renowned and emerging talent. www.macufe.co.za.

Splashy Fen

This music festival featuring some of South Africa's hottest acts is the country's longest running music festival and takes place in Underberg every Easter. www.splashyfen.co.za

RESOURCES

Arts and Culture

Dept of Arts and Culture: www.dac.gov.za
National Arts Council: www.nac.org.za
African Arts Institute: www.afai.org.za
www.artlink.co.za
www.imaginemag.co.za
www.dancedirectory.co.za
www.moviesite.co.za
www.mio.co.za

Museums

Museum Listing: www.museumsonline.co.za
South African Museums: www.sama.za.net
www.apartheidmuseum.org
www.iziko.org.za
www.nasmus.co.za
www.thebighole.co.za
www.maropeng.co.za

Travel and Accommodation

www.satourism.net
www.greenwoodguides.com
www.portfoliocollection.com
www.safarinow.com
www.sa-venues.com
www.sleeping-out.co.za
www.travelstart.co.za
www.tripadvisor.com
www.wheretostay.co.za

Sport and Recreation

Department of Sports and Recreation:
www.srsa.gov.za
Blue Flag Beaches: www.blueflag.org.za
Conservation Info: www.wessa.org.za
Sea Rescue: www.nsri.org.za
Sharks Board: www.shark.co.za
WildCard: www.wildcard.co.za
Ezemvelo Wildlife: www.kznwildlife.com

Ticket Booking Sites

www.computicket.co.za
www.itickets.co.za
www.webtickets.co.za

Spas

www.southafricanspas.co.za
www.saspaassociation.co.za
www.brookdale.co.za

Event Guides

www.whatson.co.za
www.timeout.com
www.gigcentral.co.za
www.joburg.co.za
www.durbanlive.com
www.whatsonincapetown.com

Recommended Reading

African Arts Insitute (2011) *The Migrant Artist's Handbook*. AFAI

Brett, Michael (2010) *Touring South Africa's National Parks*. Random House Struik

Map Studio (2009) *Our Top 4x4 Trips*. Map Studio

Olivier, Willie (2010) *Hiking Trails of South Africa*. Struik

Reid, Roxanne (2008) *A Walk in the Park. Travels Around South Africa*. Aardvaark Press

Various sports, travel and leisure magazines such as *Country Life, Go, Getaway* and *Responsible Traveller* are available in shops and/or online.

'There are lessons a man has to learn and there's nothing you'll learn in town the bush won't teach you better and harder.'

~ Pamela Jooste, novelist

'Everything here is just so beautiful and easy – everything but leaving.' ~ *Charlize Theron, actress*

ANNEXURE

REPRESENTATIONS ABROAD

The following listing shows the main contacts in the respective countries. Enquire there for further assistance or addresses of subordinate (honorary) consulates and representations. For countries not listed, view www.dirco.gov.za or go to www.dfa.gov.za.

Angola
Embassy in Luanda
www.saangola.org
+ 244 222 460 223

Australia
High Commission in Canberra
www.sahc.org.au
+ 61 2 6272 7300

Austria
Embassy in Vienna
www.dirco.gov.za/vienna
+ 43 1 320 6493

Belgium
Embassy in Brussels
www.southafrica.be
+32 2 285 4400

Brazil
Embassy in Brasilia
www.africadosul.org.br
+ 55 61 3312 9500

Canada
High Commission in Ottawa
www.southafrica-canada.ca
+ 1 613 744 0330

China
Embassy in Beijing
www.saembassy.org.cn
+ 86 10 8532 0000

Denmark
Embassy in Hellerup
www.southafrica.dk
+ 45 3918 0155

Finland
Embassy in Helsinki
www.southafricanembassy.fi
+ 358 9 6860 3100

France
Embassy in Paris
www.afriquesud.net
+ 33 1 5359 2323

Germany
Embassy in Berlin
www.suedafrika.org
+ 49 30 22 0730

India
High Commission in New Delhi
www.sahc-india.com
+ 91 11 2 614 9411

Indonesia
Embassy in Jakarta
www.dirco.gov.za/jakarta
+ 62 21 2991 2500

Israel
Embassy in Ramat-Gan
www.safis.co.il
+ 972 3 525 2566

Italy
Embassy in Rome
www.sudafrica.it
+ 39 06 85 2541

Korea
Embassy in Seoul
www.southafrica-embassy.or.kr
+ 82 2 2077 5900

Malaysia
High Commission in Kuala Lumpur
www.sahighcomkl.com.my
+ 60 3 2170 2400

Mozambique
High Commission in Maputo
www.dirco.gov.za/maputo
+ 258 21 243 000

Netherlands
Embassy in The Hague
www.southafrica.nl
+ 31 70 392 4501

New Zealand
High Commission in Wellington
www.sahc.org.au/consular_new-zealand.htm
+ 64 4 815 8484

Norway
Embassy in Oslo
www.dirco.gov.za/oslo
+ 47 2327 3220

Portugal
Embassy in Lisbon
www.embaixada-africadosul.pt
+ 351 21 319 2200

Russia
Embassy in Moscow
www.saembassy.ru
+ 7 495 926 11 77

Singapore
Embassy in Singapore
www.dirco.gov.za/singapore
+ 65 6339 3319

Spain
Embassy in Madrid
www.dirco.gov.za/madrid/en
+ 34 91 436 3780

Sweden
Embassy in Stockholm
www.southafrica.se
+ 46 8 24 39 50

Switzerland
Embassy in Berne
www.southafrica.ch
+ 41 31 350 13 13

Thailand
Embassy in Bangkok
www.dirco.gov.za/bangkok
+ 66 2 659 2900

Turkey
Embassy in Ankara
www.southafrica.org.tr
+ 90 312 405 6861

UAE
Embassy in Abu Dhabi
www.southafrica.ae
+ 971 2 417 6400

UK
High Commission in London
www.southafricahouseuk.com
+ 44 20 7451 7299

USA
Embassy in Washington
www.saembassy.org
+ 1 202 232 4400

FOREIGN MISSIONS

There are more than 250 foreign representations in South Africa, with most of the embassies and high commissions being located in Pretoria. Many foreign missions maintain additional consulates in Johannesburg, Cape Town and Durban. Honorary consuls may be available for many countries at other cities and towns. See www.dfa.gov.za for more countries.

Australia
www.southafrica.embassy.gov.au
012 423 6000

Austria
www.bmeia.gv.at
012 452 9155

Belgium
www.diplobel.fgov.be
012 440 3201/2

Botswana
www.mofaic.gov.bw
011 403 3748

Brazil
www.itamaraty.gov.br
012 366 5200

Canada
www.southafrica.gc.ca
012 422 3000

China
www.chinese-embassy.info
012 431 6524

Denmark
www.ambpretoria.um.dk
012 430 9340

Finland
www.finland.org.za
012 343 0275

France
www.ambafrance-rsa.org
012 425 1600

Germany
www.pretoria.diplo.de
012 427 8900

India
www.indiainsouthafrica.com
012 342 5392

Ireland
www.embassyofireland.org.za
012 452 1000

Israel
pretoria.mfa.gov.il
012 470 3511

Italy
www.ambpretoria.esteri.it
012 423 0000

Japan
www.za.emb-japan.go.jp
012 452 1500

Malaysia
www.kln.gov.my
012 342 5990

Mozambique
www.embamoc.co.za
012 401 0300

Namibia
www.namibia.org.za
012 481 9100

Netherlands
www.dutchembassy.co.za
012 425 4500

New Zealand
www.nzembassy.com
012 435 9000

Norway
www.mfa.no
012 364 3700

Portugal
www.embaixadaportugal.org.za
012 346 4285

Russian Federation
www.russianembassy.org.za
012 362 1337

Singapore
www.mfa.gov.sg/pretoria
012 430 6035

Spain
www.maec.es
012 460 0123

Swaziland
www.swazihighcom.co.za
012 344 1910

Sweden
www.swedenabroad.com
012 426 6400

Switzerland
www.eda.admin.ch/pretoria
012 452 0660

Thailand
www.thaiembassy.co.za
012 342 5648

Turkey
www.pretoria.emb.mfa.gov.tr
012 342 6053

UK
www.southafricahouseuk.com
012 421 7500

USA
southafrica.usembassy.gov
012 431 4000

Zambia
www.zambiapretoria.net
012 326 1854

BUSINESS ORGANISATIONS AND BILATERAL RELATIONS

American Chamber
www.amcham.co.za • 011 788 0265

Australian Trade Commission
www.austrade.gov.au

French-South African Chamber
www.fsacci.co.za • 011 267 5750

German-South African Chamber
www.germanchamber.co.za • 011 486 2775

Italian Chamber
www.italcham.co.za • 011 615 3906

Mozambique South Africa Chamber
www.samozacc.co.za • 076 854 8303

Netherlands South Africa Chamber
www.sanec.co.za

Nordic South African Business Association
www.nsba.co.za • 011 202 0510

Russian-South African Business Council
www.russianembassy.org.za • 012 362 1337

South Africa China Business Association
www.sacba-prc.org • 012 431 6500

Swiss South African Chamber
www.scsa.ch • 011 603 2498

Afrikaanse Handelsinstitut
www.ahi.co.za • 012 348 5440

Business Unity South Africa
www.busa.org.za • 011 784 8000

Chamber of Mines of South Africa
www.bullion.org.za • 011 498 7100

Department of Trade and Industry
www.thedti.gov.za • 012 394 9500

Minara Chamber of Commerce
www.minara.org.za • 031 208 1898

National African Federated Chamber
www.nafcoc.org.za • 011 807 5063

National Economic Development and Labour Council
www. nedlac.org.za • 011 328 4200

National Small Business Chamber
www.nsbc.org.za • 086 1726 722

Small Development Enterprise Agency
www.seda.org.za • 0860 103 703

South African Chamber
www.sacci.org.za • 011 446 3800

LARGEST CONFERENCE CENTRES & MEETING VENUES

South Africa is a popular destination for conferences and meeting venues. There are many renowned conference centres in the country. For a comprehensive listing see www.saaci.co.za.

Cape Town International Convention Centre (CTICC), *Cape Town*
www.cticc.co.za

Coca-Cola Dome, *Johannesburg*
www.coca-coladome.co.za

Expo Centre, *Johannesburg*
www.expocentrejhb.co.za

Gallagher Convention Centre, *Midrand*
www.gallagher.co.za

International Convention Centre Durban (ICC), *Durban*
www.icc.co.za

Mittah Seperepere Convention Centre, *Kimberley*
www.experiencenortherncape.com

Sandton Convention Centre, *Sandton*
www.saconvention.co.za

Stadium Management SA, *various*
www.stadiummanagement.co.za

Sun City Superbowl, *Sun City*
www.suninternational.com

Tshwane Events Centre, *Pretoria*
www.tshwane-events.co.za

MAJOR EXHIBITIONS IN SOUTH AFRICA

Africa Energy Indaba
Foremost forum for Africa's energy sector
Sandton Convention Centre
www.energyindaba.co.za

Africa Health
Biggest sub-saharan exhibition and
conference for the healthcare sector
Gallagher Convention Centre
www.africahealthexhibition.com

Automechanika
Africa's leading trade fair for the
automobile sector
www.automechanikasa.co.za

South African Book Fair
Biggest international book fair
in sub-saharan Africa
Cape Town International Convention
Centre
www.thebereed.co.za/southafricanbookfair

Design Indaba
World's top creative minds
conference and expo
Cape Town International Convention
Centre
www.designindaba.com

Meetings Africa
Africa's biggest business tourism exhibition
Sandton Convention Centre
www.meetingsafrica.co.za

Mining Indaba
World's largest mining investment event
and largest mining
Cape Town International Convention
Centre
www.miningindaba.com

Oil & Gas Summit
Leading oil and gas summit in Cape Town
Cape Town International Convention
Centre
www.southernafricaoilandgas.com

Propak Africa
Africa's largest packaging and food
processing expo
Expo Centre Johannesburg
www.propakafrica.co.za

Tourism Indaba
Africa's largest tourism exhibition
International Convention Centre Durban
www.indaba-southafrica.co.za

TRAVEL RESOURCES

Airlines Flying to/from South Africa

Air Austral
011 326 4440 • www.air-austral.com

Air Botswana
011 390 3070 • www.airbotswana.co.bw

Air France
0861 340 340 • www.airfrance.com

Air Madagascar
011 289 8222 • www.airmadagascar.com

Air Mauritius
087 151 1848 • www.airmauritius.com

Air Namibia
011 783 8022 • www.airnamibia.aero

Air Seychelles
011 326 4440 • www.airseychelles.com

Air Zimbabwe
011 390 3064 • www.airzimbabwe.aero

British Airways
011 441 8600 • www.britishairways.com

Cathay Pacific
011 700 8900 • www.cathaypacific.com

Delta
0860 018 040 • www.delta.com

Edelweiss
0860 040 506 • www.flyedelweiss.com

Egypt Air
011 537 7640 • www.egyptair.com

El Al Israel Airlines
011 620 2525 • www.elal.co.il

Emirates
0861 364 728 • www.emirates.com

Ethiopian Airlines
011 781 5950 • www.flyethiopian.com

Etihad
0860 123 150 • www.etihad.com

Jet Airways
011 616 1696 • www.jetairways.com

Kenya Airways
011 571 8832 • www.kenya-airways.com

KLM
011 961 6700 • www. klm.com

LAM Mozambique Airlines
011 622 4889 • www.lam.co.mz

Lufthansa
0861 842 538 • www.lufthansa.com

Qatar Airways
0861 861 868 • www.qatarairways.com

Quantas
0800 993 025 • www.quantas.com.au

Saudi Arabian Airlines
011 390 2178 • www.saudiairlines.com

Singapore Airlines
011 880 8560 • www.singaporeair.com

South African Airways
011 978 1000 • www.flysaa.com

Swiss International Airlines
0860 040 506 • www.swiss.com

TAAG Angola Airlines
011 450 1116 • www.taag.com

Thai Airways
011 268 2580 • www.thaiairways.com

Turkish Airlines
011 578 8000 • www.turkishairlines.com

Virgin Atlantic Airways
011 340 3400 • www.virgin-atlantic.com

Flight and Travel Bookings

www.clubmed.co.za
www.clubtravel.co.za
www.flightcentre.co.za
www.harveyworld.co.za
www.hyltonross.co.za
www.ikapa.co.za
www.pentravel.com
www.satravelcentre.com
www.statravel.co.za
www.suretravel.co.za
www.springbokatlas.com
www.thompsons.co.za
www.travelstart.co.za
www.virginholidays.co.uk

Accommodation

www.agoda.com
www.booking.com
www.greenwoodguides.com
www.hotelclub.com
www.hotelscombined.com
www.naa-sa.com
www.portfoliocollection.com
www.roomsforafrica.com
www.sa-venues.com
www.safarinow.com
www.sleeping-out.co.za
www.solomonsguide.com
www.tripadvisor.com
www.wheretostay.co.za

Hotel Groups

www.africanpridehotels.com
www.fairmont.com
www.hilton.com
www.hyatt.com
www.intercontinental.com
www.novotel.com
www.oneandonlyresorts.com
www.peermont.com
www.proteahotels.com
www.radisson.co.za
www.suninternational.com
www.sheraton.com
www.threecities.co.za
www.tsogosunhotels.com

BUSINESS RESOURCES

Major Multinational Companies

Acer Africa: www.acer.co.za
Acelor Mittal: www.acelormittal.com
Alcatel: www.alcatel-lucent.co.za
Amazon: www.amazon.co.za
AngloAmerican: www.angloamerican.co.za
AngloGold: www.anglogoldashanti.co.za
Apple: www.apple.com
Aspen: www.aspenpharma.com
Assore: www.assore.com
AstraZeneca: www.astrazeneca.com
Audi: www.audi.co.za
BASF: www.basf.co.za
Bidvest: www.bidvest.com
BHP Billiton Ltd: www.bhpbilliton.com
BMW: www.bmw.co.za
BP: www.bp.com
Bosch: www.bosch.co.za
Bridgestone: www.bridgestone.co.za
Chevron: www.chevron.com
Cisco Systems: www.cisco.com
Coca-Cola: www.cocacola.co.za
Eskom: www.eskom.co.za
Evergreen: www.evergreen-marine.com
Exxaro: www.exxaro.com
Ford: www.ford.co.za
General Electric: www.ge.com
GlencoreXstrata: www.glencorexstrata.com
General Motors: www.gmsa.com
Goodyear: www.goodyear.eu/za
Grinaker: www.grinaker-lta.co.za
Gold Fields: www.goldfields.co.za
GroupFive: www.g5.co.za
Heineken: www.heineken.com

HRG Rennies: www.renniestravel.com
Huawei: www.huawei.com
IBM: www.ibm.com
Impala Platinum: www.implats.co.za
Imperial Holdings: www.imperial.co.za
Johnson Controls:
www.johnsoncontrols.co.za
Lonmin: www.lonmin.com
MAN: www.mantruckandbus.co.za
Massmart: www.massmart.co.za
Mercedes-Benz: www.mercedes-benz.co.za
Merck: www.merck.co.za
Microsoft: www.microsoft.com
MMI Holdings: www.mmiholdings.com
Mondi: www.mondigroup.com
Naspers: naspers.com
Nestle: www.nestle.co.za
Novonordisk: www.novonordisk.com
Parsec: www.parsecgroup.com
PetroSA: www.petrosa.co.za
Remgro: www.remgro.com
Roche: www.roche.co.za
SAB Miller: www.sabmiller.com
Sanlam: www.sanlam.co.za
SAP: www.sap.com
Sasol: www.sasol.com
Siemens: www.siemens.co.za
Shoprite: www.shopriteholdings.co.za
Steinhoff: www.steinhoffinternational.com
MSA Group: www.msagroupservices.com
Unilever: www.unilever.co.za
Veolia: www.veoliawaterst.co.za
Volkswagen: www.vw.co.za

International Banks

Albaraka Bank: www.albaraka.co.za
ABN Amro Bank: www.abnamro.com
Bank of Athens: www.bankofathens.co.za
Bank of Baroda: www.bankofbaroda.com
Bank of China: www.boc.co.za
Bank of Cyprus: www.bankofcyprus.com
Barclays Bank: www.barclays.com
BNP Paribas: www.bnpparibas.com
China Construction Bank: www.ccbjhb.com
Citibank: www.citibank.com
Credit Suisse: www.creditsuisse.com
Deutsche Bank: www.db.com
Habib Overseas Bank:
www.habiboverseas.co.za
HBZ Bank: www.hbzbank.co.za

HSBC: www.hsbc.co.za
JP Morgan Chase: www.jpmorgan.com
Lloyds: www.lloydsbankinggroup.com
Mercantile Bank: www.mercantile.co.za
Merril Lynch: www.ml.com
The Bank of Tokyo-Mitsubishi UFG:
www.bk.mufg.jp
Morgan Stanley: www.morganstanley.com
Société Generale: www.sgcib.com
Standard Chartered:
www.standardchartered.co.za
State Bank of India: www.statebank.co.za
UBS: www.ubs.com
Unicredit: www.unicreditgroup.eu
Wells Fargo: www.wellsfargo.com

LOGISTICS COMPANIES

DB Schenker
www.schenker.co.za

DAL Deutsche Africa-Linien
www.dal.biz

DHL
www.dhl.co.za

Kuehne + Nagel
www.kn-portal.com

Imperial
www.imperiallogistics.co.za

Röhlig-Grindrod
www.rohlig.com

SDV Geis Logistics
www.sdv-geis.com

South African Express Line
www.sael.com

UTI
www.gouti.com

WorldNet
www.worldnetlogistics.com

COURIER SERVICES

Aramex
www.aramex.co.za

DHL
www.dhl.co.za

Fastway
www.fastway.co.za

Federal Express
www.fedex.com

Globeflight
www.globeflight.co.za

RAM
www.ramgroup.co.za

Speed Services
www.speedservices.co.za

TNT Express
www.tnt.com

UPS
www.ups.com

Worldcourier
www.worldcourier.com

TELKOM TELEPHONE SERVICE

Local Directory Enquiries: 1023
International Enquiries: 10903

080 Free Call Numbers, completely free of charge
0860 Share Call Numbers, caller pays for the local call
0861 Maxi Call Numbers, the caller pays flat rate

DIALLING CODES

The exit code for calls out of South Africa is **00**.
The country code for South Africa is **+27**

Other country codes:

Australia	+61	Mozambique	+258
Austria	+42	Netherlands	+31
Botswana	+267	New Zealand	+64
China	+86	Switzerland	+41
Cuba	+53	Turkey	+90
France	+33	UAE	+971
Germany	+49	UK	+44
India	+91	USA	+1
Italy	+39	Zimbabwe	+263

For more numbers please refer to the
International Calling Guide on www.howtocallabroad.com

CONVERSION CHARTS

Clothing Women

SA/UK	EU	US
8	34	6
10	36	8
12	38	10
14	40	12
16	42	14
18	44	16
20	46	18
22	48	20

Jackets Men

SA/UK	EU	US
36	46	36
38	48	38
40	50	40
42	52	42
44	54	44
46	56	46

Shirts Men Collar Sizes

SA/UK	EU	US
14.5	37	S
15	38	S
15.5	39	M
16	41	L
16.5	42	L
17	43	XL
17.5	44	XL
18	45	XXL

Shoes Women

SA/UK	EU	US
3	36	3.5
4	37	4.5
5	38	5.5
6	39	6.5
7	40	7
7.5	41	8
8	42	8.5

Shoes Men

SA/UK	EU	US
6	40	7.5
7	41	8
8	42	8.5
9	43	9
10	44	10.5
11	45	11.5
12	46	12.5

Measurements

South Africa uses metric measurements. Below are the most common conversions if you are used to measurements in imperial units or US volumes.

Imperial	Metric
1 stone	6.35 kg
1 pound	454 g
1 pint	568 ml
1 ounce	28 g
1 gallon	4.546 litre
1 foot	0.3 m
1 yard	0.9 m
1 mile	1.6 km

US Units	Metric
1 US liquid gallon	3.785 litre
1 quart	946 ml
1 pint	473 ml
1 cup	240 ml
1 fluid ounce	30 ml
1 tablespoon	15 ml

Paper Sizes

Size	mm	Inches
A0	841 x 1189	33.1 x 46.8
A1	594 x 841	23.4 x 33.1
A2	420 x 594	16.5 x 23.4
A3	297 x 420	11.7 x 16.5
A4	210 x 297	8.3 x 11.7
A5	148 x 210	5.8 x 8.3

Temperature

°F	°C
104	40
95	35
86	30
77	25
68	20
59	15
50	10
41	5
32	0

Oven Temperatures

°F	°C	Gas
275	140	1
300	150	2
325	165	3
350	177	4
375	190	5
400	200	6
425	220	7
450	230	8

SCHOOLS

South Africa has a wide range of excellent international, private (P) and state schools (S) in the country. Some of them offer boarding facilities and are listed below. Also refer to the various school directories mentioned in the 'Education' chapter.

International Schools

American International School
Cape Town/Western Cape
www.aisct.org

American International School
Johannesburg/Gauteng
www.aisj-jhb.com

Andrews Academy
Randburg/Gauteng
www.andrewsacademy.co.za

Ashton International College
Benoni/ Gauteng and Ballito/KwaZulu-Natal
www.ashtoncollege.co.za
www.ashtonballito.co.za

Blouberg International School
Cape Town/Western Cape
www.blouberginternational.co.za

British International College
Bryanston and Pretoria/Gauteng
www.bicollege.co.za

Cambridge Academy
eMalahleni/Mpumalanga
www.cambridge.co.za

Cape Town International School
Cape Town/Western Cape
www.isct.co.za

Charter College
Honeydew/Gauteng
www.chartercollege.co.za

Chester House
Durbanville/Western Cape
www.chesterhouse.co.za

Courtney House International School
Pretoria/Gauteng
www.courtney.co.za

Deutsche Schule Johannesburg
Johannesburg/Gauteng
www.dsj.co.za

Deutsche Schule Kapstadt
Cape Town/Western Cape
www.dsk.co.za

Deutsche Schule Pretoria
Pretoria/Gauteng
www.dspretoria.co.za

Ecole Française du Cap
Cape Town/Western Cape
www.ecolefrancaiseducap.co.za

Greenwich College
Bryanston/Gauteng
www.greenwich-college.co.za

Helderberg International School
Somerset West/Western Cape
www.helderberg.iesedu.com

International School of Hout Bay
Hout Bay/Western Cape
www.houtbay.iesedu.com

International School of South Africa
Mafikeng/North West
www.issa.co.za

Kearsney College
Durban/KwaZulu-Natal
www.kearsney.com

Lycée Jules Verne
Johannesburg/Gauteng
www.lyceejulesverne.co.za

Mountain Cambridge School
Harbeespoort/North West
www.themcs.co.za

Pretoria Chinese School
Pretoria/Gauteng
www.pretoriachineseschool.co.za

Ridgeway College
Makhado/LP
www.ridgewaycollege.co.za

St Charles College
Pietermaritzburg/KwaZulu-Natal
www.scc.za.com

St John's College
Houghton/Gauteng
www.stjohnscollege.co.za

Summerhill College
Midrand/Gauteng
www.summerhill-school.co.za

The Japanese School
Randburg/Gauteng
www.jsj.org.za

Wembley College
Greytown/KwaZulu-Natal
www.wembleycollege.co.za

Boys' Schools with Boarding Facilities

Bishops Diocesan College (P)
Cape Town/Western Cape
www.bishops.org.za

Grey College (S)
Bloemfontein/Free State
www.gc.co.za

Hilton College (P)
Hilton/KwaZulu-Natal
www.hiltoncollege.com

Jeppe High School for Boys (S)
Johannesburg/Gauteng
www.jeppeboys.co.za

Kimberley Boys' High School (S)
Kimberley/Northern Cape
www.kbhs.co.za

King Edward VII School (S)
Johannesburg/Gauteng
www.kingedwardschool.co.za

Maritzburg College (S)
Pietermaritzburg/KwaZulu-Natal
www.maritzburgcollege.org.za

Michaelhouse (P)
Balgowan/KwaZulu-Natal
www.michaelhouse.org.za

Paul Roos Gymnasium (S)
Stellenbosch/Western Cape
www.paulroos.co.za

Queen's College (P)
Queenstown/Eastern Cape
www.queenscollege.co.za

Rondebosch Boys' High School (S)
Cape Town/Western Cape
www.rondebosch.com

Selborne College (S)
East London/Eastern Cape
www.selborne.co.za

St Andrew's College (P)
Grahamstown/Eastern Cape
www.sacschool.com

St Andrew's School (S)
Bloemfontein/Free State
www.sasb.co.za

St Stithians Boys' College (P)
Johannesburg/Gauteng
www.stithian.com

South African College (S)
Cape Town/Western Cape
www.sacshigh.org.za

Girls' Schools with Boarding Facilities

Clarendon High School for Girls (S)
East London/Eastern Cape
high.clarendonschools.co.za

Diocesan School for Girls (P)
Grahamstown/Eastern Cape
www.dsgschool.com

Eunice High School (S)
Bloemfontein/Free State
www.eunice.co.za

Herschel Girls' High School (P)
Cape Town/Western Cape
www.herschel.org.za

Kimberley Girls' High School (S)
Kimberley/Northern Cape
www.kimberleygirlshigh.org.za

Pietermaritzburg Girls' High School (S)
Pietermaritzburg/KwaZulu-Natal
www.ghspmb.co.za

Potchefstroom Girls' High School (S)
Potchefstroom/North West
www.potchgirlshigh.co.za

Rhenish Girls' High Sschool (S)
Stellenbosch/Western Cape
www.rhenish.co.za

Rustenburg Girls' (S)
Cape Town/Western Cape
www.rghs.org.za

St Anne's Diocesan College (P)
Hilton/KwaZulu-Natal
www.stannes.co.za

St Catherine's Empangeni (P)
Empangeni/KwaZulu-Natal
www.saintcatherines.co.za

St John's Diocesan School (P)
Pietermaritzburg/KwaZulu-Natal
www.stjohnsdsg.com

St Mary's School (P)
Johannesburg/Gauteng
www.stmarysschool.co.za

St Michael's School (S)
Bloemfontein/Free State
www.stms.co.za

St Stitihians Girls' High School (P)
Johannesburg/Gauteng
www.stithian.com

Victoria Girls' High School (S)
Grahamstown/Eastern Cape
www.vghs.co.za

Co-educational Schools with Boarding

Bridge House (P)
Franschhoek/Western Cape
www.bridgehouse.org.za

Cornwall Hill College (P)
Pretoria/Gauteng
www.cornwall.co.za

Felixton College (P)
Empangeni/KwaZulu-Natal
www.felixtoncollege.co.za

Harriston High School (P)
Harrismith/Free State
www.harriston.co.za

Penrhyn College (P)
Mbombela/Mpumalanga
www.penryn.co.za

Stanford Lake College (P)
Magoebaskloof/Limpopo
www.stanfordlakecollege.co.za

St Dominic's School (P)
Welkom/Free State
www.dominic.co.za

St Patrick's College (P)
Kimberley/Northern Cape
www.stpatricks.co.za

Uplands College (P)
White River/Mpumalanga
www.uplandscollege.org

Woodridge College (P)
Port Elizabeth/Eastern Cape
www.woodridge.co.za

UNIVERSITIES

Cape Peninsula University of Technology (CPUT)
Cape Town/Western Cape
021 460 3955 • www.cput.ac.za

Central University of Technology (CUT)
Bloemfontein/Free State
051 507 3410 • www.cut.ac.za

Durban University of Technology (DUT)
Durban/KwaZulu-Natal
031 373 5422 • www.dut.ac.za

Nelson Mandela Metropolitan University (NMMU)
Port Elizabeth/Eastern Cape
041 504 2161 • www.nmmu.ac.za

North West University (NWU)
Potchefstroom/North West
018 299 1111 • www.nwu.ac.za

Rhodes University (RU)
Grahamstown/Eastern Cape
046 603 8217 • www.ru.ac.za

Tshwane University of Technology (TUT)
Pretoria/Gauteng
0861 102 421 • www.tut.ac.za

University of Cape Town (UCT)
Cape Town/Western Cape
021 650 2822 • www.uct.ac.za

University of Fort Hare (UFH)
Alice/Eastern Cape
043 704 7000 • www.ufh.ac.za

University of Johannesburg (UJ)
Johannesburg/Gauteng
011 559 4555 • www.uj.ac.za

University of KwaZulu-Natal (UKZN)
Durban/KwaZulu-Natal
031 260 2870 • www.ukzn.ac.za

University of Limpopo
Polokwane/Limpopo
015 268 3046 • www.ul.ac.za

University of Pretoria (UP)
Pretoria/Gauteng
012 420 3111 • www.up.ac.za

University of South Africa (UNISA)
Pretoria/Gauteng
www.unisa.ac.za

University of Stellenbosch (USB)
Stellenbosch/Western Cape
021 808 9111 • www.sun.ac.za

University of the Western Cape (UWC)
Cape Town/Western Cape
021 959 2487 • www.uwc.ac.za

University of the Witwatersrand (Wits)
Johannesburg/Gauteng
011 717 1056 • www.wits.ac.za

University of Zululand
Richards Bay/KwaZulu-Natal
035 902 6000 • www.uzulu.ac.za

Walter Sisulu University (WSU)
Buffalo City/Eastern Cape
www.wsu.ac.za

Vaal University of Technology (VUT)
Vanderbijlpark/Gauteng
016 950 9318 • www.vut.ac.za

COLLEGES

There are 50 registered and accredited public colleges with over 260 campuses in the country. They offer a variety of courses for attaining vocational certificates and diplomas and cater for a wide range of interests, such as marketing and business studies, arts, engineering, health and environmental studies. There is also a vast number of private colleges providing further and adult education. Make sure the facility you are interested in is registered with the Department of Higher Education and Training. Here is a listing of some of the largest educational facilities. (Study permits are needed for non-South African students).

Public FET Colleges

Buffalo City FET
East London/EC
www.bccollege.co.za

Central Johannesburg FET College
Johannesburg/GP
www.cjc.co.za

Coastal KZN College
Durban/KZN
www.coastalkzn.co.za

College of Cape Town
Cape Town/WC
www.cct.edu.za

East Cape Midlands College
Grahamstown/EC
www.emcol.co.za

Ekurhuleni East FET College
Springs and Benoni/GP
www.eec.edu.za

Northlink FET College
Bellville/WC
www.northlink.co.za

Umfolozi FET College
Richards Bay/KZN
www.umfolozicollege.co.za

Private Colleges and Institutions

AFDA
Film school offering courses in film production and screen design
Campuses in Johannesburg, Cape Town and Durban
www.afda.co.za

Boston City Campus
Various subjects taught in short courses, skills and degree programmes
Over 40 campus locations all over the country
www.boston.co.za

Camelot International
Part-time, full-time and post-graduate courses in health and business management
Ten campuses all over the country
www.camelotint.co.za

Damelin
Wide range of courses for lecture and correspondence studies
Campuses in over 30 locations all over the country
www.damelin.co.za

International Hotel School
Full-time, part-time and distance courses for the hospitality sector
Campuses in Johannesburg, Cape Town and Durban
www.hotelschool.co.za

Milpark Business School
Variety of courses that focus on banking, financial planning, insurance and management.
Campuses in Cape Town and Johannesburg
www.milpark.ac.za

MSC Business College
Wide range of full-time study programmes, such as social studies, engineering, IT and tourism
Campuses in over 20 locations in South Africa
www.msccollege.co.za

Varsity College
Largest private tertiary education provider in the country
Campuses in Sandton, Pretoria, Cape Town, Port Elizabeth, Durban North, Westville, Pietermaritzburg and Midrand.
www.varsitycollege.co.za

Monash South Africa
First foreign university in South Africa (wholly owned by Monash University Australia). Four faculties offer undergraduate and graduate programmes in social studies, medicine, IT and business/economics.
Campus in Johannesburg.
www.monash.ac.za

SPORT ASSOCIATIONS

Angling
Deep Sea Angling Association
www.sadsaa.co.za
Go Fishing
www.gofishing.co.za

Archery
Archery SA
www.archerysa.org

Athletics and Running
Runners World
www.runnersworld.co.za
South African Athlete
www.saathlete.com

Baseball
Baseball South Africa
www.baseballsa.com

Bowls and Bowling
Bowl South Africa
www.bowlssa.co.za

Boxing
Boxing South Africa
www.boxingsa.co.za

Bridge
South African Bridge Federation
www.sabf.co.za

Canoeing
Canoeing South Africa
www.canoesa.org.za

Chess
Chess South Africa
www.chessa.co.za
South African Women's Chess
www.sawomenschess.co.za

Cricket
Cricket South Africa
www.cricket.co.za

Cycling
Cycling South Africa
www.cyclingsa.com
Pedal Power Association
www.pedalpower.org.za

Dancing
Ballroom Dancing
www.ballroomdancing.co.za
Dance Directory
www.dancedirectory.co.za

Diving
Dive South Africa
www.divesouthafrica.com

Fencing
Amateur Fencing Association
www.safencer.co.za

Go
Go Clubs Association
www.sagoclubs.co.za

Golf
Golf Associations
www.saga.co.za
www.wgsa.co.za
Golfing South Africa
www.golfingsouthafrica.com

Handball
Play handball
www.play-handball.org

Hiking and Mountain Climbing
Mountain Club of South Africa
www.mcsa.org.za

Hockey
South Africa Hockey
www.sahockey.co.za

Horse Riding
Equestrian Association
www.saec.org.za

Ice Hockey
Ice Hockey Association
www.saicehockey.org.za

Judo
Judo South Africa
www.judosa.co.za

Karate
SA JKA Karate
www.karate.co.za

Kayaking
Paddle/Yak Sea Kayak
www.seakayak.co.za

Mountain Biking
MTB Routes
www.mtbroutes.co.za
MTB Online
www.mtbonline.co.za

Netball
Netball South Africa
www.netball-sa.co.za

Polo and Drag Hunting
South African Polo Association
www.sapolo.org.za
Cape Hunt and Polo Club
www.chpc.co.za
Rand Polo Club
www.randhunt.co.za

Rugby
Rugby Union
www.sarugby.co.za

Sailing
Sailing
www.sailing.org.za

Soccer
Football Association
www.safa.net

Squash
Squash South Africa
www.squashsa.co.za

Surf Ski
Surf Ski
www.surfski.co.za

Surfing
Surfing South Africa
www.surfingsouthafrica.co.za
www.wavescape.co.za

Walking and Running
Run/Walk for Life
www.rwfl.co.za

Waterski and Wakeboarding
Waterski Federation
www.sawaterski.co.za

Yoga
South Africa Yoga
www.yogasouthafrica.com

CULTURAL ACTIVITIES

Arts and Crafts Classes
www.artsandcraftssa.co.za
www.craftycorner.co.za

Theatre Schools
www.dramaafrica.com
www.stagecoachschools.co.za
www.kto.co.za

Music Classes
www.kindermusik.co.za
www.drumcafe.co.za

Bird Watching
www.birding.co.za
www.birdlife.org.za
www.westerncapebirding.co.za

Photographic Clubs
www.photosa.co.za
www.pssa.co.za

American Society ASSA
www.associationofamericanclubs.com

Austrian Club
www.austrianclubjohannesburg.com
www.weltbund.at

British Council
www.britishcouncil.org.za

Chinese Clubs
www.chineseforum.org.za
www.casa.za.org
www.tcagp.co.za

Danish Club
www.danish.co.za

De Nederlands Club
www.nck.co.za

French Clubs and Cultural Organisations
www.alliance.org.za
www.entraide.org.za
www.ifas.org.za
www.lesfroggies.net

German Clubs and Cultural Organisations
www.safrika.org
www.goethe.de

Greek Associations
www.ausgreeknet.com/southafrica.htm

Irish Association
www.ireland.co.za

India Club
www.indiaclub.co.za

Italian Clubs
www.icct.co.za
www.giovani.co.za
www.ladante.org
www.italy.org.za

Norwegian Club
www.norway.org.za

Portuguese Clubs
www.portuguesecape.org.za
www.portugueseforum.org.za
www.secomunidades.pt

Swiss Clubs
www.swissclub.co.za
www.swissclubjhb.co.za
www.aso.ch

Turkish Clubs
www.turquoise.org.za

SOUTH AFRICAN SLANG

Ag: Used to emphasise confusion, disappointment or irritation, meaning 'Oh no!'

Aikona: No, never

Arvie: Afternoon

Ayebo: Expression of surprise or as a seal of approval

Babbelas: Afrikaans for hangover

Bakkie: Utility vehicle or light delivery truck

Bantu: African people; can be considered offensive if used in the wrong context

Baggies: Men's long shorts used for swimming

Bergie: Homeless person, originally referring to vagrants living near Table Mountain

Bill: The account or cheque, usually at a restaurant or hotel

Bioscope: A cinema or movie theatre

Biscuit: A cookie

Bliksem: To hit or beat up; may also be used to refer to a mischievous person

Boer: Afrikaans for farmer; can be considered offensive if used in the wrong context

Bonsella: A gift, tip or bonus

Brollie: Afrikaans slang for umbrella

Bru (also bro): A friend or mate, from broer (Afrikaans)

Bucks: South African money

China: A good friend or mate

Chop: A person who is acting like an idiot

Chow: Food or 'to eat'

Cool drink (or cold drink): Carbonated soft drink or lemonade

Cossie: Short for swimming costume or bathing suit

Cheers: Informal way of saying goodbye

Chick: Depending on the context, either a sexist or affectionate term for a girl

Dassie: Rock hyrax; from Afrikaans das meaning badger

Dagga: Marijuana

Dumpie: Brown beer bottle

Dop: An alcoholic drink

Dorp: Afrikaans for village

Dos: Sleep

Deurmekaar: Afrikaans for confused, disorganised or stupid

Dinges: A thing, also called a 'thingamabob', or a 'what-you-ma-call-it'

Dummy: Baby pacifier

Dwaal: Afrikaans for confusion

Eina!: Ouch! Used to express when something is sore

Eish!: Expression of surprise

Fundi: An expert (from Xhosa umfundi)

Gatvol: Fed up

Gooi: To chuck or throw

Highway: Motorway/freeway

Gogga: An insect or bug

Granadilla: Passion fruit (Spanish), also referred to overseas as 'maracuja'

Hectic: Expression to describe extreme conditions or events

Helluva: A lot of something; the contracted version of 'a hell of a ...'

Hey: Frequently added to end a sentence: 'The wind today is rather hectic, hey?'

Hoodia: Cactus plant used by the Khoisan for its healing properties

Howzit: 'Hello, how are you?'; the contracted form of 'How is it going?'

Indaba: Conference (from Zulu/Xhosa: 'gathering to discuss important issues')

Inyanga: Traditional healer or herbalist

Isit (or izit): Response to a statement asking for confirmation, meaning 'Is it so?'

Ja: Yes

Jislaaik!: Expression of surprise or shock; 'gee wizz!'

Jol: A party or to have a good time

Just now: Soon or shortly, but not immediately

Kiff: Surfer slang, meaning awesome

Klap: Afrikaans word for a smack or a slap

Koki: A coloured felt pen; always on school stationery lists

Koppie: Afrikaans for small hill (usually in a relatively flat area)

Kraal: Enclosure for livestock or a village of huts

Kuier: Afrikaans for visit; describes a get together with friends

Kos: (from Afrikaans for food); used in 'veldkos' (food with herbs or wild plants) or 'boerekos' (farm food)

Laduma (laduuuuuuuu-ma): Used to cheer a soccer goal (from Zulu: 'it is thundering')

Lapa: Outdoor enclosure, often with thatched roof, usually with a braai or grill

Lappie: Cleaning cloth

Larny: Smart looking person, the boss or the person in charge

Lekgotla: Strategy meeting

Lekker: Afrikaans for tasty; also means enjoyable or nice

Lift: An elevator

Makaraba (or makarapa): The colourful artistic headgear worn by soccer fans

Mal: Crazy mad; used to call someone doing something really stupid

Mossie: House sparrow or small bird

Mozzie: Shortened word for a mosquito

Muti: Traditional medicine used by traditional healers

Mzansi: South Africa

Nappy: Baby diaper

Now now: Expression of time meaning 'very soon or shortly'

OBS: Old Brown Sherry, national tipple

Oke: Guy or 'bloke'

Oom: Afrikaans for uncle, used as sign of respect to refer to any older male

Pasop: Afrikaans for beware or be careful

Pavement: The sidewalk

Miggie: Bug, especially a little flying gnat

Platteland: *Afrikaans term for relatively flat, remote farmland or countryside*

Potjie: *Three-legged cast-iron pot used for cooking stew over a fire*

Pram: *Baby stroller*

Robot: *Traffic light at an intersection*

Rock up: *To arrive, usually unannounced or uninvited*

Rubbish bin: *A dust bin or garbage can*

Smaak: *To like another person or thing*

Sorry: *Used instead of 'I beg your pardon' or when sympathy needs to be expressed*

Spaza shop: *Informal township shop*

Swak: *Used to describe feeling bad, or disappointing or not good*

Stompie: *Cigarette butt*

Sangoma: *Traditional healer using special rituals and herbal medicine*

Second skins: *Lycra swimwear or shirts covering the body for sun protection*

Shame: *Expression showing sympathy, use mainly in 'Ag shame'*

Sharp (or sharp-sharp): *Used to show agreement or express enthusiasm*

Shebeen: *Informal pub or bar in the townships*

Shongololo: *Millipede*

Skinner: *To gossip*

Slap chips (or slap tjips): *Soggy French fries, usually drenched in salt and vinegar*

Skelm: *Rascal or criminal*

Skollie: *Gangster, criminal*

Skrik: *Afrikaans for fright*

Slip slops: *Simple plastic beach footwear or sandals, worn extensively in summer*

Smokes: *Cigarettes*

So long: *'In the meantime' as in 'I will go so long'*

Sommer: *'Just because' or for no particular reason*

Takkies: *Running or sports shoes, trainers or sneakers*

Tannie: *Afrikaans for auntie but also used as sign of respect for an older female*

Taxi: *Refers to either a traditional metered taxi or a minibus taxi*

Tom: *Money*

Toppie: *Old man*

Toyi-toyi: *Traditional dance used during strikes or protest marches*

Trek: *To move or pull*

Tsotsi: *A gangster*

Veld (felt): *Open grassland. From the Dutch for field*

Velskoen: *Afrikaans for field shoes; simple, unworked lace up leather shoes*

Voetsek: *Crude Afrikaans word for 'go away'; often used when talking to a dog*

Vrot: *Afrikaans for rotten*

Vuvuzela: *Plastic horn used at soccer matches*

Witblits: *Homebrewed brandy, moonshine or 'aqua vita'*

Woes: *Used to describe being cross, wound up, aggressive. (Afrikaans: vicious, wild)*

Yebo: *Yes*

HOW TO SAY

Hello		
	Afrikaans	Hallo
	isiZulu & siSwati	Sawubona (greeting one person), Sanibonani (greeting a group of people)
	isiXhosa	Molo (greeting one person), Molweni (greeting a group of people)
	Sepedi, Sesotho & Setswana	Dumela (greeting one person), Dumelang (greeting a group of people)
	Tshivenda	Ndaa (greeting a man), Aa (greeting a woman)
	Xitsonga	Avuxeni

Good bye		
	Afrikaans	Totsiens
	isiZulu	Hamba kahle
	isiXhosa	Sala kakuhle
	Sepedi	Gabotse
	Sesotho & Setswana	Sala hantle

How are you?		
	Afrikaans	Hoe gaan dit?
	isiZulu & isiXhosa	Kunjani?
	Sepedi & Setswana	Phela jwang?
	Sesotho	O phela jwang?

Thank you		
	Afrikaans	Dankie
	isiZulu	Ngiyabonga
	isiXhosa	Enkosi
	Sepedi	Ke la leboga

Yes		
	Afrikaans	Ja
	isiZulu	Yebo
	isiXhosa	Ewe
	Sepedi, Setswana & Sesotho	Ee

No		
	Afrikaans	Nee
	isiZulu	Cha
	isiXhosa	Hayi
	Sepedi	Aowa
	Sesotho & Setswana	Thjee

MOVING CHECKLIST

Four months before your move

- [ ] Arrange for health checks at your dentist and doctor.
- [ ] Start your vaccination program if your records are not up to date.
- [ ] Organise your financial and personal documents.
- [ ] Start your research on moving companies.

Three months before your move

- [ ] Sort through all your belongings.
- [ ] Donate, arrange for storage or throw away things you will not need.
- [ ] Notify your child's school and ask to have transfer records prepared.
- [ ] Collect information about schools at your destination and start with applications.
- [ ] Apply for your permits such as temporary residency permit, work permit or study permit.

Two months before your move

- [ ] Order moving supplies like boxes, tape and bubble wrap if you are not using a removal company.
- [ ] Get quotes from removal companies for your move and appoint one.
- [ ] Book your flights and temporary accommodation.
- [ ] Fill in change of address documents from the post office if you want to have your mail forwarded to your company or a South African post office box.
- [ ] Apply for a post office box at the South African post office or the private mail service PostNet.

One month before your move

- [ ] Confirm arrangements with your moving company and know what you will have to pack yourself.
- [ ] Remember to keep valuables separate and take photos of valuable items.
- [ ] Prepare a comprehensive inventory of your valuable and favourite items for insurance purposes.
- [ ] Arrange for your medical records to be transferred or collect them from your doctor.
- [ ] Organise a farewell party, possibly arrange for catering.
- [ ] Make a plan where to stay the last days should your furniture be moved before your actual departure day.
- [ ] Notify the insurance companies, banks and utilities of your departure and change of address.
- [ ] Find a buyer for your car or arrange a last check up at your garage before the move.
- [ ] Cancel newspaper and magazine subscriptions.
- [ ] Cancel grocery or milk deliveries.

Two weeks before your move

☐ Reconfirm arrangements with your moving company.

☐ Obtain health certificates for your pets.

One week before your move

☐ Empty your safe-deposit box at the bank and arrange for a safe you can take with you on your move.

☐ Start packing your suitcases.

☐ Get your prescription medicine and organise for enough supply for the next month.

☐ Collect school records for children.

A couple of days before your move

☐ Defrost your freezer and empty out your fridge.

☐ Reconfirm you flights and moving arrangements.

Moving day/s

☐ Be present when the movers pack, and keep all the suitcases and travel items in a separate area.

☐ Keep a list of what the movers put into each box and label them accordingly.

☐ Check and sign the mover's inventory and condition list.

☐ Keep one copy of the inventory and take it along with your documents.

☐ Ensure the address and contact numbers are correct on the landing bill.

☐ Hand over the keys of your home to the new owners, landlord or rental agency.

Duty-free Goods

All travellers to South Africa can bring certain consumable goods duty-free or VAT-free in accompanied baggage. The following allowances are available per person.

*Allowances for alcohol and tobacco are only applicable to persons over 18 years.

Duty-free Goods	Maximum Amount
Tobacco*	250 g
Cigarettes*	200
Cigars*	20
Perfume	50 ml
Eau de Toilette	250 ml
Wine*	2 litres
Other alcohol*	1 litres

TIME ZONES

The whole of South Africa lies on one time zone, the South African Standard Time, or SAST which is two hours ahead of the UTC (Co-ordinated Universal Time, formerly GMT). The SAST also applies to Swaziland and Lesotho. There is no daylight saving time in South Africa, however due to the vast distances from east to west, the sun rises later and sets later in the Western Cape and western parts of the Northern Cape than in other provinces. South African Standard Time, Central Africa Time, West Africa Summer Time and Eastern European Time are all two hours ahead of the UTC.

Deduct from SA time		Add to SA time	
Berlin*	- 1 hr	Helsinki	+ 1 hr
London	- 2 hrs	Moscow	+ 2 hrs
Casablanca	- 2 hrs	Islamabad	+ 3 hrs
Buenos Aires	- 5 hrs	Delhi	+ 3.5 hrs
New York*	- 6 hrs	Jakarta	+ 5 hrs
Mexico City*	- 7 hrs	Beijing	+ 6 hrs
Calgary	- 8 hrs	Tokyo	+ 7 hrs
Los Angeles*	- 9 hrs	Sydney	+ 8 hrs
Anchorage	- 10 hrs	Auckland	+ 10 hrs

*Daylight saving times may apply, if so, add +1 hr to times mentioned above.

SOME RENAMED TOWNS

North West
Klerksdorp
Matlosana
Mafikeng/Mafeking
Mahikeng
Potchefstroom
Tlokwe

Eastern Cape
Umtata
Mthatha
Dutywa
Idutywa
Bisho
Bhisho

Mpumalanga
Machadodorp
eNtokozweni
Blyde River
Molatse River
Nelspruit
Mbombela
Piet Retief
Mkhondo
Witbank
eMalahleni

Gauteng
Pretoria
Tshwane

Limpopo
Warmbaths
Bela-Bela
Pietersburg
Polokwane
Potgietersrus
Mokopane
Naboomspruit
Mookgophong
Nylstroom
Modimolle

KwaZulu-Natal
Stanger
KwaDukuza

Ellisras
Lephalale
Louis Trichardt
Makhado
Messina
Musina
Duiwelskloof
Modjadjiskloof

SPEED

Km/h	30	40	50	60	70	80	90	100	110	120
Miles/hr	19	25	31	37	43	50	56	62	69	75

DISTANCES

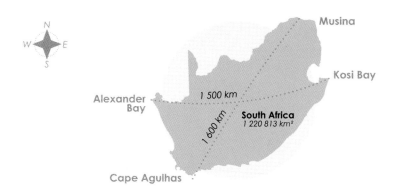

DISTANCE CHART (In Kilometres)

	Bloemfontein	Cape Town	Durban	East London	George	Johannesburg	Kimberley	Musina	Nelspruit	Phalaborwa	Pietermaritzburg	Polokwane	Port Elizabeth	Pretoria	Richards Bay	Upington
Bloemfontein	•	998	628	546	764	396	175	955	754	952	578	727	676	454	775	576
Cape Town	998	•	1660	1042	436	1405	960	1957	1779	1940	1544	1736	756	1463	1769	821
Durban	628	1660	•	667	1240	598	842	1081	689	910	77	929	927	656	182	1243
East London	546	1042	667	•	630	992	722	1530	1214	1391	594	1323	300	1050	849	958
George	764	436	1240	630	•	1168	734	1719	1509	1686	1173	1499	330	1226	1487	857
Johannesburg	396	1405	598	992	1168	•	467	552	358	535	503	331	1062	58	594	875
Kimberley	175	960	842	722	734	467	•	1026	832	1009	748	798	763	525	905	401
Musina	955	1957	1081	1530	1719	552	1026	•	513	340	1004	221	1620	494	1014	1296
Nelspruit	754	1779	689	1214	1509	358	832	513	•	221	675	315	1373	328	585	1144
Phalaborwa	952	1940	910	1391	1686	535	1009	340	221	•	797	204	1524	477	806	1279
Pietermaritzburg	578	1544	77	594	1173	503	748	1004	675	797	•	811	854	561	259	1149
Polokwane	727	1736	929	1323	1499	331	798	221	315	204	811	•	1393	273	821	1075
Port Elizabeth	676	756	927	300	330	1062	763	1620	1373	1524	854	1393	•	1119	1098	902
Pretoria	454	1463	656	1050	1226	58	525	494	328	477	561	273	1119	•	680	813
Richards Bay	775	1769	182	849	1487	594	905	1014	585	806	259	821	1098	680	•	1313
Upington	576	821	1243	958	857	875	401	1296	1144	1279	1149	1075	902	813	1313	•

(Source: www.aa.co.za)

This map and all other maps in this book are for illustrative purposes only. Accurate maps are available from either the local AA or South African Tourism offices. In addition, maps can be purchased in most local bookstores, petrol stations or supermarkets.

BIBLIOGRAPHY

Automobile Association (AA) (2009) *Key Guide to South Africa*. Johannesburg: AA Publishing

Biko, Hlumelo (2013) *The Great African Society*. Johannesburg: Johnathan Ball

Brett, Michael (2011) *DK Eyewitness South Africa*. Johannesburg: Penguin

Briggs, Philip (2011) *South Africa Highlights*. United Kingdom: Bradt Publishers Guilford

Bristow, David (2011) *Been There, Done That*. Cape Town: Struik

Campbell, Derryn (2010) *Awesome Souh Africa*. Durban: Awesome SA Publishers

Crwys-Williams, Jennifer (2012) *In the Words of Nelson Mandela*. Johannesburg: Penguin

FIFA *2010 When the World Cup Came to South Africa*. FIFA World Cup Committee

Flanagan, Neil & Finger (2010) *Just about Everything a Manager Needs to Know in South Africa*. Cape Town: Zebra Press

Fraser, Sean (2005) *South Africa*. Cape Town: Struik

George, Richard & Slabert, Denise & Wildman, Kim (2006) *Offbeat South Africa*. Cape Town: Struik

Hall, Edward T (1989) *Beyond Culture*. New York: Anchor Press

Harrison, Ian & Joyce, Peter (2005) *The Book of Firsts*. Johannesburg: Jonathan Ball

Hofstede, Geert (2004) *Culture and Organizations*. New York: McGraw Hill

Holt-Biddle, David (2012) *Culture Smart! South Africa*. London: Kuperard

Irwin, Rachel (2007) *Culture Shock – Negotiating Feelings in the Field*. In: Fielding Emotions

Lundy, Guy & Visser, Wayne (2003) *South Africa – Reasons to Believe!* Onrus River: Aardvark Press

Marais, Jacques (2012) *The Adventure Guide of South Africa*. Pretoria: Lapa Publishers

Michler, Ian & Van Schaik, Tessa (2009) *South Africa – The Insider's Guide*. Cape Town: Random Struik

Naidoo, Beverley (2008) *Journey to Jo'burg - Modern South African Stories*. New York: HarperCollins

Ngcobo, Ndumiso (2007) *Some of my Best Friends are White*. Cape Town: Two Dogs Press

Ngwenya, Jabulile Bongiwe & Slabbert, Denise & Hopkins, Pat (2009) *The South African Fact Book*. Johannesburg: Penguin

Oberg, Kalervo (1970) *Culture Shock – Adjustment to New Cultural Environments*. In: Practical Anthopology 7.

Richmond, Simon et al. (2002) *South Africa, Lesotho & Swaziland*. Melbourne: Lonely Planet Publications

Strieman, Mercia (2009) *On the Ball – Getting to Know You Before 2010*. Cape Town

Stuart, Chris & Mathilde (2012) *National Parks and Nature Reserves*. Cape Town: Struik

Sycholt, August (2009) *Ecoguide – South African Destinations*. Pretoria: Briza Publications

Tishkoff, Sarah (2009) *The Genetic Structure and History of Africans and African Americans*. In: Science Magazine

Van Lill, Dawid (2013) *See South Africa*. Cape Town: Human & Rousseau

Wills, Mike & Zapiro (2013) *Vuvuzela Nation - SA Sports 1995–2013*. Johannesburg: Jacana

Websites

www.awesomesouthafrica.co.za
www.expatcapetown.com
www.gcis.gov.za
www.joburgexpat.com
www.sagoodnews.co.za
www.sahistory.org.za
www.smartcape.org.za
www.southafrica.info
www.southafrica.net
www.statssa.gov.za
www.worldbank.org

IMAGE CREDITS

The authors would like to thank the following people for permission to use their photographs in this book:

Abbreviations Key:
SAT: South Africa Tourism
KZNT: KwaZulu-Natal Tourism
TNW: Tourism North West
SSK: Shutterstock
wiki: Wikimedia Commons
GL: Go Limpopo
MC: Mediaclub
GW: Graeme Williams
CK: Chris Kirchhoff
DC: Derryn Campbell
RC: Rose Collingwood
RG: Regina Gräff

1: SAT; 12: Luke Schmidt/SSK; 13: SAT; 14: Valroe/wiki, wiki, wiki; 15: wiki, ANC, MSU.edu; 16: ndr.org.za, wiki; 17: sahistory.org.za, sahistory.org.za, Kristen Opaliski/wiki, fstockphoto/SSK, SSK; 20: Marco Schmitt/wiki, Michael Clarke/wiki, GW/MC; 21: OU, Brian Snelson/wiki, Mary Alexander/MC; 22: Government SA/flickr, Government SA/flickr; 23: Government SA/flickr; TNW, Government SA/flickr; 24: Soweto Gospel Choir; 25: constitutionhill.org.za; 26: SAT, helplesotho.org, SAT; 27: SAT, KZNT, Walter Callens/flickr; 28: Warenski/flickr, DC; 29: Warren Rohner/flickr; 33: Tim Giddings/wiki, KZNT, gauteng.net; 34: gauteng.net; 35: RG; 36: Vincent van Osten/SSK; 37: Dennis Donohue/SSK; 39: Harm Kruyshaar/SSK; David Maskell, Di Jones/flickr; 40: KZNT, SAT, Roger de la Harpe/SAT, SAT; 41: SAT, Dr. Thomas Wagner/wiki, SSK, SSK; 42: SSK, SSK, Neil Moultrie/SAT, SSK, SSK; 44: DC, GL, GL, Tourism North West, GL; 45: Paul Manning/wiki, G. Goddard, Chad Rosentha/wiki, SSK, DC; 51: Daleen Loest/SSK, Jerome Bon/flickr, Franschoek Wine Route/MC; 52: SSK; 54: RG, MAN, Franschhoek Wine Route/MC; 55: SSK, SSK, SAT, SSK; 56: SSK; 58: DC; 60: VWSA/MC, DC, SSK; 61: Tiffindell, SSK, SSK, Rian Saunders/flickr; 62: Kay Africa/wiki; 64: SAT; 65: SSK; 66: SSK, GW/MC, SAT; 67: SSK, Dietmar Temps/SSK, Malcolm Manners/flickr, SSK; 68: SSK; 70: Dylan Harbour/wiki; 72: SAT, gauteng.net, joburg.org.za; 73: CK/MC, SAT, Rotational/wiki, maropeng.org.za; 74: SSK, 76: SSK; 78: SSK, Sasol/MC, SAT; 79: SSK, SAT, GW/MC, SSK; 80: GW/MC; 82: SSK; 84: SAT, GW/MC, SSK; 85: TNW, Inna Felker/SSK, TNW, TNW; 86: SSK; 88: Walter Knirr/Durban Tourism; 90: Durban Tourism, KZNT, SSK; 91: SSK, KZNT, KZNT; 92: KZNT; 94: GL; 96: SSK, SSK, GL; 97: Legends, SSK, SAT, GL; 98: SSK; 100: SSK; 102: SSK, GW/MC, SSK; 103: Ossewas/wiki, SSK, Attila Jandi/SSK, SAT; 104: SSK; 108: SAT; 109: Anke van Wyk/SSK; 110: Dylan Harbour/wiki; 115: SAT; 116: Bfluff/wiki; 118: RG; 120: Aero Icarus/wiki; 121: SSK; 123: Durban Tourism; 124: RG; 129: DC; 130: DC; 132: SSK; 133: SSK; 134: SSK; 146: RG; 147: SSK; 148: SSK; 156: Joachim Huber/wiki, SSK, SSK; 158: Brookdale; 159: SSK; 165: Milpark; 168: SSK; 169: Gautrain/MC, SAT; 170: Sasol/MC; 173: SAT; 176: Photo360/SSK; 177: Hein van Hoersten/SAT; 182: CK/MC; 183: VWSA/MC; 186: SAT; 187: DC; 188: Chris Welsh/wiki; 196: VWSA/MC; 197: Sasol/MC; 205: SSK; 206: Jamie Wilson/SSK; 208: Michaelhouse; 209: Blouberg International School; 212: Blouberg International School; 215: DC; 217: Adrian Frith/wiki; 218: DC; 222: Inna Felker/SSK; 223: SAT; 224: SSK, SSK, RC; 225: Jon Mountjoy/flickr, RC, RC; 226: RG; 227: Robert Bosch/MC; 228: Scott McLean/flickr, Jan Braai, DC, DC; 229: DC, DC; 230: SAT; 231: National Braai Day/flickr, amarula.com, DC; 232: SAT; 234: KZNT, RG, Jan Braai; 236: SAT; 237: SAT; 244: DC, DC, RG, SAT; 245: DC, SSK, GL, GW/MC; 248: DC; 249: SAT; 250: Soweto Gospel Choir; 251: KZNT; 252: fstockfoto/SSK; 254: SAT, SAT, Brookdale; 255: meunierd/SSK; 256: DC; 257: SAT, Jeroen Looye/flickr, SSK; 258: KevinD6C/flickr, Lira/macufe.co.za, Kim Novacki/flickr

Created and written by
Regina Gräff
Derryn Campbell

Editors
Moray Comrie and Cheryl Knupp

Designer
Rose Collingwood

Printed and bound by ABC Press, Cape Town

Published by Awesome SA Publishers, Durban

First Edition 2014

ISBN 978-0-620-57656-7

If you want to know more about this book or any other Awesome SA publications, visit www.awesomesa.co.za or phone +27 (0)82 786 8450 or email info@awesomesa.co.za.

Books are available in bulk to corporations and institutions. For more information, please contact the publisher.

Acknowledgements

This book is a collaborative effort pulling together Regina's idea and concept for an expat guide book and Derryn's passion for sharing information about her awesome home country. Creating this book was a journey full of adventures and discoveries.

We owe much to the hard work and creativity of our talented designer. Thus the foremost thanks go to Rose, who, with lots of patience, managed to transform our plain manuscript into this unique book. Many thanks go also to Cheryl and Moray, our editors, who not only gave sound and knowledgeable input but also much helpful advice. Thanks to our proofreader, Kelly Norwood-Young, for checking the book meticulously prior to going to print.

Thank you to South Africa Tourism and various tourism bodies for their friendly support and encouragement of our project. We are very grateful for the insights and input we received from the headmasters of various schools as well as lawyers, bankers, doctors and many other specialists in their respective fields who generously supported us during our research.

We cherish the friendships of fellow South Africans and 'South Africans at heart', people of many nations, who believe in this awesome country. We appreciate all the valuable input from the followers of our blogs and newsletters. Thank you for sharing your insights with us over the years and providing ongoing encouragement and support.

Last but not least, a huge, heartfelt thank you goes to our family and friends, particularly our husbands and children. We appreciate all your encouragement and your belief in us and our project. Without you, we never would have enjoyed the journey as much as we did.

INDEX

USEFUL NUMBERS

National Emergency Call Centre Fire, Police, Ambulance	107
Cellphone National Emergency Number Fire, Police, Ambulance	112
Police Flying Squad	10 111
Ambulance	10 177
ER 24 Ambulance	084 124
Netcare Ambulance	082 911
Lifeline	0861 322 322
Women Abuse	0800 150 150
Childline	0800 055 555
Poisons Info Centre	021 689 5227
Alcoholics Anonymous	0861 435 722
Suicide Crisis Line	0800 567 567
Aids Line	0800 012 322
Crime Stop	0860 010 111
ID Theft Hotline	0860 101 248

PERSONAL DATA

Name: _____ Cell: _____
Passport Number: _____ ID Number: _____

In Case of Emergency Contact
Name: _____
Tel: _____ Cell: _____

Next of Kin
Name: _____
Tel: _____ Cell: _____

Family Doctor
Name: _____
Tel: _____ Cell: _____

Medical Aid
Account Holder: _____ Account Number: _____
Tel: _____ Email: _____

Banking
Bank: _____ Account Holder: _____
Bank Code: _____ Account Number: _____
Tel: _____ Email: _____

Car
Registration: _____
Insurance Name: _____ Insurance Number: _____
Service Centre: _____ Email: _____

Childcare/Au Pair
Name: _____ ID Number: _____
Tel: _____ Cell: _____

Domestic Help
Name: _____ ID Number: _____
Tel: _____ Cell: _____
Next of Kin: _____ Contact: _____

Name: _____ ID Number: _____
Tel: _____ Cell: _____
Next of Kin: _____ Contact: _____

School
Name: _____ Contact Person: _____
Tel: _____ Email: _____

Name: _____ Contact Person: _____
Tel: _____ Email: _____

Name: _____ Contact Person: _____
Tel: _____ Email: _____

NOTES